# THE COLOR
## OF LAW

# THE COLOR OF LAW

## A FORGOTTEN HISTORY OF HOW OUR GOVERNMENT SEGREGATED AMERICA

### RICHARD ROTHSTEIN

LIVERIGHT PUBLISHING CORPORATION
*A Division of* W. W. Norton & Company
INDEPENDENT PUBLISHERS SINCE 1923
NEW YORK • LONDON

3650159

Frontispiece: *Pittsburgh, 1940. President Franklin D. Roosevelt hands keys to the 100,000th family to receive lodging in the federal government's public housing program. Most projects were for whites only.*

For information about permission to reproduce selections from this book, write to Permissions, Liveright Publishing Corporation, a division of W. W. Norton & Company, Inc., 500 Fifth Avenue, New York, NY 10110

For information about special discounts for bulk purchases, please contact W. W. Norton Special Sales at specialsales@wwnorton.com or 800-233-4830

Manufacturing by LSC Communications, Harrisonburg, VA
Book design by Brooke Koven
Production manager: Anna Oler

ISBN 978-1-63149-285-3

Liveright Publishing Corporation,
500 Fifth Avenue, New York, N.Y. 10110
www.wwnorton.com

W. W. Norton & Company Ltd.,
15 Carlisle Street, London W1D 3BS

1 2 3 4 5 6 7 8 9 0

# CONTENTS

# PREFACE

WHEN, FROM 2014 TO 2016, riots in places like Ferguson, Baltimore, Milwaukee, or Charlotte captured our attention, most of us thought we knew how these segregated neighborhoods, with their crime, violence, anger, and poverty came to be. We said they are "*de facto* segregated," that they result from private practices, not from law or government policy.

*De facto* segregation, we tell ourselves, has various causes. When African Americans moved into a neighborhood like Ferguson, a few racially prejudiced white families decided to leave, and then as the number of black families grew, the neighborhood deteriorated, and "white flight" followed. Real estate agents steered whites away from black neighborhoods, and blacks away from white ones. Banks discriminated with "redlining," refusing to give mortgages to African Americans or extracting unusually severe terms from them with subprime loans. African Americans haven't generally gotten the educations that would enable them to earn sufficient incomes to live in white suburbs, and, as a result, many remain concentrated in urban neighborhoods. Besides, black families prefer to live with one another.

All this has some truth, but it remains a small part of the truth, submerged by a far more important one: until the last quarter of the twentieth century, racially explicit policies of federal, state, and local governments defined where whites and African Americans should live. Today's residential segregation in the North, South, Midwest, and West is not the unintended consequence of individual choices and of otherwise well-meaning law or regulation but of unhidden public policy that explicitly segregated every metropolitan area in the United States. The policy was so systematic and forceful that its effects endure to the present time. Without our government's purposeful imposition of racial segregation, the other causes—private prejudice, white flight, real estate steering, bank redlining, income differences, and self-segregation—still would have existed but with far less opportunity for expression. Segregation by intentional government action is not *de facto*. Rather, it is what courts call *de jure*: segregation by law and public policy.

Residential racial segregation by state action is a violation of our Constitution and its Bill of Rights. The Fifth Amendment, written by our Founding Fathers, prohibits the federal government from treating citizens unfairly. The Thirteenth Amendment, adopted immediately after the Civil War, prohibits slavery or, in general, treating African Americans as second-class citizens, while the Fourteenth Amendment, also adopted after the Civil War, prohibits states, or their local governments, from treating people either unfairly or unequally.

The applicability of the Fifth and Fourteenth Amendments to government sponsorship of residential segregation will make sense to most readers. Clearly, denying African Americans access to housing subsidies that were extended to whites constitutes unfair treatment and, if consistent, rises to the level of a serious constitutional violation. But it may be surprising that residential segregation also violates the Thirteenth Amendment. We typically think of the Thirteenth as only abolishing slavery. Section 1 of the Thirteenth Amendment does so, and Section 2 empowers Congress to enforce Section 1. In 1866, Congress enforced the abolition of slavery by passing a Civil Rights Act, prohibiting actions that it deemed perpetuated the characteristics of slavery. Actions that made African Americans second-class citizens, such as racial discrimination in housing, were included in the ban.

In 1883, though, the Supreme Court rejected this congressional interpretation of its powers to enforce the Thirteenth Amendment.

The Court agreed that Section 2 authorized Congress to "to pass all laws necessary and proper for abolishing all badges and incidents of slavery in the United States," but it did not agree that exclusions from housing markets could be a "badge or incident" of slavery. In consequence, these Civil Rights Act protections were ignored for the next century.

Today, however, most Americans understand that prejudice toward and mistreatment of African Americans did not develop out of thin air. The stereotypes and attitudes that support racial discrimination have their roots in the system of slavery upon which the nation was founded. So to most of us, it should now seem reasonable to agree that Congress was correct when it determined that prohibiting African Americans from buying or renting decent housing perpetuated second-class citizenship that was a relic of slavery. It also now seems reasonable to understand that if government actively *promoted* housing segregation, it failed to abide by the Thirteenth Amendment's prohibition of slavery and its relics.

This interpretation is not far-fetched. Indeed, it is similar to one that was eventually adopted by the Supreme Court in 1968 when it effectively rejected its 1883 decision. In 1965, Joseph Lee Jones and his wife, Barbara Jo Jones, sued the Alfred H. Mayer Company, a St. Louis developer, who refused to sell them a home solely because Mr. Jones was black. Three years later, the Supreme Court upheld the Joneses' claim and recognized the validity of the 1866 Civil Rights Act's declaration that housing discrimination was a residue of slave status that the Thirteenth Amendment empowered Congress to eliminate.

Yet because of an historical accident, policy makers, the public, and even civil rights advocates have failed to pay much attention to the implications of the *Jones v. Mayer* decision. Two months before the Supreme Court announced its ruling, Congress adopted the Fair Housing Act, which was then signed into law by President Lyndon B. Johnson. Although the 1866 law had already determined that housing discrimination was unconstitutional, it gave the government no powers of enforcement. The Fair Housing Act provided for modest enforcement, and civil rights groups have used this law, rather than the earlier statute, to challenge housing discrimination.

*Joseph Lee and Barbara Jo Jones. Their successful 1968 law-suit established that housing discrimination is a badge of slavery.*

But when they did so, we lost sight of the fact that housing discrimination did not become unlawful in 1968; it had been so since 1866. Indeed, throughout those 102 years, housing discrimination was not only unlawful but was the imposition of a badge of slavery that the Constitution mandates us to remove.

*The Color of Law* is concerned with consistent government policy that was employed in the mid-twentieth century to enforce residential racial segregation. There were many specific government actions that prevented African Americans and whites from living among one another, and I categorize them as "unconstitutional." In doing so, I reject the widespread view that an action is not unconstitutional until the Supreme Court says so. Few Americans think that racial segregation in schools was constitutional before 1954, when the Supreme Court prohibited it. Rather, segregation was always unconstitutional, although a misguided Supreme Court majority mistakenly failed to recognize this.

Yet even if we came to a nationally shared recognition that government policy has created an unconstitutional, *de jure*, system of residential segregation, it does not follow that litigation can remedy this situation. Although most African Americans have suffered under this *de jure* system, they cannot identify, with the specificity a court case requires, the particular point at which they were victimized. For example, many African American World War II veterans did not apply for government-guaranteed mortgages for suburban purchases because they knew that the Veterans Administration would reject them on account of their race, so applications were pointless. Those veterans then did not gain wealth from home equity appreciation as did white veterans, and their descendants could then not inherit that wealth as did white veterans' descendants. With less inherited wealth, African Americans today are generally less able than their white peers to afford to attend good colleges. If one of those African American descendants now learned that the reason his or her grandparents were forced to rent apartments in overcrowded urban areas was that the federal government unconstitutionally and unlawfully prohibited banks from lending to African Americans, the grandchild would not have the standing to file a lawsuit; nor would he or she be able to name a particular party from whom damages could be recovered. There is generally no *judicial* remedy for a policy that the Supreme Court wrongheadedly approved. But this does not mean that there is no constitutionally required remedy for such violations. It is up to the people, through our elected representatives, to enforce our Constitution by implementing the remedy.

By failing to recognize that we now live with the severe, enduring effects of *de jure* segregation, we avoid confronting our constitutional obligation to reverse it. If I am right that we continue to have *de jure* segregation, then desegregation is not just a desirable policy; it is a constitutional as well as a moral obligation that we are required to fulfill. "Let bygones be bygones" is not a legitimate approach if we wish to call ourselves a constitutional democracy.

Racial segregation in housing was not merely a project of southerners in the former slaveholding Confederacy. It was a nationwide project of the federal government in the twentieth century, designed and implemented by its most liberal leaders. Our system of official segregation was not the result of a single law that consigned African Americans to designated neighborhoods. Rather, scores of racially explicit laws, regulations, and government practices combined to create a nationwide system of urban ghettos, surrounded by white suburbs. Private discrimination also played a role, but it would have been considerably less effective had it not been embraced and reinforced by government.

Half a century ago, the truth of *de jure* segregation was well known, but since then we have suppressed our historical memory and soothed ourselves into believing that it all happened by accident or by misguided private prejudice. Popularized by Supreme Court majorities from the 1970s to the present, the *de facto* segregation myth has now been adopted by conventional opinion, liberal and conservative alike.

A turning point came when civil rights groups sued to desegregate Detroit's public schools. Recognizing that you couldn't desegregate schools if there were few white children in Detroit, the plaintiffs argued that a remedy had to include the white suburbs as well as the heavily African American city. In 1974, by a 5–4 vote, the Supreme Court disagreed. The majority reasoned that because government policy in the suburbs had not segregated Detroit's schools, the suburbs couldn't be included in a remedy. Justice Potter Stewart explained that black students were concentrated in the city, not spread throughout Detroit's suburbs, because of "unknown and perhaps unknowable factors such as in-migration, birth rates, economic changes, or cumulative acts of private racial fears." He concluded: "The Constitution simply does not allow federal courts to attempt to change that situation unless and until it is shown that the State, or its political subdivisions, have contributed to cause the situation to exist. No record has been made in this case showing that the racial composition of the Detroit school population or that residential patterns within Detroit and in the surrounding areas were in any significant measure caused by governmental activity."

Most disturbing about Justice Stewart's observation was that the civil rights plaintiffs did offer evidence to prove that residential patterns within Detroit and in the surrounding areas were in significant measure caused by governmental activity. Although the trial judge agreed with this argument, Justice Stewart and his colleagues chose to ignore it, denying that such evidence even existed.*

This misrepresentation of our racial history, indeed this willful blindness, became the consensus view of American jurisprudence, expressed again in a decision written by Chief Justice John Roberts in 2007. His opinion prohibited school districts in Louisville and Seattle from accounting for a student's race as part of modest school integration plans. Each district permitted students to choose which school they would attend, but if remaining seats in a school were limited, the district admitted students who would contribute to the school's racial balance. In other words, black students would get preference for admission to mostly white schools, and white students would get preference for mostly black ones.

The chief justice noted that racially homogenous housing arrangements in these cities had led to racially homogenous student bodies in neighborhood schools. He observed that racially separate neighborhoods might result from "societal discrimination" but said that remed-

---

* From this evidence, federal district court judge Stephen J. Roth, in his opinion that was overruled by the Supreme Court, concluded: "The policies pursued by both government and private persons and agencies have a continuing and present effect upon the complexion of the community—as we know, the choice of a residence is a relatively infrequent affair. For many years FHA and VA openly advised and advocated the maintenance of 'harmonious' neighborhoods, *i.e.*, racially and economically harmonious. The conditions created continue." Judge Roth urged that to acknowledge that other factors were also involved, we "need not minimize the effect of the actions of federal, state and local governmental officers and agencies, and the actions of loaning institutions and real estate firms, in the establishment and maintenance of segregated residential patterns—which lead to school segregation."

ying discrimination "not traceable to [government's] own actions" can never justify a constitutionally acceptable, racially conscious, remedy. "The distinction between segregation by state action and racial imbalance caused by other factors has been central to our jurisprudence. . . . Where [racial imbalance] is a product not of state action but of private choices, it does not have constitutional implications." Because neighborhoods in Louisville and Seattle had been segregated by private choices, he concluded, school districts should be prohibited from taking purposeful action to reverse their own resulting segregation.

Chief Justice Roberts himself was quoting from a 1992 opinion by Justice Anthony Kennedy in a case involving school segregation in Georgia. In that opinion Justice Kennedy wrote: "[V]estiges of past segregation by state decree do remain in our society and in our schools. Past wrongs to the black race, wrongs committed by the State and in its name, are a stubborn fact of history. And stubborn facts of history linger and persist. But though we cannot escape our history, neither must we overstate its consequences in fixing legal responsibilities. The vestiges of segregation . . . may be subtle and intangible but nonetheless they must be so real that they have a causal link to the *de jure* violation being remedied. It is simply not always the case that demographic forces causing population change bear any real and substantial relation to a *de jure* violation."

The following pages will refute this too-comfortable notion, expressed by Justice Kennedy and endorsed by Chief Justice Roberts and his colleagues, that wrongs committed by the state have little causal link to the residential segregation we see around us. *The Color of Law* demonstrates that racially explicit government policies to segregate our metropolitan areas are not vestiges, were neither subtle nor intangible, and were sufficiently controlling to construct the *de jure* segregation that is now with us in neighborhoods and hence in schools. The core argument of this book is that African Americans were unconstitutionally denied the means and the right to integration in middle-class neighborhoods, and because this denial was state-sponsored, the nation is obligated to remedy it.

Many legal scholars are properly skeptical of the distinction between *de jure* and *de facto* segregation. Where private discrimination is pervasive, they argue, discrimination by public policy is indistinguishable from "societal discrimination." For example, if it becomes a community norm for whites to flee a neighborhood where African Americans were settling, this norm can be as powerful as if it were written into law. Both public policy discrimination and societal discrimination express what these scholars term "structural racism," in which many if not most institutions in the country operate to the disadvantage of African Americans. It is pointless, these scholars argue, to try to distinguish the extent to which these institutions' racially disparate impact originated with private or public discrimination. Government has an obligation, they say, to remedy structural racism regardless of its cause decades ago.

These scholars may be right, but in this book I don't take their approach. Rather, I adopt the narrow legal theory of Chief Justice Roberts, his predecessors, his colleagues, and their likely successors. They agree that there is a constitutional obligation to remedy the effects of government-sponsored segregation, though not of private discrimination. I will take them at their word. Where *The Color of Law* differs is not with their theory but with their facts. For those who, like the Court, believe that the Constitution requires a remedy for government-sponsored segregation, but that most segregation doesn't fall into this category, I hope to show that Justice Roberts and his colleagues have their facts wrong. Most segregation *does* fall into the category of open and explicit government-sponsored segregation.

B efore I begin, some notes about word usage: I will frequently refer (indeed, I've already done so) to things *we* have done, or things *we* should do. *We* means all of us, the American community. This is not a book about whites as actors and blacks as victims. As citizens in this democracy, we—all of us, white, black, Hispanic, Asian, Native American, and others—bear a collective responsibility to enforce our Constitution and to rectify past violations whose effects endure. Few of us may be the direct descendants of those who perpetuated a segregated system or those who were its most exploited victims. African Americans cannot await rectification of past wrongs as a gift, and white Americans collectively do not owe it to African Americans to rectify them. We, all of us, owe this to ourselves. As American citizens, whatever routes we or our particular ancestors took to get to this point, we're all in this together now.

Over the past few decades, we have developed euphemisms to help us forget how we, as a nation, have segregated African American citizens. We have become embarrassed about saying *ghetto*, a word that accurately describes a neighborhood where government has not only concentrated a minority but established barriers to its exit. We don't hesitate to acknowledge that Jews in Eastern Europe were forced to live in ghettos where opportunity was limited and leaving was difficult or impossible. Yet when we encounter similar neighborhoods in this country, we now delicately refer to them as the *inner city*, yet everyone knows what we mean. (When affluent whites gentrify the same geographic areas, we don't characterize those whites as *inner city* families.) Before we became ashamed to admit that the country had circumscribed African Americans in ghettos, analysts of race relations, both African American and white, consistently and accurately used *ghetto* to describe low-income African American neighborhoods, created by public policy, with a shortage of opportunity, and with barriers to exit. No other term succinctly describes this combination of characteristics, so I use the term as well.*

---

\* In 1948, Robert Weaver, long before becoming the first African American to serve in the cabinet, wrote a book called *The Negro Ghetto* that documented how government segregated the nation. In 1965, Kenneth B. Clark, the social psychologist whose research was relied upon by the Supreme Court in *Brown v. Board of Education*, published *Dark Ghetto*, which described the lack of opportunity in New York City's Harlem. In 1968, the Kerner Commission (the National Advisory Committee on Civil Disorders) published its influential report that concluded: "[W]hite society is deeply implicated in the ghetto. White institutions created it, white institutions maintain it, and white society condones it." A definitive scholarly study of how public policy segregated Chicago is *Making the Second Ghetto*, published in 1983 by Arnold R. Hirsch. A similar study of Cleveland, *A Ghetto Takes Shape: Black Cleveland, 1870–1930*, was published by Kenneth L. Kusmer in 1978. One of the more important books on American race relations of the past decade or more is Michelle Alexander's *The New Jim Crow*, published in 2010. She uses the term *ghetto* frequently.

We've developed other euphemisms, too, so that polite company doesn't have to confront our history of racial exclusion. When we consider problems that arise when African Americans are absent in significant numbers from schools that whites attend, we say we seek *diversity*, not racial integration. When we wish to pretend that the nation did not single out African Americans in a system of segregation specifically aimed at them, we diffuse them as just another *people of color*. I try to avoid such phrases.

Because our majority culture has tended to think of African Americans as inferior, the words we've used to describe them, no matter how dignified they seem when first employed, eventually sound like terms of contempt. African Americans react and insist on new terminology, which we eventually accept until it too seems to connote inferiority. So at the beginning of the twentieth century, America's subordinated race was called *colored*. Later, we came to think of it as *Negro*, first with a lowercase and then with a capital N. It was replaced by *black*, a term that has had a seemingly permanent currency. Today *African American* strikes us as most appropriate. In these pages, it's the term I'll use most frequently, but I will sometimes use *black* as well. Occasionally, in describing historical events, I will refer to *Negroes*, intending the same respect that it enjoyed in those earlier periods.

This shifting of terminology should not distract us from this underlying truth: We have created a caste system in this country, with African Americans kept exploited and geographically separate by racially explicit government policies. Although most of these policies are now off the books, they have never been remedied and their effects endure.

# THE COLOR OF LAW

*Richmond, California, 1948. African Americans worked together with whites in a Ford assembly plant but were barred from living in white neighborhoods.*

# 1

## IF SAN FRANCISCO, THEN EVERYWHERE?

WE THINK OF the San Francisco Bay Area as one of the nation's more liberal and inclusive regions. If the federal, state, and local governments explicitly segregated the population into distinct black and white neighborhoods in the Bay Area, it's a reasonable assumption that our government also segregated metropolitan regions elsewhere and with at least as much determination—which is why I became particularly interested in the government's racial policies in San Francisco and its environs in the twentieth century.

Across the Bay from the city itself is Richmond, a town with the region's greatest concentration of African Americans. During World War II, Richmond hosted the most extensive shipbuilding complex in the nation; later it was best known as the site of a large oil refinery. There I met Frank Stevenson in 2013, after reading an oral history that he had recorded for the National Park Service. I called on him at his Richmond home.

# I

ONE OF seven brothers, Mr. Stevenson was born in 1924 in Lake Providence, Louisiana, a town that *Time* magazine once called "the poorest place in America." But he was privileged compared to most other black youths in the South at the time. His father, a pastor, owned the land on which his First Baptist Church sat, so unlike many other southern black men in the early twentieth century, he didn't have to sharecrop for white farmers. The Stevensons grew cotton and corn for sale and raised hogs and fowl, hunted, and maintained a vegetable garden for their own sustenance.

Through the seventh grade Frank attended a one-room schoolhouse in his father's church, with a single teacher who lived with the family. If Frank were to continue, he would have had to get to a high school in town, too far to walk. In rural Louisiana in the early 1930s, the school year for African Americans was much shorter than for whites, because children like Frank were expected to hire out when planting or harvesting was to be done. "Actually," Mr. Stevenson recalled, "they didn't care too much whether you were going to school or not, if you were black. . . . White school would be continued, but they would turn the black school out because they wanted the kids to go to work on the farm. . . . Lots of times these white guys would . . . come to my dad and ask him to let us work for them one or two days of the week."

During this time, Franklin Roosevelt's New Deal, first with industry codes and then with the Fair Labor Standards Act, prohibited child labor and established minimum wages of about twelve dollars a week in the South, rising to twenty-five cents an hour in 1938. But to pass such economic legislation, Roosevelt needed the votes of southern congressmen and senators, who agreed to support economic reform only if it excluded industries in which African Americans predominated, like agriculture. The Stevenson brothers were each paid only fifty cents a day to work in white farmers' fields.

After finishing seventh grade, Frank Stevenson followed his older brothers and found work in New Orleans, delivering food to workers in the shipyards. Later he had jobs that were typically reserved for African Americans: carrying cement, laying rails, and loading or unloading freight, including, once World War II began, dangerous ammunition. He followed his brother Allen to California, eventually settling at the age of nineteen in Richmond. At first the shipyards and other war industries attempted to operate only with white men, but as the war dragged on, unable to find a sufficient number to meet their military orders, they were forced to hire white women, then black men, and eventually black women as well.

From 1940 to 1945, the influx of war workers resulted in Richmond's population exploding from 24,000 to more than 100,000. Richmond's black population soared from 270 to 14,000. Like Frank Stevenson, the typical African American settling in Richmond had a seventh-grade education, which made these migrants an elite; their educational attainment was greater than that of African Americans in the southern states they left behind.

With such rapid population growth, housing could not be put up quickly enough. The federal government stepped in with public housing. It was officially and explicitly segregated. Located along railroad tracks and close to the shipbuilding area, federally financed housing for African Americans in Richmond was poorly constructed and intended to be temporary. For white defense workers, government housing was built farther inland, closer to white residential areas, and some of it was sturdily constructed and permanent. Because Richmond had been overwhelmingly white before the war, the federal government's decision to segregate public housing established segregated living patterns that persist to this day.

The Richmond police as well as the housing authority pressed the city recreation department to forbid integrated activities, so where projects for whites and projects for blacks shared recreational and sports facilities, the authority designated special hours for African American use. The authority maintained separate social programs for whites and blacks—Boy and Girl Scout troops and movie screenings, for example. A policy of segregation was adopted, explained the authority's director, for the purpose of "keeping social harmony or balance in the whole community." Another housing authority official insisted that "Negroes from the South would rather be by themselves."

Twenty projects with 24,000 units (for both races) built in Richmond during this period barely met the need. For white workers, the federal government created a "war guest" program in which it leased spare rooms from Richmond's white families so workers could move in as tenants. The government also issued low-interest loans for white homeowners to remodel and subdivide their residences.

Consistent with this policy, the federal government recruited one of the nation's leading mass production developers, David Bohannon, to create Rollingwood, a new Richmond suburb. Federal officials approved bank loans to finance construction, requiring that none of Rollingwood's 700 houses be sold to an African American. The government also specified that each Rollingwood property must have an extra bedroom with a separate entrance to accommodate an additional white war worker.

Although African Americans, with fewer private options, were more dependent on public housing than whites, the Richmond Housing Authority's segregated projects did less to alleviate the housing shortage for African American than for white families. Not surprisingly, units for African Americans included many doubled-up families and illegal sublets. By 1947, when Richmond's black population had increased to 26,000, half still lived in temporary war housing. As the government financed whites to abandon these apartments for permanent homes in suburbs like Rollingwood, vacancies in white projects were made available to African Americans. Gradually black families became almost the only tenants of Richmond public housing, except for three permanent projects of sturdily constructed units that had been assigned to whites, most of whom didn't want to leave. By 1950, the city's ghetto had expanded with more than three-fourths of Richmond's black population living in war projects.

For black workers like Frank Stevenson who couldn't squeeze

into the limited number of public housing units, there were no "war guest" or other supplemental government programs. Mr. Stevenson, like many African Americans in Richmond who did not get into the segregated public projects, lived in North Richmond, an unincorporated area for which the city provided no services. He boarded with an elderly woman with whom he traded maintenance for rent.

Other black war workers in North Richmond, not as fortunate as Frank Stevenson, remained in cardboard shacks, barns, tents, or even open fields. Black workers who earned steady wages at war industries could save to buy small plots in unincorporated North Richmond, but because the federal government refused to insure bank loans made to African Americans for housing, standard construction was unaffordable.* Some built their own dwellings with orange crates or scrap lumber scoured from the shipyards. By the early 1950s, some 4,000 African Americans in North Richmond were still living in these makeshift homes.

During the war the government also collaborated with private groups to segregate Richmond. The United Services Organization (USO) maintained separate black and white clubs in Richmond for military personnel and also operated separate black and white Travelers Aid services for newly arrived war workers. On one occasion in 1943, the USO proposed a service center for African Americans on property that was available in a white neighborhood. The local newspaper, the *Richmond Independent*, protested; a petition drive in opposition to the plan ensued, and the city council prevented the plan from going forward. Although the USO was and is a private organization, it was organized by President Roosevelt (who held the title of honorary chairman), benefited from the use of government buildings for some of its clubs, coordinated its services with the War Department, and had a congressional charter. Along with the city council's action, this tight federal government nexus rendered

---

* Throughout, I use the term *bank* loosely to include not only banks but also savings and loans, credit unions, and mortgage-originating companies. However, the discussion in Chapter 7 about federal and state regulators of banks includes only those lending institutions that are heavily regulated by government.

the USO's practice of segregation in Richmond (and elsewhere) an aspect of *de jure* segregation.

To ensure that no African Americans migrated to Richmond unless they were essential to the war effort, the city's police stopped African American men on the street and then arrested and jailed them if they couldn't prove they were employed. So after joining his older brother Allen in Richmond, Frank Stevenson quickly located a job at a Ford Motor assembly plant that had been taken over by the government for the manufacture of military jeeps and the refurbishing of damaged tanks.

In the 1930s, the Ford plant had a sign in front, "No Mexican or Black Workers Wanted," but when Frank Stevenson arrived in 1944, his services were badly needed. Three years earlier, the United Auto Workers (UAW) had forced Henry Ford to the bargaining table, and at the war's end, a union contract prevented Ford Motor from firing African Americans to make way for returning white veterans or for white workers who had been laid off from military production in places like the shipyards. So in 1945, when the army gave up control of the plant and the Ford Motor Company began to make cars again, black workers who had been hired during the war were able to stay on with secure industrial jobs.

Ford had established the plant in 1931 after Richmond offered the company tax incentives to lure its northern California assembly operations. The city had a deepwater port—that's why it became a shipbuilding center during the war—and Ford found the site attractive because it was accessible both to ocean freighters and to railroads. The company could inexpensively transport parts from Detroit to Richmond for assembly into cars and light trucks and then ship the completed vehicles from Richmond to dealers in northern California and Hawaii. The Richmond plant was two stories tall, with conveyor belts moving parts and subassemblies from one floor to the other.

When they were first hired during the war, black workers were assigned only to the lowest and most strenuous job classifications, but the union fought to open more skilled assignments to African Americans. Frank Stevenson seems to have been among the most ambitious and talented, and within a decade of being employed, he was sufficiently skilled to fill in when workers at different workstations were at lunch. "I was smart enough," Mr. Stevenson says, "to go to the other jobs on my break and say, 'Let me see what you do.' That's why they made me a utility man."

In the 1950s, as the postwar consumer boom created growing demand for automobiles, Ford's Richmond plant had no room to expand. Highways made undeveloped rural areas accessible, and land was cheap, allowing Ford the opportunity to spread out and eliminate the inefficiencies of multistory buildings. So in 1953, the company announced it would close its Richmond plant and reestablish operations in a larger facility fifty miles south, in Milpitas, a suburb of San Jose, rural at the time. (Milpitas is part of what we now call Silicon Valley.) Ford purchased a 160-acre site from the Western Pacific Railroad, which had bought 1,700 acres in hopes of attracting industrial facilities for a rail hub.

Union leaders met with Ford executives and negotiated an agreement permitting all 1,400 Richmond plant workers, including the approximately 250 African Americans, to transfer to the new facility. Once Ford's plans became known, Milpitas residents incorporated the town and passed an emergency ordinance permitting the newly installed city council to ban apartment construction and allow only single-family homes. Developers then set to work, creating subdivisions of inexpensive single-family houses for workers not only at Ford but at the other plants that Western Pacific had drawn to the area.

The builders went to the Federal Housing Administration (FHA) for approval of their subdivision plans, and then used these approvals to get banks to issue low-interest loans to finance construction. If the houses conformed to its specifications, the federal government then guaranteed mortgages to qualified buyers without a further property appraisal.* Although banks would generally make mortgage loans to affluent buyers without government involvement, they usually shied away from making loans to working-class families unless the mort

---

* The Veterans Administration "guaranteed" mortgages, while the Federal Housing Administration "insured" them. The distinction is of no importance for understanding *de jure* segregation, and I use the terms interchangeably.

gages were insured. With reduced risk, banks offered lower interest rates, making ownership more affordable to working-class families. For veterans, government approval also usually meant that no down payment was required. As in Rollingwood ten years earlier, one of the federal government's specifications for mortgages insured in Milpitas was an openly stated prohibition on sales to African Americans.

Because Milpitas had no apartments, and houses in the area were off-limits to black workers—though their incomes and economic circumstances were like those of whites on the assembly line—African Americans at Ford had to choose between giving up their good industrial jobs, moving to apartments in a segregated neighborhood of San Jose, or enduring lengthy commutes between North Richmond and Milpitas. Frank Stevenson bought a van, recruited eight others to share the costs, and made the drive daily for the next twenty years until he retired. The trip took more than an hour each way.

Of Frank Stevenson and his eight carpoolers, only one was ever able to move farther south, closer to the plant, and he was not able to do so until the late 1960s. He found a home in Hayward, a town about halfway between Richmond and Milpitas that had also previously been closed to African Americans.

As the civilian housing shortage eased after the war and more government-subsidized suburbs like Rollingwood were built for white working-class families, Richmond itself became a predominantly black city. As the black population of North Richmond swelled, African Americans began to break into the south Richmond housing market. Soon, south Richmond as well became part of Richmond's ghetto. In 1970, after his daughters finished high school, Frank Stevenson was finally able to buy his first home in the southern, previously whites-only section of the city.

## II

AT THE end of World War II, Stanford University in Palo Alto, south of San Francisco, recruited Wallace Stegner to teach creative writing. Stanford's offer followed the publication in 1943 of Stegner's widely acclaimed semiautobiographical novel, *The Big Rock Candy Mountain*. Years later Stegner would go on to win the Pulitzer Prize and the National Book Award, but when he arrived in Palo Alto with his family immediately after the war, his financial resources were modest.

Like the rest of the country, the Stanford area was suffering from a housing shortage: during the war, with all available material and labor reserved for military use, the government had prohibited civilian housing construction, except for projects designated for the defense industry in towns like Richmond. Stegner joined and then helped to lead a cooperative of middle- and working-class families who were all unable to find available housing. For the most part, college professors were not highly paid; the co-op included others of similar economic status—public school teachers, city employees, carpenters, and nurses. Of the first 150 families to join, three were African American.

Calling itself the Peninsula Housing Association of Palo Alto, the co-op purchased a 260-acre ranch adjacent to the Stanford campus and planned to build 400 houses as well as shared recreational facilities, a shopping area, a gas station, and a restaurant on commonly owned land. But banks would not finance construction costs nor issue mortgages to the co-op or to its members without government approval, and the FHA would not insure loans to a cooperative that included African American members. The cooperative's board of directors, including Stegner, recommended against complying with the demand that the cooperative reconstitute itself as an all-white organization, but the membership, attempting to appease the government, voted in January 1948 by a narrow 78–75 margin to compromise. The co-op proposed to include a quota system in its bylaws and deeds, promising that the proportion of African Americans in the Peninsula Housing Association would not exceed the proportion of African Americans in California's overall population.

This concession did not appease government officials, and the project stalled. Stegner and other board members resigned; soon afterward the cooperative was forced to disband because it could not obtain financing without government approval. In 1950, the association sold its land to a private developer whose FHA agreement specified that no properties be sold to African Americans. The builder then constructed individual homes for sale to whites in "Ladera," a subdivision that still adjoins the Stanford campus.

# III

OVER THE next few years, the number of African Americans seeking jobs and homes in and near Palo Alto grew, but no developer who depended on federal government loan insurance would sell to them, and no California state-licensed real estate agent would show them houses. But then, in 1954, one resident of a whites-only area in East Palo Alto, across a highway from the Stanford campus, sold his house to a black family.

Almost immediately Floyd Lowe, president of the California Real Estate Association, set up an office in East Palo Alto to panic white families into listing their homes for sale, a practice known as blockbusting. He and other agents warned that a "Negro invasion" was imminent and that it would result in collapsing property values. Soon, growing numbers of white owners succumbed to the scaremongering and sold at discounted prices to the agents and their speculators. The agents, including Lowe himself, then designed display ads with banner headlines—"Colored Buyers!"— which they ran in San Francisco newspapers. African Americans, desperate for housing, purchased the homes at inflated prices. Within a three-month period, one agent alone sold sixty previously white-owned properties to African Americans. The California real estate commissioner refused to take any action, asserting that while regulations prohibited licensed agents from engaging in "unethical practices," the exploitation of racial fear was not within the real estate commission's jurisdiction. Although the local real estate board would ordinarily "blackball" any agent who sold to a nonwhite buyer in the city's white neighborhoods (thereby denying the agent access to the multiple listing service upon which his or her business depended), once wholesale blockbusting began, the board was unconcerned, even supportive.

At the time, the Federal Housing Administration and Veterans Administration not only refused to insure mortgages for African Americans in designated white neighborhoods like Ladera; they also would not insure mortgages for whites in a neighborhood where African Americans were present. So once East Palo Alto was integrated, whites wanting to move into the area could no longer obtain government-insured mortgages. State-regulated insurance companies, like the Equitable Life Insurance Company and the Prudential Life Insurance Company, also declared that their policy was not to issue mortgages to whites in integrated neighborhoods. State insurance regulators had no objection to this stance. The Bank of America and other leading California banks had similar policies, also with the consent of federal banking regulators.

Within six years the population of East Palo Alto was 82 percent black. Conditions deteriorated as African Americans who had been excluded from other neighborhoods doubled up in single-family homes. Their East Palo Alto houses had been priced so much higher than similar properties for whites that the owners had difficulty making payments without additional rental income. Federal and state housing policy had created a slum in East Palo Alto.

With the increased density of the area, the school district could no longer accommodate all Palo Alto students, so in 1958 it proposed to create a second high school to accommodate the expanding student population. The district decided to construct the new school in the heart of what had become the East Palo Alto ghetto, so black students in Palo Alto's existing integrated building would have to withdraw, creating a segregated African American school in the eastern section and a white one to the west. The board ignored pleas of African American and liberal white activists that it draw an east-west school boundary to establish two integrated secondary schools.

In ways like these, federal, state, and local governments purposely created segregation in every metropolitan area of the nation. If it could happen in liberal San Francisco, then indeed, it not only could but did happen everywhere. That the San Francisco region was segregated by government policy is particularly striking because, in contrast to metropolitan areas like Chicago, Detroit, Cleveland, or Baltimore, northern California had few African Americans before migrants like Frank Stevenson arrived during World War II in search of jobs. The government was not following preexisting racial patterns; it was imposing segregation where it hadn't previously taken root.*

---

* If you inquire into the history of the metropolitan area in which you live, you will probably find ample evidence of how the federal, state, and local governments unconstitutionally used housing policy to create or reinforce segregation in ways that still survive.

*Detroit, 1943. A family moves into the segregated Sojourner Truth public housing project, having withstood equivocation by federal officials and rioting by white neighborhood residents.*

# 2

# PUBLIC HOUSING, BLACK GHETTOS

THE PURPOSEFUL USE of public housing by federal and local governments to herd African Americans into urban ghettos had as big an influence as any in the creation of our *de jure* system of segregation.

Most Americans have an image of public housing: groups of high-rise towers with few amenities like playgrounds or parks, packed next to one another in central city neighborhoods, plagued by crime and drugs, and filled with black (or Hispanic) mothers and their children. It's a mostly inaccurate image even today,* but it couldn't be further from the reality of public housing when it began in the mid-twentieth century. At that time public housing was mostly for working- and lower-middle-class white families. It was not heavily

---

* In New York City an unusually large share of public housing units are in high-rise buildings, but there high-rises are inhabited by people of all races, ethnicities, and social classes. This is not true elsewhere. Most public housing projects consist of garden apartments, low-rise walk-ups, and single-family homes or townhouses. The federal government stopped funding high-rise public housing in the 1970s, and the share of units in high-rises has been steadily declining.

subsidized, and tenants paid the full cost of operations with their rent. Public housing's original purpose was to give shelter not to those too poor to afford it but to those who could afford decent housing but couldn't find it because none was available.

In New York City, for example, from World War II to 1955, the housing authority constructed twenty large unsubsidized projects for middle-class families, all of whom paid rent that covered the housing cost. Many projects were attractive low-rise (six-story) developments, with trees, grassy areas, and park benches. In addition to giving priority to veterans, the authority maintained a list of twenty-one disqualifying factors for prospective tenants, including irregular employment history, single-parent family or an out-of-wedlock birth, criminal record, narcotic addiction, mental illness, poorly behaved children, poor housekeeping habits, and lack of sufficient furniture. To ensure that undesirable tenants were not accepted, the housing authority sent agents to inspect the condition in which applicants kept their previous homes (often shared with relatives). Couples had to show a marriage license before their application was accepted. The Boston Housing Authority had similar requirements for its middle-class projects for white families.

# I

THE FEDERAL government first developed housing for civilians—living quarters on military bases had long been in existence—during World War I, when it built residences for defense workers near naval shipyards and munitions plants. Eighty-three projects in twenty-six states housed 170,000 white workers and their families. African Americans were excluded, even from projects in northern and western industrial centers where they worked in significant numbers. Federal policy sometimes imposed racial segregation where it hadn't previously been established, forcing African Americans into overpopulated slums. When the war ended, the government sold off its existing projects to private real estate firms and canceled those that were not complete.

Beginning with the Great Depression of the 1930s and into

the early 1950s, working- and middle-class white as well as African American families faced a serious housing shortage. In the Depression only the affluent could afford to purchase homes or rent new apartments, so builders couldn't be induced to provide housing for others. World War II exacerbated the shortage because all construction material was appropriated for military purposes. Working- and lower-middle-class families doubled up with relatives, stayed in apartments that were too small for their growing families, or remained in emergency Quonset huts that had been put up toward the end of the war for returning veterans.

In response, President Franklin D. Roosevelt's New Deal created the nation's first public housing for civilians who were not engaged in defense work. Race determined the program's design. The administration constructed separate projects for African Americans, segregated buildings by race, or excluded African Americans entirely from developments.

Segregation in the administration's housing programs followed a pattern that was established by New Deal construction, employment, and jobs agencies. An early initiative was the Tennessee Valley Authority (TVA), created in 1933 to bring jobs and economic growth to a region whose suffering during the Depression had been unusually severe. In Norris, Tennessee, where the TVA was headquartered, the government developed a model village with 500 comfortable homes, leased to employees and construction workers. The village, though, was open only to whites, while the TVA housed its African American workers in shoddy barracks some distance away. A TVA official explained that the town was being reserved for whites because "Negroes do not fit into the program."

Other New Deal agencies shared this commitment to residential segregation. The Civilian Conservation Corps (CCC) established work camps for jobless youth and young adults. These camps were segregated not just in the South but often in the North as well. In New Jersey, for example, Governor Harold Hoffman refused to allow any camps for African American corps members because of what he termed "local resentment." The national CCC director, Robert Fechner, implemented a policy never to "force colored companies on localities that have openly declared their opposition to them." Initially, local administrators integrated some camps in western and midwestern states, but federal officials ordered racial segregation in these camps, too.

Many state and local governments refused to permit even segregated African American CCC camps within their borders. Federal officials accommodated these demands, locating camps for African Americans on nearby army bases or on national forest or park land. In Gettysburg, Pennsylvania, an African American CCC unit was assigned to work alongside a white one to restore the historic battleground. The white unit was housed near the town itself, but the town's residents objected to having the African American crew living in the vicinity, so the CCC set up a camp for the African American crew some twenty miles away.

## II

WHERE HOUSING was not merely the byproduct of a New Deal economic development or jobs program, like the TVA or CCC, but was the direct object of Roosevelt administration reform, segregation was even more rigid. New Deal housing efforts were initially created as a project of the Public Works Administration (PWA), established in 1933 shortly after Roosevelt took office. The PWA's goal was to alleviate a national housing shortage while creating jobs in construction. Secretary of the Interior Harold Ickes, who directed the effort, had been president of the Chicago branch of the National Association for the Advancement of Colored People (NAACP) in the 1920s and was one of the administration's few liberals on racial matters.

Although most officials intended public housing for middle- and working-class white families, Ickes's efforts resulted in African Americans occupying one-third of the units, an unprecedented government commitment to the housing needs of African Americans. But Ickes did not propose to integrate PWA developments. Of the PWA's forty-seven projects, seventeen were assigned to African Americans. Six others were segregated by building. The rest were for whites only.

Ickes established a "neighborhood composition rule": federal housing projects should reflect the previous racial composition of their neighborhoods. Projects in white areas could house only white tenants, those in African American areas could house only African American tenants, and only projects in already-integrated neighborhoods could house both whites and blacks. In Birmingham, Alabama, the PWA built a project restricted to African Americans in a neighborhood that the city had zoned for black residence only. The federal government took a similar approach in Miami, where it agreed to segregate housing for African Americans in areas that the city's planners had designated exclusively for black residents. A Miami civic leader explained to federal administrators that the sites were chosen to "remove the entire colored population" from places that had been reserved for white occupancy.

Despite its nominal rule of respecting the prior racial composition of neighborhoods—itself a violation of African Americans' constitutional rights—the PWA segregated projects even where there was no previous pattern of segregation. At the time, many urban neighborhoods contained both black and white (mostly immigrant) low-income families. The neighborhoods were integrated because workers of both races needed to live close to the downtown factory jobs to which they walked.*

The PWA designated many integrated neighborhoods as either white or black and then used public housing to make the designation come true—by installing whites-only projects in mixed neighborhoods it deemed "white" and blacks-only projects in those it deemed "colored."

The first PWA project, the Techwood Homes in Atlanta, opened in 1935. It was built on land cleared by demolishing the Flats, a low-income integrated neighborhood adjacent to downtown that had

---

* West Oakland, California, for example, was integrated—mostly white, but with a small black population—because the Pullman Company hired only African Americans as sleeping car porters. Oakland was the western rail terminus for intercontinental trains; the porters had to live close to the station. For similar reasons, African American baggage handlers in other cities also integrated downtown neighborhoods.

included 1600 families, nearly one-third of whom were African American. The PWA remade the neighborhood with 604 units for white families only. The Techwood project not only created a segregated white community, it also intensified the segregation of African American families who, evicted from their homes, could find new housing only by crowding into other neighborhoods where African Americans were already living. Some families evicted from the Flats settled in a segregated development, also created by the federal government, that later opened on the west side. But because public housing was intended not for poor but for lower-middle-class families, many of those displaced from the Flats had incomes that were insufficient to qualify. Instead, many had to double up with relatives or rent units created when other African American families subdivided their houses. A result of the government program, therefore, was the increased population density that turned the African American neighborhoods into slums.

In 1934, the city of St. Louis proposed to raze the DeSoto-Carr area, a tenement neighborhood on the near north side whose population was split nearly evenly between whites and African Americans. For the cleared site, the city proposed a whites-only low-rise project. When the federal government objected to the city's failure to accommodate African Americans, St. Louis agreed to a blacks-only project as well. In the end, St. Louis built a segregated development for African Americans in the DeSoto-Carr area, while it demolished another previously integrated neighborhood south of downtown to build a separate project for whites.

Across the Northeast and the Midwest, the PWA imposed segregation on integrated communities. In Cleveland, for example, the Central neighborhood had been a packed but racially mixed tenement community, housing African Americans along with Italian and Eastern European immigrants. Langston Hughes, the African American poet, playwright, and novelist, recounts in his autobiography that when he attended Central High School in the late 1910s, he dated a Jewish girl and his best friend was Polish. Over the next fifteen years, white families began to leave the Central neighborhood, and African Americans arrived. Yet many whites remained.

Despite the neighborhood's biracial history, the PWA constructed two segregated projects, one for African Americans (the Outhwaite Homes) and one for whites (the Cedar-Central apartments). Although there previously had been ethnic and racial clusters in the neighborhood, the PWA solidified its racial segregation. The PWA also built a third Cleveland project, Lakeview Terrace, developed, as its name suggests, in a more scenic location; it was exclusively for whites. Like many other PWA projects for white families—but rarely like those for African Americans—Lakeview Terrace included a community center, playgrounds, and plentiful green space, and it was decorated with murals.

PWA projects also concentrated African Americans in low-income neighborhoods in Detroit, Indianapolis, Toledo, and New York where, for example, the PWA created two segregated projects: the Williamsburg Homes in a white neighborhood was for whites, and the Harlem River Houses in a black neighborhood was for African Americans. Of the twenty-six projects built in the Northeast and Midwest, sixteen were reserved for whites, eight for African Americans, and two were internally segregated.

In 1937, Congress ended the PWA program of direct federal construction of public housing and required localities wanting such projects to establish their own agencies that could then build housing with federal subsidies provided by the newly created U.S. Housing Authority (USHA). The authority continued the policy of claiming to respect existing neighborhood racial characteristics while in practice creating new racially homogenous communities. The USHA manual warned that it was undesirable to have projects for white families "in areas now occupied by Negroes" and added: "The aim of the [local housing] authority should be the preservation rather than the disruption of community social structures which best fit the desires of the groups concerned." The manual stated that projects in previously integrated areas should be open to mixed occupancy, but this standard, like that of the PWA, was rarely honored.

The first USHA-funded projects were built in Austin, Texas, largely because of aggressive promotion by its congressman, Lyndon Johnson. Segregated projects were constructed for African Americans in East Austin's black neighborhood and for whites on the Westside. As elsewhere, the projects were used to create a more rigid segregation than had previously existed. Austin's city planners had recently developed a proposal that included shifting African Americans who were scattered throughout the city to a single Eastside ghetto; the public housing plan advanced this scheme.

Rosewood Courts, Austin's Eastside project for African Americans, was built on land obtained by condemning Emancipation Park, the site of an annual festival to commemorate the abolition of slavery. The park had been privately owned by a neighborhood association, the Travis County Emancipation Organization, and residents protested the condemnation of this community institution in which they took great pride. But their objections had no effect, despite the availability of other vacant land.

Certainly, many urban areas already had distinct African American neighborhoods when the PWA or USHA came on the scene; federal agencies cannot be charged with sole responsibility for segregation. But they reinforced it. In Chicago, for example, a substantial African American population in segregated neighborhoods predated the Depression. The PWA constructed four projects in that city. Two, the Julia C. Lathrop and Trumbull Park Homes for white families, were in previously all-white communities. African American families were assigned to the Ida B. Wells Homes in an African American neighborhood. The Jane Addams Houses, in a mostly white area that had some African Americans, was called "integrated": the PWA gave about 3 percent of the Jane Addams units to African Americans but segregated them in a designated section within the project.

It would be going too far to suggest that cities like these would have evolved into integrated metropolises were it not for New Deal public housing. But it is also the case that the federal government's housing rules pushed these cities into a more rigid segregation than otherwise would have existed. The biracial character of many neighborhoods presented opportunities for different futures than the segregated ones that now seem so unexceptional. Yet those opportunities were never seized.

# III

As THE nation prepared for war in 1940, Congress adopted the Lanham Act to finance housing for workers in defense industries. Lanham Act projects played a particularly important role in segregating urban areas—like Frank Stevenson's Richmond—where few African Americans had previously lived. In some cities, the government provided war housing only for whites, leaving African Americans in congested slums and restricting their access to jobs. In other cities, like Richmond, war housing was created for African American workers as well, but it was segregated. By the war's end, the Lanham Act had combined with PWA and USHA programs to create or solidify residential racial segregation in every metropolitan area they had touched.

When construction of civilian public housing resumed, it continued to promote segregation. Local governments, with federal support, were responsible for its racial character. Segregation violated constitutional rights whether it was federal, state, or local government that insisted upon it. The examples that follow—from the Northeast, Midwest, and Pacific Coast—reflect a racial design that prevailed throughout the country during the war and its aftermath.

In 1941, Boston began building the West Broadway project, designated for white middle-class occupancy only. It remained almost entirely white, with only a few token African Americans, until a legal complaint by civil rights groups in 1962 forced the city to cease excluding qualified African American applicants. Another Boston project from the 1940s, Mission Hill, had two sections: Mission Hill itself and across the street, the Mission Hill Extension. In 1962, 1,024 families, not one of them African American, lived in Mission Hill. At the Mission Hill Extension, 500 of 580 families were African American. Five years later, after Boston agreed to desegregate the developments, Mission Hill was still 97 percent white while the Mission Hill Extension had increased to 98 percent African American. One observer reported, "In the rental office there are two windows, one for Mission Hill and one for the Extension, and except for the absence of two signs saying

'white' and 'colored' it might be Birmingham, Alabama. There is liter-
ally a line of whites and a line of Negroes paying their rent."

Cambridge, home of Harvard University and the Massachusetts
Institute of Technology, also required segregation in its housing
projects. In 1935, the Cambridge Housing Authority, in coopera-
tion with the PWA, demolished a low-income tenement neighborhood that had been integrated, mostly by African Americans and
European immigrants. There the authority built Newtowne Court,
restricted to white tenants. Later, in 1940, local and federal agencies
again worked together to establish Washington Elms, an adjoining
segregated project for African Americans.

In Detroit, a substantial population of African Americans had
arrived during World War I seeking jobs in munitions plants;
most lived in racially separate neighborhoods. Shortly before
the United States entered World War II in 1941, the government
commissioned a bomber plant in Willow Run, a previously undeveloped suburban area with no preexisting racial housing arrangement. Nonetheless, when the government built a new community
for the workers, its policy was that only whites could live there.

At the time, the Federal Works Agency (FWA) had also been
given responsibility for constructing temporary housing for war
workers. Clark Foreman, its director, proposed a Detroit development, the Sojourner Truth Homes, for African Americans. The
project was in the district of Democratic Congressman Rudolph
Tenerowicz, who persuaded his colleagues that funding for the
agency should be cut off unless Foreman was fired and the Sojourner
Truth units were assigned only to whites.

The director of the Federal Housing Administration supported
Tenerowicz, stating that the presence of African Americans in the
area would threaten property values of nearby residents. Foreman was
forced to resign. The Federal Works Agency then proposed a different project for African Americans on a plot that the Detroit Housing
Commission recommended, in an industrial area deemed unsuitable
for whites. It soon became apparent that this site, too, would provoke
protests because it was not far enough away from a white neighborhood. First Lady Eleanor Roosevelt protested to the president. The

FWA again reversed course and assigned African Americans to the Sojourner Truth project. Whites in the neighborhood rioted, leading to one hundred arrests (all but three were African Americans) and thirty-eight hospitalizations (all but five were African Americans).

Following the war, Detroit's politicians mobilized white voters by stirring up fear of integration in public housing. Mayor Edward Jeffries's successful 1945 reelection campaign warned that projects with African Americans could be located in white neighborhoods if his opponent, Dick Frankensteen, won. Jeffries's literature proclaimed, "Mayor Jeffries Is Against Mixed Housing." One leaflet, distributed in white neighborhoods but pretending to be addressed to African Americans, suggested that a vote for Frankensteen would bring black families to white communities. It read:

NEGROES CAN LIVE ANYWHERE
WITH FRANKENSTEEN MAYOR.

NEGROES – DO YOUR DUTY NOV. 6.

By the late 1940s, as white families increasingly found shelter in the private market, more African American than white families remained dependent on public housing. Projects built for whites ran the danger of having vacant units that only African Americans would want to fill. In 1948 and 1949, the Detroit City Council held hearings on twelve proposed projects, seven of which were to be situated in outlying (predominantly white) areas. If approved, they would have set Detroit on a hard-to-reverse trajectory of residential integration. But Jeffries's successor, Albert Cobo, who had also campaigned against "Negro invasions" in public housing, vetoed eight of the twelve, including all seven in the white neighborhoods. Only projects in predominantly African American areas were approved, further solidifying the city's segregation.

In northern California, Richmond was not the only community in which the government created segregation. The San Francisco Housing Authority, in 1942, constructed a massive development to house 14,000 workers and their families at the Hunters Point Naval

Shipyard and began to assign apartments on a nondiscriminatory first-come, first-served basis. The navy objected, insisting that integration would cause racial conflict among workers and interfere with ship repair. Local officials bowed to the navy's demand and moved African American tenants to separate sections.

Because discrimination by landlords left African American migrant war workers facing a greater housing shortage than whites, the authority's policy resulted in many vacant units in the white sections while black war workers' housing needs went unmet. The San Francisco Housing Authority attempted to recruit white tenants by placing advertisements in light-rail commuter cars, despite the long waiting lists of African Americans for apartments. This combination of vacant white units and waiting lists for black units increasingly characterized public housing nationwide.

San Francisco created five other projects during the war years, all segregated. Four were for whites only and were in white neighborhoods—Holly Courts, Potrero Terrace, Sunnydale, and Valencia Gardens. The fifth, Westside Courts in the Western Addition, was exclusively for African Americans.

The Western Addition had been a mixed community, including a large Japanese American population. But when the federal government relocated Japanese-origin families to internment camps, their residences were vacated, and African Americans were able to rent them, making this one of the few San Francisco neighborhoods where African Americans could find housing. By placing a segregated project in this integrated area, the housing authority propelled its transition to almost all-black. The authority seemed to follow a principle that if a neighborhood had even a few African American residents, it should become an African American neighborhood.

In 1942, the San Francisco authority announced its resolve to maintain segregation by unanimously adopting a resolution: "In the selection of tenants . . . [we shall] not insofar as possible enforce the commingling of races, but shall insofar as possible maintain and preserve the same racial composition which exists in the neighborhood where a project is located." One commissioner resigned in protest of the policy (which replicated the neighborhood composition rule that Harold Ickes had adopted). Responding to protests by civil rights groups and African American residents, the authority said it would cease discriminating, but by 1944 only five white families resided in the Westside Courts' 136 units, and no African Americans lived in the other developments. A housing authority commissioner explained that in Westside Courts "[w]e deliberately allowed a few white families to go in so as not to establish a purely Negro project." By the end of World War II, over one-third of San Francisco's African Americans, barred from private housing almost everywhere in the city, were residing in segregated public projects either in the Western Addition or in temporary Hunters Point barracks.

The only integrated war project in the Bay Area was one that housed shipyard workers in Marin County, across the Golden Gate Bridge from the city. The project was not integrated purposely; the first buildings were dormitories for single men, and the shipyard's rapid expansion left no time to separate the races. As workers flooded in, officials could barely keep up, just handing out blankets and pillows and assigning rooms that were available. Perhaps to their surprise, the officials found that integration presented few problems among the workers, so the biracial character of the project was maintained when workers' families arrived. After a few years, however, private housing in the area became available to whites, and the Marin project, too, became predominantly African American.

The waffling of San Francisco's elected leaders and housing administrators about whether to segregate public projects, like similar waffling in Boston and elsewhere, makes sense only if these officials knew that the segregation they imposed was wrong, if not unconstitutional. In 1949 the San Francisco Board of Supervisors adopted a resolution requiring "nonsegregation" for future housing projects and for filling vacancies on a nondiscriminatory basis. But the city's housing authority voted to reject the new policy, and as a result, all public housing construction was suspended. A compromise was eventually reached—the housing authority agreed not to discriminate in future projects, while maintaining its segregation policy in those already in existence. When the authority proceeded in 1952 to build one of its already-planned projects for whites only, the NAACP took it to court.

The case went to trial in 1953. The housing authority's chairman testified that the agency's intent was to "localize occupancy of Negroes" in the Western Addition and ensure that no African Americans would reside in projects inhabited by whites. The authority's executive secretary then made this concession: although projects in white neighborhoods would remain all white, the authority would admit more white applicants to its nearly all-black Westside Courts project and to Hunters Point (where black and white tenants remained segregated by building). It was a meaningless concession because whites were unlikely to apply to reside in Westside Courts now that they had rapidly increasing opportunities to move to the suburbs. Only a decision to assign African Americans to the all-white projects would have promoted integration, but such a proposal was not on offer by the authority. Temporary war units at Hunters Point still housed African Americans twenty-five years after the war ended. Although most whites had left Hunters Point by then, few African Americans could find homes or apartments elsewhere in the city or its environs.

The judge's decision was an NAACP victory: he ruled that the authority's policy violated the Fourteenth Amendment. A California appeals court upheld the finding, instructing San Francisco to abandon segregation and assign black families to projects outside the Western Addition. With contempt for the spirit of the court order, the authority established three new public housing projects in other areas that by then had few white residents, ensuring that segregation in these neighborhoods would be reinforced. Moreover, the California decision was not widely imitated. Nationwide, segregation in public housing remained the rule.

## IV

HARRY TRUMAN became president upon Roosevelt's death in 1945. By the time he was elected in his own right in 1948, the lack of civilian housing had reached a crisis. The millions of returning World War II veterans and their baby boom families needed shelter, and there was a severe shortage. In 1949, Truman proposed a new public housing effort. Conservative Republicans had long opposed any government involvement in the private housing market; they had supported the Lanham Act as a war measure only because it contained a commitment that all federal housing for war workers would be demolished or taken over by localities after hostilities ceased. To defeat Truman's bill, they attempted to saddle the legislation with an amendment prohibiting segregation and racial discrimination in public housing. The conservatives knew that if such an amendment were adopted, southern Democrats would kill the legislation. Without the amendment, the southerners would support public housing as they had other progressive economic legislation throughout the Roosevelt and Truman administrations, provided the bills did not challenge segregation. Many southern Democrats particularly wanted public housing for white constituents in their own districts and states.

Liberals, led by Minnesota Senator Hubert Humphrey and Illinois Senator Paul Douglas, had to choose between enacting a segregated public housing program or no program at all. On the Senate floor, Douglas proclaimed: "I should like to point out to my Negro friends what a large amount of housing they will get under this act. . . . I am ready to appeal to history and to time that it is in the best interests of the Negro race that we carry through the housing program as planned rather than put in the bill an amendment which will inevitably defeat it." The Senate and House rejected the proposed integration amendments, and the 1949 Housing Act was adopted, permitting local authorities to continue to design separate public housing projects for blacks and whites or to segregate blacks and whites within projects.

Whether such segregation was in anyone's best interests is doubtful. True, without the public housing, tens of thousands of African Americans would have had to remain in tenements that were out of compliance with the most minimal municipal building and health codes. But with the segregated projects, African Americans became more removed from mainstream society than ever, packed into high-rise ghettos where community life was impossible, where access to jobs and social services was more difficult, and where supervision of adolescents and even a semblance of community policing was impractical.

The NAACP, for one, was unwilling to sacrifice integration for more housing and supported the 1949 integration amendment, despite its cynical sponsorship. So did a few congressional radicals, led by Vito Marcantonio of New York, who argued on the House floor that "you have no right to use housing against civil rights. . . . Housing is advanced in the interest of the general welfare and in the interest of strength[en]ing democracy. When you separate civil rights from housing you weaken that general welfare."

In the wake of Congress's repudiation of integration, government administrators reiterated a commitment to segregation, insisting that they could not impose by regulation what Congress specifically rejected. The director of the federal Division of Slum Clearance justified the use of redevelopment funds to demolish black neighborhoods and replace them with housing for whites, saying "it does not appear reasonable to assume that . . . we can impose an anti-segregation requirement . . . in light of the Congressional intention as evidenced by its vote on [the amendment]."

With funds from the 1949 act, massive segregated high-rise projects were constructed nationwide, including the Robert Taylor and Cabrini Green Homes in Chicago, Rosen Homes and Schuylkill Falls in Philadelphia, Van Dyke Houses in New York City, and the Pruitt-Igoe towers in St. Louis. Although public housing was rapidly becoming a program exclusively for African Americans, working-class whites were accommodated in places where they still needed housing. The Igoe towers, for example, were initially reserved for whites only, while Pruitt was for African Americans. Black families were accepted in Igoe only when whites could no longer be found to fill vacancies.

In about a dozen states (among them California, Iowa, Minnesota, Virginia, and Wisconsin), the few suburban officials who may have wanted integrated developments were prevented by state constitutional amendments, adopted in the 1950s, that required a local referendum before building a low-income family public housing project. Middle-class white communities then systematically vetoed public housing proposals. A lower federal court found such referenda requirements unconstitutional because their racial motivation was so obvious—referenda were not required, for example, for low-income senior citizen housing. But in 1971 the Supreme Court ruled otherwise, upholding the referendum provisions on the grounds that they preserved democratic decision making.

In 1952, its last year in office, the Truman administration had adopted a new "racial equity formula" that required local housing authorities that practiced segregation to build separate projects to house low-income black families in proportion to their need, an attempt to address a pervasive situation in which large numbers of white-designated units remained vacant while African Americans stayed impatiently on overflowing waiting lists.

Dwight D. Eisenhower succeeded Truman as president in 1953, becoming the first Republican to hold the office in twenty years. A political realignment, with Republicans becoming more conservative than northern Democrats on matters of racial equality, was under way. Soon the new administration began to reverse the few halting steps toward nondiscrimination that the Roosevelt and Truman administrations had taken or considered. Following the Supreme Court's 1954 decision invalidating "separate but equal" public education, Berchmans Fitzpatrick, general counsel of the Housing and Home Finance Agency, stated that the decision did not apply to housing. In 1955, President Eisenhower's housing administrator told a congressional committee that the government should not "move too precipitously" to eliminate racial segregation from federal programs. The administration formally abolished a policy (it had never been enforced) that African Americans and whites receive public housing of equal quality. It also ended even nominal adherence to requirements that local housing authorities give priority to the neediest applicants, regardless of race, and that the net supply of housing available to African Americans not be reduced by demolition projects.

In the 1950s some housing authorities built scatter-site rather than concentrated units, having recognized that high-rise ghettos for the poor aggravated residents' desperation and generated more crime. They also hoped that scattered units would provoke less opposition from whites. In the mid-1970s, the federal government began to recommend that cities use their public housing funds this way. Yet most cities, Chicago and Philadelphia being extreme examples, continued to situate public housing in predominantly low-income African American neighborhoods. A few municipalities did begin to use funds for scatter-site projects, but these were typically cities with small low-income African American populations.

Public housing authorities not only continued to choose segregated sites for new developments but made efforts to segregate existing projects where integration might have been tolerated. In 1960, for example, the Housing Authority of Savannah evicted all white families from its integrated Francis Bartow project, creating an all-black complex. The authority justified its policy by observing that with national (and local) housing shortages abating, whites could easily find homes elsewhere and African Americans needed the public projects more.

In 1984, investigative reporters from the *Dallas Morning News* visited federally funded developments in forty-seven metropolitan areas. The reporters found that the nation's nearly ten million public housing tenants were almost always segregated by race and that every predominantly white-occupied project had facilities, amenities, services, and maintenance that were superior to what was found in predominantly black-occupied projects.

## V

BY THE 1960's, when few white families were still living in urban public housing, civil rights groups had little remaining reason to challenge the discriminatory assignment of tenants. Instead, their focus shifted to opposing the placement of what had become predominantly African American projects in already-segregated neighborhoods, increasing residents' racial isolation.

In 1976 the Supreme Court adopted lower court findings that the Chicago Housing Authority (CHA), with the complicity of federal housing agencies, had unconstitutionally selected sites to maintain the city's segregated landscape. Although the authority had suggested tracts that would integrate white neighborhoods, each project was subject to veto by the alderman in whose ward it was proposed. In his ruling, the district judge who originally heard the case wrote, "No criterion, other than race, can plausibly explain the veto of over 99½% of the housing units located on the White sites which were originally selected on the basis of CHA's expert judgment and at the same time the rejection of only 10% or so of the units on Negro sites."

In the years leading up to the final ruling, the City of Chicago had blocked efforts by the CHA and the Department of Housing and Urban Development (HUD) to comply with consent decrees and lower court decisions. In 1971, for example, CHA officials identified land for new projects that included some predominantly white areas. Unlike the high-rises the agency had built to concentrate public housing in a black ghetto, these proposals were for low-rise, scatter-site housing. But they still would have had African American tenants. Mayor Richard J. Daley rejected the proposal, saying that public housing should not go where it was not "accepted."

In defending HUD before the Supreme Court, President Gerald Ford's solicitor general, Robert Bork, expressed the government's opposition to placing public housing in white areas: "There will be an enormous practical impact on innocent communities who have to bear the burden of the housing, who will have to house a plaintiff class from Chicago, which they wronged in no way." Thus the federal government described nondiscriminatory housing policy as punishment visited on the innocent.

The Supreme Court rejected Bork's objection, upholding lower court orders that HUD must henceforth construct apartments in predominantly white areas of Chicago and its suburbs. The CHA-HUD response was to cease building public housing altogether. Yet even if the CHA, HUD, and the City of Chicago itself had complied with the Supreme Court's decision and built units in the city's white communities, it mostly would have been too late. The litigation had dragged on for years, during which time most of the vacant land in white neighborhoods that could have been used for scatter-site housing had been developed. Following the Supreme Court decision, the separation of African American from other families in Chicago increased. As whites in integrated urban neighborhoods departed for the suburbs, the Chicago area's share of African Americans living in all-black areas grew.

Other federal court decisions or settlements—in Baltimore, Dallas, San Francisco, Yonkers, and elsewhere—also recognized that HUD or local governments had created or perpetuated segregation. In Miami, for example, African Americans eligible for public housing were assigned to distinct projects while eligible whites were given vouchers for rentals of private apartments to subsidize their dispersal throughout the community. It was not until 1998 that civil rights groups won a requirement that vouchers be offered to African Americans as well—too late to reverse the city's segregation. In most other cities, court orders and legal settlements were also not sufficient to undo the segregation that federal, state, and local government had created and abetted.

# VI

FROM THE beginning, the real estate industry bitterly fought public housing of any kind and had support from Republicans in Congress. Industry lobbyists insisted that socialism in housing was a threat to private enterprise, a difficult argument to make when, from the 1930s to the end of World War II, private enterprise had been unwilling or unable to build dwellings affordable for working- and middle-class families. But once the housing shortage eased, the real estate lobby was successful in restricting public housing to subsidized projects for the poorest families only. New federal and local regulations set forth strict upper-income limits for families in public housing. Beginning in about 1950, many middle-class families, white and black, were forced out under these new rules, although many would have preferred to stay in the low-rise, scatter-site, and well-maintained projects that mostly characterized pre-1949 public dwellings.

This policy change, mostly complete by the late 1960s, ensured that integrated public housing would cease to be possible. It transformed public housing into a warehousing system for the poor. The condition of public projects rapidly deteriorated, partly because housing authority maintenance workers and their families had to leave the buildings where they worked when their wages made them ineligible to live there, and partly because the loss of middle-class rents resulted in inadequate maintenance budgets. The federal government had required public housing to be made available only to families who needed substantial subsidies, while the same government declined to provide sufficient subsidies to make public housing a decent place to live. The loss of middle-class tenants also removed a constituency that had possessed the political strength to insist on adequate funds for their projects' upkeep and amenities. As a result, the condition and then the reputation of public housing collapsed. By 1973 the changeover was mostly complete. President Richard Nixon announced that public housing should not be forced on white communities that didn't want it, and he reported to Congress that many public housing projects were "monstrous, depressing places—rundown, overcrowded, crime-ridden."

Throughout the mid-twentieth century, government housing projects frequently defined the racial character of neighborhoods that endured for many years afterward. Reflecting on public housing in his state, Carey McWilliams, who had been California's housing commissioner in the early years of World War II, later wrote that "the federal government [had] in effect been planting the seeds of Jim Crow practices throughout the region under the guise of 'respecting local attitudes.'" We can only wonder what our urban areas would look like today if, instead of creating segregation where it never, or perhaps barely, existed, federal and local governments had pushed in the opposite direction, using public housing as an example of how integrated living could be successful.

# LOOK At These Homes NOW!

An entire block ruined by negro invasion. Every house marked "X" now occupied by negroes. ACTUAL PHOTOGRAPH OF 4300 WEST BELLE PLACE.

## SAVE YOUR HOME! VOTE FOR SEGREGATION!

 73

*St. Louis, 1916. Leaflet urging voters to adopt a referendum that prohibited African Americans from moving onto predominantly white blocks.*

# 3

# RACIAL ZONING

WE LIKE TO think of American history as a continuous march of progress toward greater freedom, greater equality, and greater justice. But sometimes we move backward, dramatically so. Residential integration declined steadily from 1880 to the mid-twentieth century, and it has mostly stalled since then.

## I

AFTER THE Civil War, liberated slaves dispersed throughout the United States, seeking work and to escape the violence of the postwar South. For several decades many lived relatively peacefully in the East, the Midwest, and the West. But in 1877 the disputed presidential election of the previous autumn was resolved in a compromise that gave the Republican candidate, Rutherford B. Hayes, the White House. In return for southern Democratic support of their presidential candidate, Republicans agreed to withdraw federal troops who had been protecting African Americans in the defeated Confederacy. The period of black liberation known as Reconstruction then came to an end. In the South, the former slaveholding aristocracy renewed African Americans' subjugation. Supported by a campaign of violence against the newly emancipated slaves, southern states adopted segregation statutes—Jim Crow laws. Denied the right to vote, segregated in public transportation, schools, and private accommodations, and victimized by lynching and other forms of brutality, African Americans in the South were reduced again to a lower-caste status. Plantation owners redefined their former slaves as sharecroppers to maintain harsh and exploitative conditions.

Events in the African American town of Hamburg, in the Edgefield District of South Carolina, were typical of many others across the former Confederacy where white paramilitary groups mobilized to regain control of state governments. Their aim was simple: prevent African Americans from voting. In July 1876, a few months before the election that gave the presidency to Hayes, a violent rampage in Hamburg abolished the civil rights of freed slaves. Calling itself the Red Shirts, a collection of white supremacists killed six African American men and then murdered four others whom the gang had captured. Benjamin Tillman led the Red Shirts; the massacre propelled him to a twenty-four-year career as the most vitriolic racist in the U.S. Senate.

Following the massacre, the terror did not abate. In September, a "rifle club" of more than 500 whites crossed the Savannah River from Georgia and camped outside Hamburg. A local judge begged the governor to protect the African American population, but to no avail. The rifle club then moved on to the nearby hamlet of Ellenton, killing as many as fifty African Americans. President Ulysses S. Grant then sent in federal troops, who temporarily calmed things down but did not eliminate the ongoing threats.

Employers in the Edgefield District told African Americans they would be fired, and landowners threatened black sharecroppers with eviction if they voted to maintain a biracial state government. When the 1876 election took place, fraudulent white ballots were cast; the total vote in Edgefield substantially exceeded the entire voting age population. Results like these across the state gave segregationist Democrats the margin of victory they needed to seize control of South Carolina's government from the black-white coalition that had held office during Reconstruction. Senator Tillman later bragged that "the leading white men of Edgefield" had decided "to seize the first opportunity that the Negroes might offer them to provoke a riot and teach the Negroes a lesson."

Although a coroner's jury indicted Tillman and ninety-three other Red Shirts for the murders, they were never prosecuted and continued to menace African Americans. Federal troops never again came to offer protection. The campaign in Edgefield was of a pattern followed not only in South Carolina but throughout the South.

With African Americans disenfranchised and white supremacists in control, South Carolina instituted a system of segregation and exploitation that persisted for the next century. In 1940, the state legislature erected a statue honoring Tillman on the capitol grounds, and in 1946 Clemson, one of the state's public universities, renamed its main hall in Tillman's honor. It was in this environment that hundreds of thousands of African Americans fled the former Confederacy in the first half of the twentieth century.*

## II

As the Jim Crow atmosphere intensified in the South, fear (turning to hatred) of African Americans began to spread beyond that region. Throughout the country, whites came to assume black perversity and inferiority. Consider a state as seemingly improbable as Montana where African Americans thrived in the post–Civil War years. In the early 1900s they were systematically expelled from predominantly white communities in the state. Public officials supported and promoted this new racial order.

The removal of African Americans was gradual. By 1890, black

---

* Only in 2015, after the murder of nine black church members by a white supremacist youth in Charleston, did the trustees of Clemson adopt a resolution dissociating themselves from Tillman's "campaign of terror against African Americans in South Carolina that included intimidation and violence." But the trustees can't take his name off the hall unless the state legislature authorizes it, and the legislature has not done so.

settlers were living in every Montana county. By 1930, though, eleven of the state's fifty-six counties had been entirely cleared of African Americans, and in the other counties few remained. The African American population of Helena, the state capital, peaked at 420 (3.4 percent) in 1910. It was down to 131 by 1930, and only 45 remained by 1970. By 2010 the 113 African Americans in Helena comprised less than half of one percent of the city's population.

At the turn of the twentieth century, African Americans in Helena had included an established middle-class community, alongside those who came as laborers or to work on the railroads and in Montana's mines. The police officer assigned to patrol one of Helena's wealthiest white neighborhoods was an African American. Helena's African Methodist Episcopal Church was important enough in 1894 to host its denomination's western regional conference. The city had black newspapers, black-owned businesses, and a black literary society that sometimes drew one hundred attendees to hear presentations by poets, playwrights, and essayists. But in 1906, Helena's prosecuting attorney expressed the new attitude of public authorities when he announced, "It is time that the respectable white people of this community rise in their might and assert their rights." Helena's newspaper called the prosecutor's statement masterful and eloquent. Three years later Montana banned marriages between blacks and whites.

During this era many towns across the country adopted policies forbidding African Americans from residing or even from being within town borders after dark. Although the policies were rarely formalized in ordinances, police and organized mobs enforced them. Some towns rang bells at sundown to warn African Americans to leave. Others posted signs at the town boundaries warning them not to remain after sundown.

A 1915 newspaper article in Glendive, Montana, was headlined "Color Line Is Drawn In Glendive." It noted that the town's policy was that "the sun is never allowed to set on any niggers in Glendive" and boasted that the town's black population was now a "minus quantity." The town of Roundup posted a sign banning African Americans from remaining overnight. In Miles City a once-substantial African American community was forced to flee by white mob violence. In 1910, 81

African Americans comprised 2 percent of the Miles City population. Today it has only 25, or 0.3 percent.

## III

THE IMPOSITION of a new African American subordination eventually spread to the federal government as well. In Washington, D.C., in the late nineteenth and early twentieth centuries, African Americans in the federal civil service had been making great progress; some rose to positions whose responsibilities included supervising white office workers and manual laborers. This came to an end when Woodrow Wilson was elected president in 1912. Although he had served as president of Princeton University in New Jersey, and then as governor of that state, his origins were in the South, and he was an uncompromising believer in segregation and in black inferiority. At Princeton, for example, he refused to consider African Americans for admission.

In 1913, Wilson and his cabinet approved the implementation of segregation in government offices. Curtains were installed to separate black and white clerical workers. Separate cafeterias were created. Separate basement toilets were constructed for African Americans. Black supervisors were demoted to ensure that no African American oversaw a white employee. One official responsible for implementing segregation was the assistant secretary of the navy: Franklin Delano Roosevelt. He might or might not have been enthusiastic about segregation, but it was an aspect of the changing national political culture in which he matured and that he did not challenge.

## IV

IN THIS early-twentieth-century era, when African Americans in the South faced terror that maintained them in subjugation, when African Americans throughout the nation were being driven from small towns where they had previously enjoyed a measure of integration and safety, and when the federal government had abandoned its African American civil servants, we should not be surprised to learn that there was a new dedication on the part of public officials to ensure that white families' homes would be removed from proximity to African Americans in large urban areas.

Unlike public housing, which was primarily a federal program with some local participation, government policies to isolate white families in all-white urban neighborhoods began at the local level. As African Americans were being driven out of smaller midwestern and western communities like those in Montana, many other cities, particularly in southern and border states, already had large black populations that couldn't be expelled. Instead, many of these cities adopted zoning rules decreeing separate living areas for black and white families.

The first to do so was Baltimore, which in 1910 adopted an ordinance prohibiting African Americans from buying homes on blocks where whites were a majority and vice versa. Milton Dashiel, the lawyer who drafted Baltimore's ordinance, explained:

> Ordinarily, the negro loves to gather to himself, for he is very gregarious and sociable in his nature. But those who have risen somewhat above their fellows appear to have an intense desire to leave them behind, to disown them, as it were, and get as close to the company of white people as circumstances will permit them.

The segregation ordinance, he said, was needed to prevent this.

The troubles Baltimore encountered in applying the ordinance reflected just how integrated some areas of the city were. Soon after it adopted the ordinance, the city pursued twenty prosecutions to evict wrong-race residents. Judges had to grapple with such questions as whether an African American should be allowed to buy a home on a block that was evenly divided between white and black. A white homeowner moved out while his house was being repaired but then couldn't move back because the block was 51 percent black. An African American pastor of a church with an African American congregation complained to the mayor that because his church was on a mostly white block, the pastor who succeeded him would be forbidden to move into the parsonage. Eventually, the ordinance was revised so that it applied only to blocks that were entirely white or black, leaving Baltimore's integrated blocks unaffected.

Many southern and border cities followed Baltimore and adopted similar zoning rules: Atlanta, Birmingham, Dade County (Miami), Charleston, Dallas, Louisville, New Orleans, Oklahoma City, Richmond (Virginia), St. Louis, and others. Few northern cities did so; before the Great Migration stimulated by the First World War, most northern urban black populations were still small. Nonetheless support for these segregation ordinances was widespread among white political and opinion leaders. In 1915, *The New Republic*, still in its infancy but already an influential magazine of the Progressive movement, argued for residential racial segregation until Negroes ceased wanting to "amalgamate" with whites—which is to say, ceased wanting to engage in relationships that produced mixed-race children. The article's author apparently did not realize that race amalgamation in the United States was already considerably advanced, resulting from the frequent rapes of slaves by white masters.

In 1917, the Supreme Court overturned the racial zoning ordinance of Louisville, Kentucky, where many neighborhoods included both races before twentieth-century segregation. The case, *Buchanan v. Warley*, involved an African American's attempt to purchase property on an integrated block where there were already two black and eight white households. The Court majority was enamored of the idea that the central purpose of the Fourteenth Amendment was not to protect the rights of freed slaves but a business rule: "freedom of contract." Relying on this interpretation, the Court had struck down minimum wage and workplace safety laws on the grounds that they interfered with the right of workers and business owners to negotiate individual employment conditions without government interference. Similarly, the Court ruled that racial zoning ordinances interfered with the right of a property owner to sell to whomever he pleased.

Many border and southern cities ignored the *Buchanan* decision. One of the nation's most prominent city planners, Robert Whitten, wrote in a 1922 professional journal that notwithstanding the *Buchanan* decision, "[e]stablishing colored residence districts has removed one of the most potent causes of race conflict." This, he added, was "a sufficient justification for race zoning. . . . A reasonable segregation is normal, inevitable and desirable." Whitten then went ahead and designed a zoning ordinance for Atlanta, advising city officials that "home neighborhoods had to be protected from any further damage to values resulting from inappropriate uses, including the encroachment of the colored race." The zone plan drafted by Whitten and published by the Atlanta City Planning Commission in 1922 explained that "race zoning is essential in the interest of the public peace, order and security and will promote the welfare and prosperity of both the white and colored race." The zoning law divided the city into an "R-1 white district" and an "R-2 colored district" with additional neighborhoods undetermined.

Challenged in court, Atlanta defended its law by arguing that the *Buchanan* ruling applied only to ordinances identical to Louisville's. Atlanta's was different, its lawyers contended, because it designated whole neighborhoods exclusively for black or white residence, without regard to the previous majority-race characteristics of any particular block. The lawyers also claimed that the Louisville decision didn't apply because Atlanta's rules addressed only where African Americans and whites could live, not who could purchase the property. The Georgia Supreme Court rejected this argument in 1924, finding Whitten's plan unconstitutional, but Atlanta officials continued to use the racial zoning map to guide its planning for decades to come.

Other cities continued to adopt racial zoning ordinances after *Buchanan*, insisting that because their rules differed slightly from Louisville's, the Court's prohibition didn't apply. In 1926, Indianapolis adopted a regulation permitting African Americans to move to a white area only if a majority of its white residents gave their written consent, although the city's legal staff had advised that the ordinance was unconstitutional. In 1927, the Supreme Court overturned a similar New Orleans law that required a majority vote of opposite-race neighbors.

Richmond, Virginia, attempted a sly evasion of *Buchanan*. In 1924, the state adopted a law banning interracial marriage, so the city then prohibited anyone from residing on a street where they were ineligible to marry a majority of those already living there. Municipal lawyers told federal courts that *Buchanan* did not apply because their city's racial zoning law was solely intended to prevent intermarriage and its interference with residential property rights was incidental. In 1930 the Supreme Court rejected this reasoning.

Birmingham, like Atlanta, defended a racial zoning law with claims that *Buchanan* banned only sales of property to persons of the other race, not residence in an other-race district; the city also argued that threats to peace were so imminent and severe if African Americans and whites lived in the same neighborhoods that the need to maintain order should trump the constitutional rights involved. After a lower court banned Birmingham's ordinance in 1947, the city claimed that the ban applied only to the single piece of property involved in the court case, then increased criminal penalties for future violations. The city commission (council) president stated that "this matter goes beyond the written law, in the interest of . . . racial happiness." Birmingham continued to administer its racial zoning ordinance until 1950, when a federal appeals court finally struck it down.

In Florida, a West Palm Beach racial zoning ordinance was adopted in 1929, a dozen years after *Buchanan*, and was maintained until 1960. The Orlando suburb of Apopka adopted an ordinance banning blacks from living on the north side of the railroad tracks and whites from living on the south side. It remained in effect until 1968. Other cities, like Austin and Atlanta, continued racial zoning without specific ordinances by designating African American areas in official planning documents and using these designations to guide spot zoning decisions. Kansas City and Norfolk continued this practice until at least 1987.

But in cities that respected *Buchanan* as the law, segregationist officials faced two distinct problems: how to keep lower-income African Americans from living near middle-class whites and how to keep middle-class African Americans from buying into white middle-class neighborhoods. For each of these conditions, the federal and local governments developed distinct solutions.

# V

IN 2014, police killed Michael Brown, a young African American man in Ferguson, a suburb of St. Louis. Protests followed, some violent, and subsequent investigations uncovered systematic police and government abuse of residents in the city's African American neighborhoods. The reporting made me wonder how the St. Louis metropolitan area became so segregated. It turns out that economic zoning—with a barely disguised racial overlay—played an important role.

To prevent lower-income African Americans from living in neighborhoods where middle-class whites resided, local and federal officials began in the 1910s to promote zoning ordinances to reserve middle-class neighborhoods for single-family homes that lower-income families of all races could not afford. Certainly, an important and perhaps primary motivation of zoning rules that kept apartment buildings out of single-family neighborhoods was a social class elitism that was not itself racially biased. But there was also enough open racial intent behind exclusionary zoning that it is integral to the story of *de jure* segregation. Such economic zoning was rare in the United States before World War I, but the *Buchanan* decision provoked urgent interest in zoning as a way to circumvent the ruling.

St. Louis appointed its first plan commission in 1911 and five years later hired Harland Bartholomew as its full-time planning engineer. His assignment was to categorize every structure in the city—single-family residential, multifamily residential, commercial, or industrial—and then to propose rules and maps to prevent future multifamily, commercial, or industrial structures from impinging on single-family neighborhoods. If a neighborhood was covered with single-family houses with deeds that prohibited African American occupancy, this was taken into consideration at plan commission meetings and made it almost certain that the neighborhood would be zoned "first-residential," prohibiting future construction of anything but single-family units and helping to preserve its all-white character.

According to Bartholomew, an important goal of St. Louis zoning was to prevent movement into "finer residential districts . . . by colored people." He noted that without a previous zoning law, such neighborhoods have become run-down, "where values have depreciated, homes are either vacant or occupied by colored people." The survey Bartholomew supervised before drafting the zoning ordinance listed the race of each building's occupants. Bartholomew attempted to estimate where African Americans might encroach so the commission could respond with restrictions to control their spread.

The St. Louis zoning ordinance was eventually adopted in 1919, two years after the Supreme Court's *Buchanan* ruling banned racial assignments; with no reference to race, the ordinance pretended to be in compliance. Guided by Bartholomew's survey, it designated land for future industrial development if it was in or adjacent to neighborhoods with substantial African American populations.

Once such rules were in force, plan commission meetings were consumed with requests for variances. Race was frequently a factor. For example, one meeting in 1919 debated a proposal to reclassify a single-family property from first-residential to commercial because the area to the south had been "invaded by negroes." Bartholomew persuaded the commission members to deny the variance because, he said, keeping the first-residential designation would preserve homes in the area as unaffordable to African Americans and thus stop the encroachment.

On other occasions, the commission changed an area's zoning from residential to industrial if African American families had begun to move into it. In 1927, violating its normal policy, the commission authorized a park and playground in an industrial, not residential, area in hopes that this would draw African American families to seek housing nearby. Similar decision making continued through the middle of the twentieth century. In a 1942 meeting, commissioners explained they were zoning an area in a commercial strip as multifamily because it could then "develop into a favorable dwelling district for Colored people." In 1948, commissioners explained they were designating a U-shaped industrial zone to create a buffer between African Americans inside the U and whites outside.

In addition to promoting segregation, zoning decisions contributed to degrading St. Louis's African American neighborhoods into slums. Not only were these neighborhoods zoned to permit industry, even polluting industry, but the plan commission permitted taverns, liquor stores, nightclubs, and houses of prostitution to open in African American neighborhoods but prohibited these as zoning violations in neighborhoods where whites lived. Residences in single-family districts could not legally be subdivided, but those in industrial districts could be, and with African Americans restricted from all but a few neighborhoods, rooming houses sprang up to accommodate the overcrowded population.

Later in the twentieth century, when the Federal Housing Administration (FHA) developed the insured amortized mortgage as a way to promote homeownership nationwide, these zoning practices rendered African Americans ineligible for such mortgages because banks and the FHA considered the existence of nearby rooming houses, commercial development, or industry to create risk to the property value of single-family areas. Without such mortgages, the effective cost of African American housing was greater than that of similar housing in white neighborhoods, leaving owners with fewer resources for upkeep. African American homes were then more likely to deteriorate, reinforcing their neighborhoods' slum conditions.

# VI

LOCAL OFFICIALS elsewhere, like those in St. Louis, did not experiment with zoning in isolation. In the wake of the 1917 *Buchanan* decision, the enthusiasm of federal officials for economic zoning that could also accomplish racial segregation grew rapidly. In 1921 President Warren G. Harding's secretary of commerce, Herbert Hoover, organized an Advisory Committee on Zoning to develop a manual explaining why every municipality should develop a zoning ordinance. The advisory committee distributed thousands of copies to officials nationwide. A few months later the committee published a model zoning law. The manual did not give the creation of racially homogenous neighborhoods as the reason why zoning should become such an important priority for cities, but the advisory committee was composed of outspoken segrega- tionists whose speeches and writings demonstrated that race was one basis of their zoning advocacy.

One influential member was Frederick Law Olmsted, Jr., a for- mer president of the American City Planning Institute and of the American Society of Landscape Architects. During World War I, Olmsted Jr. directed the Town Planning Division of the federal gov- ernment's housing agency that managed or built more than 100,000 units of segregated housing for workers in defense plants. In 1918, he told the National Conference on City Planning that good zoning policy had to be distinguished from "the legal and constitutional question" (meaning the *Buchanan* rule), with which he wasn't con- cerned. So far as policy went, Olmsted stated that "in any housing developments which are to succeed, . . . racial divisions . . . have to be taken into account. . . . [If] you try to force the mingling of people who are not yet ready to mingle, and don't want to mingle," a development cannot succeed economically.

Another member of the advisory committee was Alfred Bett- man, the director of the National Conference on City Planning. In 1933 President Franklin D. Roosevelt appointed him to a National Land Use Planning Committee that helped to establish planning commissions in cities and states throughout the country. Planning (i.e., zoning) was necessary, Bettman and his colleagues explained, to "maintain the nation and the race."

The segregationist consensus of the Hoover committee was reinforced by members who held positions of leadership in the National Association of Real Estate Boards, including its president, Irving B. Hiett. In 1924, two years after the advisory committee had published its first manual and model zoning ordinance, the association followed up by adopting a code of ethics that included this warning: "a realtor should never be instrumental in introducing into a neighborhood . . . members of any race or nationality . . . whose presence will clearly be detrimental to property values in that neighborhood."

Other influential zoning experts made no effort to conceal their expectation that zoning was an effective means of racial exclusion. Columbia Law School professor Ernst Freund, the nation's leading authority on administrative law in the 1920s, observed that preventing "the coming of colored people into a district" was actually a "more powerful" reason for the spread of zoning during the previous decade than creation of single-family districts, the stated justification for zoning. Because the *Buchanan* decision had made it "impossible to find an appropriate legal formula" for segregation, Freund said that zoning masquerading as an economic measure was the most reasonable means of accomplishing the same end.

Secretary Hoover, his committee members, and city planners across the nation believed that zoning rules that made no open reference to race would be legally sustainable—and they were right. In 1926, the Supreme Court for the first time considered the constitutionality of zoning rules that prohibited apartment buildings in single-family neighborhoods. The decision, arising from a zoning ordinance in a Cleveland suburb, was a conspicuous exception to the Court's rejection of regulations that restricted what an owner could do with his property. Justice George Sutherland, speaking for the Court, explained that "very often the apartment house is a mere parasite, constructed in order to take advantage of the open spaces and attractive surroundings created by the residential character of the district" and that apartment houses in single-family districts "come very near to being nuisances." In reaching this decision, the Supreme Court had to overrule the findings of a district judge who would have preferred to uphold the zoning ordinance but could not pretend ignorance of its true racial purpose, a violation of *Buchanan*. The judge explained, "The blighting of property values and the congesting of the population, whenever the colored or certain foreign races invade a residential section, are so well known as to be within the judicial cognizance."

In the years since the 1926 Supreme Court ruling, numerous white suburbs in towns across the country have adopted exclusionary zoning ordinances to prevent low-income families from residing in their midst. Frequently, class snobbishness and racial prejudice were so intertwined that when suburbs adopted such ordinances, it was impossible to disentangle their motives and to prove that the zoning rules violated constitutional prohibitions of racial discrimination. In many cases, however, like Secretary Hoover's experts, localities were not always fastidious in hiding their racial motivations.

The use of zoning for purposes of racial segregation persisted well into the latter half of the twentieth century. In a 1970 Oklahoma case, the segregated town of Lawton refused to permit a multiunit development in an all-white neighborhood after residents circulated a petition in opposition. They used racial appeals to urge citizens to sign, although the language of the petition itself did not mention race. The sponsors of the apartment complex received anonymous phone calls that expressed racial antagonism. In a subsequent lawsuit, the only member of the planning commission who voted to allow the project testified that bias was the basis of other commissioners' opposition. Although the commission did not use race as the reason for denying the permit, a federal appeals court found that the stated reasons were mere pretexts. "If proof of a civil rights violation depends on an open statement by an official of an intent to discriminate, the Fourteenth Amendment offers little solace to those seeking its protection," the court concluded.

Yet the appeals court view did not prevail in other cases. A few years later, in 1977, the Supreme Court upheld a zoning ordinance in Arlington Heights, a suburb of Chicago, that prohibited multiunit development anywhere but adjacent to an outlying commercial area. The ordinance ensured that few, if any, African Americans could reside in residential areas. The city council had adopted its zoning ordinance at a meeting where members of the public urged action for racially discriminatory reasons. Letters to the local newspaper urged support for the ordinance as a way to keep African Americans out of white neighborhoods. But despite the openly racial character of community sentiment, the Supreme Court said the ordinance was constitutional because there was no proof that the council members themselves had adopted the ordinance to exclude African Americans specifically and not exclude all lower-income families, regardless of race.

My purpose, however, is not to argue courtroom standards of proof. I am interested in how we got to the systematic racial segregation we find in metropolitan areas today, and what role government played in creating these residential patterns. We can't prove what was in council members' hearts in Arlington Heights or anywhere else, but in too many zoning decisions the circumstantial evidence of racial motivation is persuasive. I think it can fairly be said that there would be many fewer segregated suburbs than there are today were it not for an unconstitutional desire, shared by local officials and by the national leaders who urged them on, to keep African Americans from being white families' neighbors.

# VII

THE USE of industrial, even toxic waste zoning, to turn African American neighborhoods into slums was not restricted to St. Louis. It became increasingly common as the twentieth century proceeded and manufacturing operations grew in urban areas. The pattern was confirmed in a 1983 analysis by the U.S. General Accounting Office (GAO), concluding that, across the nation, commercial waste treatment facilities or uncontrolled waste dumps were more likely to be found near African American than white residential areas.

Studies by the Commission for Racial Justice of the United Churches of Christ and by Greenpeace, conducted at about the same time as the GAO report, concluded that race was so strong a statistical predictor of where hazardous waste facilities could be found that there was only a one-in-10,000 chance of the racial distribution of such sites occurring randomly, and that the percentage of minorities living near incinerators was 89 percent higher than the national median. Skeptics of these data speculated that African Americans moved to such communities after these facilities were present. But while this may sometimes have been the case—after all, most African Americans had limited housing choices—it cannot be the full explanation: neighborhoods with proposed incinerators, not those already built, had minority population shares that were much higher than the shares in other communities.

Decisions to permit toxic waste facilities in African American areas did not intend to intensify slum conditions, although this was the result. The racial aspect of these choices was a desire to avoid the deterioration of white neighborhoods when African American sites were available as alternatives. The welfare of African Americans did not count for much in this policy making. Oftentimes, as in St. Louis, zoning boards made explicit exceptions to their residential neighborhood rules to permit dangerous or polluting industry to locate in African American areas.

In Los Angeles, for example, a black community became established in the South Central area of the city in the 1940s. The neighborhood had some industry, but its nonresidential character was more firmly entrenched when the city began a process of "spot" rezoning for commercial or industrial facilities. Automobile junkyards became commonplace in the African American neighborhood. In 1947, an electroplating plant explosion in this newly developing ghetto killed five local residents (as well as fifteen white factory workers) and destroyed more than one hundred homes. When later that year the pastor of an African American church protested a rezoning of property adjacent to his church for industrial use, the chairman of the Los Angeles City Council's planning committee, responsible for the rezoning, responded that the area had now become a "business community," adding, "Why don't you people buy a church somewhere else?"

For the most part, courts have refused to reject toxic siting decisions without proof of explicit, stated intent to harm African Americans because of their race. In a 1979 Houston case, an African American community that already had a disproportionately high number of hazardous waste sites protested the addition of another. A federal judge found that the proposal was "unfortunate and insensitive" but refused to ban it without proof of explicit racial motivation. A 1991 case arose in Warren County, North Carolina, whose overall population was about half white and half African American. The county had three existing landfills, all in African American areas. When a new landfill was proposed for a white area, residents protested, and county officials did not issue a permit. But when another was proposed, this time in an African American area, county officials ignored residents' protests and approved the land-fill. A federal judge upheld the county's decision, finding that there was a discriminatory impact but no explicit racial intent.

In 1991, the Environmental Protection Agency issued a report confirming that a disproportionate number of toxic waste facilities were found in African American communities nationwide. President Bill Clinton then issued an executive order requiring that such disparate impact be avoided in future decisions. The order did not, however, require any compensatory actions for the existing toxic placements.

The frequent existence of polluting industry and toxic waste plants in African American communities, along with subdivided homes and rooming houses, contributed to giving African Americans the image of slum dwellers in the eyes of whites who lived in neighborhoods where integration might be a possibility. This, in turn, contributed to white flight when African Americans attempted to move to suburbs.

Zoning thus had two faces. One face, developed in part to evade a prohibition on racially explicit zoning, attempted to keep African Americans out of white neighborhoods by making it difficult for lower-income families, large numbers of whom were African Americans, to live in expensive white neighborhoods. The other attempted to protect white neighborhoods from deterioration by ensuring that few industrial or environmentally unsafe businesses could locate in them. Prohibited in this fashion, polluting industry had no option but to locate near African American residences. The first contributed to creation of exclusive white suburbs, the second to creation of urban African American slums.

*Detroit, 1941. The Federal Housing Administration required a developer to build a wall separating his whites-only project from nearby African American residences.*

# 4

## "OWN YOUR OWN HOME"

EXCLUSIONARY ZONING ORDINANCES could be, and have been, successful in keeping low-income African Americans, indeed all low-income families, out of middle-class neighborhoods. But for those wanting to segregate America, zoning solved only half the problem. Zoning that created neighborhoods of only single-family homes could not keep out middle-class African Americans. Herbert Hoover's seemingly race-neutral zoning recommendations could not prevent African Americans who could afford to live in expensive communities from doing so.

Frequently, the African Americans who attempted to pioneer the integration of white middle-class neighborhoods were of higher social status than their white neighbors, and they were rarely of lower status. The incident that provoked Baltimore to adopt its racial zoning ordinance in 1910 was a prominent African American lawyer moving onto a majority white block. Economic zoning without racial exclusion could not have prevented Frank Stevenson or his African American co-workers from moving into Milpitas subdivisions where many of their white Ford union brothers were settling.

To ban Frank Stevenson and his friends, different tools were needed. The federal government developed them in full contempt of its constitutional obligations. First, the government embarked on a scheme to persuade as many white families as possible to move from urban apartments to single-family suburban homes. Then, once suburbanization was under way, the government, with explicit racial intent, made it nearly impossible for African Americans to follow.

I

THE FEDERAL government's policy of racial exclusion had roots earlier in the twentieth century. The Wilson administration took the initial steps. Terrified by the 1917 Russian revolution, government officials came to believe that communism could be defeated in the United States by getting as many white Americans as possible to become homeowners—the idea being that those who owned property would be invested in the capitalist system. So in 1917 the federal Department of Labor promoted an "Own-Your-Own-Home" campaign, handing out "We Own Our Own Home" buttons to schoolchildren and distributing pamphlets saying that it was a "patriotic duty" to cease renting and to build a single-family unit. The department printed more than two million posters to be hung in factories and other businesses and published newspaper advertisements throughout the country promoting single-family ownership—each one had an image of a white couple or family.

Here, too, Secretary of Commerce Herbert Hoover played an important role. Upon assuming office in 1921, he not only developed a campaign to encourage exclusionary zoning, but to complement that effort, he also headed up a new Better Homes in America organization. Although it was nominally private, Hoover served as president. The executive director was James Ford, who had overseen Frederick Law Olmsted, Jr., when he designed the whites-only public housing program during World War I. The chairman of its advisory council was Vice President Calvin Coolidge, and a member was the president of the American Construction Council, Franklin D. Roosevelt.

Hoover boasted that the organization was "practically directed by the Department," which published a pamphlet, "How to Own Your Own Home," and conducted other promotional activities. It sponsored forums in communities across the nation on the benefits of property ownership, including how to avoid "racial strife." Such strife, Better Homes representatives probably told audiences, could be avoided by moving to single-family houses away from African Americans in urban areas. In 1923, another department publication promoted ethnic and racial homogeneity by urging potential home buyers to consider the "general type of people living in the neighborhood" before making a purchase.

Later, as president, Hoover asserted that it was "self-evident" that "every thrifty family has an inherent right to own a home." He convened the President's Conference on Home Building and Home Ownership, hoping, in the depths of the Depression, to revive housing construction and sales. In his opening address, he told the conference that single-family homes were "expressions of racial longing" and "[t]hat our people should live in their own homes is a sentiment deep in the heart of our race."

On the eve of the conference, Better Homes in America published *The Better Homes Manual*, a compendium of housing recommendations from the organization's leaders. James Ford explained that apartments were the worst kind of housing, frequently overcrowded because of the "ignorant racial habit" of African Americans and European immigrants. John Gries, director of the president's conference, and James S. Taylor, chief of the Department of Commerce's housing division, listed thirty items a prospective purchaser should consider. In the midst of the advice—such as use a dependable real estate expert, and make sure there is good transportation to work— was item number nineteen: "Buy partnership in the community. 'Restricted residential districts' may serve as protection against persons with whom your family won't care to associate, provided the restrictions are enforced and are not merely temporary." There was little doubt about who the persons to be avoided might be.

The conference documents themselves, written and endorsed by some of the nation's most prominent racial segregationists, clarified what restricted residential districts should accomplish. One member of the conference planning committee was Frederick Ecker, president of the Metropolitan Life Insurance Company, who chaired a committee on financing homeownership. His report, adopted and published by the federal government, recommended that zoning laws be supplemented by deed restrictions to prevent "incompatible owner- ship occupancy"—a phrase generally understood to mean prevention of property sales to African Americans. Under Ecker's leadership, a few years after the conference concluded, Metropolitan Life developed the largest planned community in the nation, Parkchester in New York City, from which African Americans were barred. When one apartment was sublet to a black family, Ecker had them evicted.

The Hoover conference's committee on planning new subdivisions included Robert Whitten, who had designed Atlanta's racial zoning scheme in 1922 that flouted the Supreme Court's *Buchanan* decision. Another was Lawrence Stevenson, president-elect of National Association of Real Estate Boards, which had recently adopted its ethics rule prohibiting agents from selling homes to African Americans in white neighborhoods. The committee was headed by Harland Bartholomew, who ten years earlier had led the St. Louis Plan Commission in using zoning to evade *Buchanan*, while enforcing segregation.

One of the conference's thirty-one committees was devoted to Negro housing. Its report was written by the prominent social scientist, Charles S. Johnson, with help from other African American experts. It documented violence against African Americans who attempted to live in previously white neighborhoods but issued no call for measures to prevent this. With just a hint of disapproval, it described court permission for zoning and other legal devices to impose segregation. It concluded by recommending "the removal of legislation restrictive of Negro residence" and "that Negroes follow the trend in urban communities and move out into subdivisions in which modern homes can be built." The report did not address the inconsistency of such proposals with the conference's endorsement of residential segregation. Most of Johnson's report was devoted to recommending improvements in the quality of urban apartments where African Americans were forced to live in northern cities.

The Johnson report on Negro housing garnered little attention, and the federal government's insistence that African Americans be excluded from single-family suburbs became more explicit during the New Deal. As with the public housing programs of the PWA, federal promotion of homeownership became inseparable from a policy of racial segregation.

## II

ALTHOUGH THE federal government had been trying to persuade middle-class families to buy single-family homes for more than fourteen years, the campaign had achieved little by the time Franklin D. Roosevelt took office in 1933. Homeownership remained prohibitively expensive for working- and middle-class families: bank mortgages typically required 50 percent down, interest-only payments, and repayment in full after five to seven years, at which point the borrower would have to refinance or find another bank to issue a new mortgage with similar terms. Few urban working- and middle-class families had the financial capacity to do what was being asked.

The Depression made the housing crisis even worse. Many property-owning families with mortgages couldn't make their payments and were subject to foreclosure. With most others unable to afford homes at all, the construction industry was stalled. The New Deal designed one program to support existing homeowners who couldn't make payments, and another to make first-time homeownership possible for the middle class.

In 1933, to rescue households that were about to default, the administration created the Home Owners' Loan Corporation (HOLC). It purchased existing mortgages that were subject to imminent foreclosure and then issued new mortgages with repayment schedules of up to fifteen years (later extended to twenty-five years). In addition, HOLC mortgages were amortized, meaning that each month's payment included some principal as well as interest, so when the loan was paid off, the borrower would own the home. Thus, for the first time, working- and middle-class homeowners could gradually gain equity while their properties were still mortgaged. If a family with an amortized mortgage sold its home, the equity (including any appreciation) would be the family's to keep.

HOLC mortgages had low interest rates, but the borrowers still were obligated to make regular payments. The HOLC, therefore, had to exercise prudence about its borrowers' abilities to avoid default. To assess risk, the HOLC wanted to know something about the condition of the house and of surrounding houses in the neighborhood to see whether the property would likely maintain its value. The HOLC hired local real estate agents to make the appraisals on which refinancing decisions could be based. With these agents required by their national ethics code to maintain segregation, it's not surprising that in gauging risk HOLC considered the racial composition of neighborhoods. The HOLC created color-coded maps of every metropolitan area in the nation, with the safest neighborhoods colored green and the riskiest colored red. A neighborhood earned a red color if African Americans lived in it, even if it was a solid middle-class neighborhood of single-family homes.

For example, in St. Louis, the white middle-class suburb of Ladue was colored green because, according to an HOLC appraiser in 1940, it had "not a single foreigner or negro." The similarly middle-class suburban area of Lincoln Terrace was colored red because it had "little or no value today . . . due to the colored element now controlling the district." Although the HOLC did not always decline to rescue homeowners in neighborhoods colored red on its maps (i.e., redlined neighborhoods), the maps had a huge impact and put the federal government on record as judging that African Americans, simply because of their race, were poor risks.

To solve the inability of middle-class renters to purchase single-family homes for the first time, Congress and President Roosevelt created the Federal Housing Administration in 1934. The FHA insured bank mortgages that covered 80 percent of purchase prices, had terms of twenty years, and were fully amortized. To be eligible for such insurance, the FHA insisted on doing its own appraisal of the property to make certain that the loan had a low risk of default. Because the FHA's appraisal standards included a whites-only requirement, racial segregation now became an official requirement of the federal mortgage insurance program. The FHA judged that properties would probably be too risky for insurance if they were in racially mixed neighborhoods or even in white neighborhoods near black ones that might possibly integrate in the future.

When a bank applied to the FHA for insurance on a prospective loan, the agency conducted a property appraisal, which was also likely performed by a local real estate agent hired by the agency. As the volume of applications increased, the agency hired its own appraisers, usually from the ranks of the private real estate agents who had previously been working as contractors for the FHA. To guide their work, the FHA provided them with an *Underwriting Manual*. The first, issued in 1935, gave this instruction: "If a neighborhood is to retain stability it is necessary that properties shall continue to be occupied by the same social and racial classes. A change in social or racial occupancy generally leads to instability and a reduction in values." Appraisers were told to give higher ratings where "[p]rotection against some adverse influences is obtained," and that "[i]mportant among adverse influences . . . are infiltration of inharmonious racial or nationality groups." The manual concluded that "[a]ll mortgages on properties protected against [such] unfavorable influences, to the extent such protection is possible, will obtain a high rating."

The FHA discouraged banks from making any loans at all in urban neighborhoods rather than newly built suburbs; according to the *Underwriting Manual*, "older properties . . . have a tendency to accelerate the rate of transition to lower class occupancy." The FHA favored mortgages in areas where boulevards or highways served to separate African American families from whites, stating that "[n]atural or artificially established barriers will prove effective in protecting a neighborhood and the locations within it from adverse influences, . . . includ[ing] prevention of the infiltration of . . . lower class occupancy, and inharmonious racial groups."

The FHA was particularly concerned with preventing school desegregation. Its manual warned that if children "are compelled to attend school where the majority or a considerable number of the pupils represent a far lower level of society or an incompatible racial element, the neighborhood under consideration will prove far less stable and desirable than if this condition did not exist," and mortgage lending in such neighborhoods would be risky.

Subsequent editions of the *Underwriting Manual* through the 1940s repeated these guidelines. In 1947, the FHA removed words like "inharmonious racial groups" from the manual but barely pretended that this represented a policy change. The manual still specified lower valuation when "compatibility among the neighborhood occupants" was lacking, and to make sure there was no misunderstanding, the FHA's head told Congress that the agency had no right to require nondiscrimination in its mortgage insurance program. The 1952 *Underwriting Manual* continued to base property valuations, in part, on whether properties were located in neighborhoods where there was "compatibility among the neighborhood occupants."

FHA policy in this regard was consistent. In 1941, a New Jersey real estate agent representing a new development in suburban Fanwood, about twenty miles west of Newark, attempted to sell twelve properties to middle-class African Americans. All had good credit ratings, and banks were willing to issue mortgages if the FHA would approve. But the agency stated that "no loans will be given to colored developments." When banks told the real estate agent that without FHA endorsement they would not issue the mortgages, he approached the Prudential Life Insurance Company, which also said that although the applicants were all creditworthy, it could not issue mortgages unless the FHA approved. Today, Fanwood's population remains 5 percent black in a county with a black population of about 25 percent.

In 1958, a white San Francisco schoolteacher, Gerald Cohn, purchased a house with an FHA-guaranteed mortgage in the Elmwood district of Berkeley. By the closing date, Mr. Cohn wasn't ready to move in and, while keeping up his mortgage payments, rented the house to a fellow teacher, Alfred Simmons, an African American. The Berkeley chief of police asked the Federal Bureau of Investigation (FBI) to inquire how Mr. Simmons had managed to get into this all-white community. The bureau questioned Gerald Cohn's neighbors in San Francisco but failed to find evidence that he had obtained his mortgage under false pretenses—in other words, that he had never intended to occupy his Berkeley home but had always planned to rent to an African American. The FBI referred the case to the U.S. attorney, who refused to prosecute because no law had been broken. The FHA, however, then blacklisted Mr. Cohn, advising him that he would be "denied the benefits of participation in the FHA insurance program" and never again be able to obtain a government-backed mortgage. The director of the San Francisco FHA office wrote to him, "This is to advise you that any application for mortgage insurance under the programs of this Administration submitted by you or any firm in which you have ten per cent interest, will be rejected on the basis of an Unsatisfactory Risk Determination made by this office on April 30, 1959."

In thousands of communities between Fanwood and Berkeley, FHA policy was the same, with very few exceptions: no guarantees for mortgages to African Americans, or to whites who might lease to African Americans, regardless of the applicants' creditworthiness.

## III

A FEW years ago I received a note from Pam Harris, a schoolteacher in Georgia who had heard a radio program where I discussed the history of neighborhood racial segregation. As it happened, Ms. Harris' family traces its roots to Hamburg, South Carolina, the town where white terror persuaded many African Americans to seek safety and security in the North. Her family story, like that of Frank Stevenson, exposes how *de jure* segregation operated to establish the racial divisions we know today.

Ms. Harris told me about a great-uncle, Leroy Mereday, who was born in Hamburg fourteen years after the Red Shirt massacre. His father worked in the brickyards, and Leroy himself became a blacksmith, shoeing horses for the cavalry in France in World War I. There he caught the attention of railroad tycoon August Belmont II, who was serving in the U.S. Army's supply department. A passionate horse racer, he had built the Belmont Race Track on Long Island, New York. Impressed with Leroy Mereday's skill, Belmont asked him to work at his track. Mr. Mereday went on to have a successful career there, shoeing Man o' War, among other great thoroughbreds.

He found lodging in Hempstead, not far from the racetrack, and soon sent for a younger brother, Charles, who in turn persuaded brothers Arthur and Robert, sister Lillie, and their parents to come north. Charles recruited several classmates to join them. The extended Mereday family and other Hamburg refugees all initially lived on a single street in Hempstead, an early African American settlement on Long Island.

Robert Mereday, the youngest of the brothers, played the saxophone and in the 1930s was part of a well-known jazz ensemble. During World War II the federal government sponsored the United Service Organizations (USO) to support the troops and workers in defense plants, and he joined a USO band that entertained workers at the Grumman Aircraft plant in Bethpage, Long Island. The contacts Robert Mereday made there led to the company hiring him as one of its first African American employees. Grumman, like the Ford Motor Company in Richmond, California, had exhausted the supply of white workers available to meet its military contracts and had begun to recruit African Americans for the first time.

At Grumman, Robert Mereday was able to save money to start a trucking business when the war ended. He bought inexpensive army surplus trucks and repurposed them himself for heavy hauling. In 1946, when William Levitt was building houses for returning veterans in Roslyn, Long Island, the Mereday company got work hauling cement blocks that lined the development's cesspools. Soon Levitt began to develop the massive Levittown subdivision nearby, and Robert Mereday won a contract to deliver drywall to the construction site. His business expanded to half a dozen trucks; when several nephews returned from military service, they joined the company.

Robert Mereday had a solid middle-class income in the late 1940s and was able to pay his nephews decently. He had married and was raising a family, but Levitt and other subdivision developers would not sell homes to any of the Meredays or to other African Americans who were helping to build the nation's suburbs. African

Americans did not lack the necessary qualifications; the Meredays' economic circumstances were similar to those of the white workers and returning veterans who became Levittowners. But as Robert Mereday's son later recalled, his father and most other relatives didn't bother to file applications, although the Levittown homes were attractive and well designed: "It was generally known that black people couldn't buy into the development. When you grow up and live in a place, you know what the rules are."

Nonetheless one nephew who worked for the trucking business tried. Like most of those who moved into Levittown, Vince Mereday was a veteran. He'd been in the navy during World War II, stationed at the Great Lakes Naval Training Center outside Chicago. Just before the war, Secretary of the Navy Frank Knox had told President Roosevelt he would resign if the navy were forced to take African Americans in roles other than their traditional ones in food service and as personal servants to officers. However, when it became widely known that the most heroic American sailor at Pearl Harbor was Private Dorie Miller, an African American kitchen worker—he had run through flaming oil to carry his ship's captain to safety and then grabbed a machine gun and shot down Japanese aircraft—public pressure forced Knox to accede. At Great Lakes, however, African American recruits were not permitted to train with whites, and the navy established a segregated training camp for them. Vince Mereday passed tests to be a pilot, but because African Americans were barred from entering flight training, he was assigned to mechanic duty for the war's duration.

After the Japanese surrender in 1945, Vince Mereday went to work for his uncle delivering material to Levittown. When he attempted to buy a house in the development, his application was refused. Instead he bought a house in an almost all-black neighboring suburb, Lakeview. Although Levittowners could buy property with no down payments and low-interest Veterans Administration (VA) mortgages, Vince Mereday had to make a substantial down payment in Lakeview and get an uninsured mortgage with higher market interest rates. His experiences of discrimination in the navy and in the housing market permanently embittered him.

William Levitt's refusal to sell a home to Vince Mereday was not a mere reflection of the builder's prejudicial views. Had he felt differently and chosen to integrate Levittown, the federal government would have refused to subsidize him. In the decades following World War II, suburbs across the country—as in Milpitas and Palo Alto and Levittown—were created in this way, with the FHA administering an explicit racial policy that solidified segregation in every one of our metropolitan areas.

# IV

AFTER WORLD War II, the newly established VA also began to guarantee mortgages for returning servicemen. It adopted FHA housing policies, and VA appraisers relied on the FHA's *Underwriting Manual*. By 1950, the FHA and VA together were insuring half of all new mortgages nationwide.

The FHA had its biggest impact on segregation, not in its discriminatory evaluations of individual mortgage applicants, but in its financing of entire subdivisions, in many cases entire suburbs, as racially exclusive white enclaves. Frank Stevenson was not denied the opportunity to follow his job to Milpitas because the FHA refused to insure an individual mortgage for him. Vince Mereday was not denied the opportunity to live in Levittown because a VA appraiser considered his individual purchase too risky for a mortgage guarantee. Rather, in these and thousands of other locales, mass-production builders created entire suburbs with the FHA- or VA-imposed condition that these suburbs be all white. As Frank Stevenson and Robert Mereday understood, and as Vince Mereday learned, African Americans need not bother to apply.

Levittown was a massive undertaking, a development of 17,500 homes. It was a visionary solution to the housing problems of returning war veterans—mass-produced two-bedroom houses of 750 square feet sold for about $8,000 each, with no down payment required. William Levitt constructed the project on speculation; it was not a case in which prospective purchasers gave the company funds with which to construct houses. Instead, Levitt built the houses and then sought customers. He could never have amassed the capital for such an enormous undertaking without the FHA and the VA. But during the World War II years and after, the government had congressional authority to guarantee bank loans to mass-production builders like Levitt for nearly the full cost of their proposed subdivisions. By 1948, most housing nationwide was being constructed with this government financing.

Once Levitt had planned and designed Levittown, his company submitted drawings and specifications to the FHA for approval. After the agency endorsed the plans, he could use this approval to negotiate low-interest loans from banks to finance its construction and land-acquisition costs. The banks were willing to give these concessionary loans to Levitt and to other mass-production builders because FHA preapproval meant that the banks could subsequently issue mortgages to the actual buyers without further property appraisal needed. Instead of local FHA appraisers taking the *Underwriting Manual* and going out to inspect the individual properties for which mortgage insurance was sought—there was, after all, nothing but empty land to inspect—the FHA almost automatically insured mortgages for the eventual buyers of the houses, based on its approval of the preconstruction plans. The banks, therefore, were exposed to little risk from issuing these mortgages.

For Levittown and scores of such developments across the nation, the plans reviewed by the FHA included the approved construction materials, the design specifications, the proposed sale price, the neighborhood's zoning restrictions (for example, a prohibition of industry or commercial development), and a commitment not to sell to African Americans. The FHA even withheld approval if the presence of African Americans in *nearby* neighborhoods threatened integration. In short, the FHA financed Levittown on condition that, like the Richmond suburb of Rollingwood during the war, it be all white, with no foreseeable change in its racial composition.

*The Veterans Administration subsidized the "Sunkist Gardens" development in Southeast Los Angeles in 1950, for white veterans only.*

The FHA's involvement was so pervasive that full-time government inspectors were stationed at the construction sites where Levittown and similar projects were being built. As William Levitt testified before Congress in 1957, "We are 100 percent dependent on Government."

In 1960, a New Jersey court concluded that Levitt's project in that state was so dependent on the FHA that it was "publicly assisted housing" and that it therefore could not refuse to sell to African Americans under New Jersey law. The court opinion included a detailed description of the numerous ways in which the FHA directed the project's design, construction, and financing, as well as Levitt's acknowledgment of his dependence on government involvement. The case had no national consequences because the order to sell to African Americans was based on New Jersey, not federal, law.

Although Levittown came to symbolize postwar suburbanization, Levittown was neither the first nor the only such development financed by the FHA and VA for white families. Metropolitan areas nationwide were suburbanized by this government policy. The first was Oak Forest, built in 1946 on Houston's northwest side. Shortly thereafter Prairie Village in Kansas City mushroomed, also financed with FHA guarantees. The extraordinary growth of California and the West in the decades following World War II was financed on a racially restricted basis by the federal government: Westlake, a 1950 development in Daly City, south of San Francisco; Lakewood, south of Los Angeles, constructed between 1949 and 1953 and only slightly smaller than Levittown; Westchester, also south of Los Angeles and developed by Kaiser Community Homes, an offshoot of the wartime shipbuilding company; and Panorama City, in the San Fernando Valley—all were FHA whites-only projects.

## V

A St. Louis story illustrates how stark the FHA policy could be. Charles Vatterott was an area builder who obtained advance FHA guarantees for a subdivision of single-family homes in western St. Louis County. Vatterott called his development St. Ann and intended it to be a community for lower-middle-class Catholics, particularly returning war veterans. He began construction in 1943, and while he made a special effort to recruit Catholics, he did not prohibit sales to non-Catholic whites—he barred only blacks, as the FHA required.

Vatterott had relatively moderate attitudes on racial matters and believed that the housing needs of African Americans should also be addressed but in separate projects. So after completing St. Ann, he constructed a subdivision for African Americans—De Porres, in the town of Breckenridge Hills, a few miles away from St. Ann. He intended to sell to African Americans whose incomes and occupations, from truck drivers to chemists, were similar to those of St. Ann buyers. These were the kinds of potential purchasers who, if they were white, could have bought into St. Ann or any of the many other subdivisions developed throughout St. Louis County in the postwar period.

But because De Porres was intended for African Americans, Vatterott could not get FHA financing for it. As a result, the construction was shoddier and the house design skimpier than it had been in St. Ann. Because potential buyers were denied FHA or VA mortgages, many of the homes were rented. Vatterott set up a special savings plan by which families without FHA or VA mortgages could put aside money toward a purchase of their homes. But unlike St. Ann residents, the De Porres savers could not accumulate equity during this process. The De Porres development for African Americans also lacked the community facilities—parks and playgrounds—that Vatterott had built into the St. Ann subdivision.

# VI

WHEN THE FHA rejected proposals for projects like De Porres that might house African Americans or otherwise threaten future integration, the agency didn't mask the racial bases of its decisions. In 1940, for example, a Detroit builder was denied FHA insurance for a project that was near an African American neighborhood. He then constructed a half-mile concrete wall, six feet high and a foot thick, separating the two neighborhoods, and the FHA then approved the loan. Occasionally, FHA mortgage holders did default, and the agency repossessed the property and resold it. To make certain that such resale did not undermine its segregation policy, the FHA contracted with real estate brokers who refused to sell to African Americans.

On rare occasions, the FHA approved loans for segregated African American developments. In 1954, responding to a severe housing shortage for African Americans and hoping to dampen civil rights protests, New Orleans mayor DeLesseps S. Morrison begged the FHA to insure a development for middle-class black professionals and promised the agency that no units would be sold to whites. The New Orleans NAACP chapter protested the creation of a segregated housing development. The agency ignored the protest, and the development eventually consisted of one thousand homes for African Americans only, surrounding a park and golf course and adjoining a similar FHA-insured development for whites only. In 1955 an FHA spokesman toured fifty cities where he addressed African American audiences, boasting of New Orleans's achievements and telling his listeners that such segregated projects were "the type of thing [the] FHA wanted."

A pattern emerges from these examples. Government's commitment to separating residential areas by race began nationwide following the violent suppression of Reconstruction after 1877. Although the Supreme Court in 1917 forbade the first wave of policies—racial segregation by zoning ordinance—the federal government began to recommend ways that cities could evade that ruling, not only in the southern and border states but across the country. In the 1920s a Harding administration committee promoted zoning ordinances that distinguished single-family from multifamily districts. Although government publications did not say it in as many words, committee members made little effort to hide that an important purpose was to prevent racial integration. Simultaneously, and through the 1920s and the Hoover administration, the government conducted a propaganda campaign directed at white middle-class families to persuade them to move out of apartments and into single-family dwellings. During the 1930s the Roosevelt administration created maps of every metropolitan area, divided into zones of foreclosure risk based in part on the race of their occupants. The administration then insured white homeowners' mortgages if they lived in all-white neighborhoods into which there was little danger of African Americans moving. After World War II the federal government went further and spurred the suburbanization of every metropolitan area by guaranteeing bank loans to mass-production builders who would create the all-white subdivisions that came to ring American cities.

In 1973, the U.S. Commission on Civil Rights concluded that the "housing industry, aided and abetted by Government, must bear the primary responsibility for the legacy of segregated housing. . . . Government and private industry came together to create a system of residential segregation."

*Daly City, California, 1949. FHA district director D. C. McGinness drives a spike to inaugurate construction of a shopping center, part of the segregated Westlake housing development.*

# 5

## PRIVATE AGREEMENTS, GOVERNMENT ENFORCEMENT

BEFORE THE FHA sponsored whites-only suburbanization in the mid-twentieth century, many urban neighborhoods were already racially exclusive. Property owners and builders had created segregated environments by including language both in individual home deeds and in pacts among neighbors that prohibited future resales to African Americans. Proponents of such restrictions were convinced that racial exclusion would enhance their property values and that such deeds were mere private agreements that would not run afoul of constitutional prohibitions on racially discriminatory state action. The FHA adopted both of these theories.

But when the Supreme Court ruled in 1948 that racial clauses in deeds and mutual agreements, if truly private, could not depend on the power of government to enforce them, the FHA and other federal agencies evaded and subverted the ruling, preserving state-sponsored segregation for at least another decade.

# I

As EARLY as the nineteenth century, deeds in Brookline, Massachusetts, forbade resale of property to "any negro or native of Ireland." Such provisions spread throughout the country in the 1920s as the preferred means to evade the Supreme Court's 1917 *Buchanan* racial zoning decision.

The deed clauses were part of what are commonly termed "restrictive covenants," lists of obligations that purchasers of property must assume. The obligations included (and still do include) such matters as what color the owner promises to paint the outside window trim and what kind of trees the owner commits to plant in front. For the first half of the twentieth century, one commonplace commitment in this long list was a promise never to sell or rent to an African American. Typical restrictive language read like this from a 1925 covenant on a property in suburban northern New Jersey:

> There shall not be erected or maintained without the written consent of the party of the first part on said premises, any slaughter house, smith shop, forge furnace, steam engine, brass foundry, nail, iron or other foundry, any manufactory of gunpowder, glue, varnish, vitriol, or turpentine, or for the tanning dressing or preparing of skins, hides or leather, or for carrying on any noxious, dangerous or offensive trade; all toilet outhouses shall be suitably screened, no part of said premises shall be used for an insane, inebriate or other asylum, or cemetery or place of burial or for any structure other than a dwelling for people of the Caucasian Race.

Almost all such documents created exceptions for live-in household or childcare workers, like this passage from a 1950 covenant on property in the Westlake subdivision of Daly City, California:

> The real property above described, or any portion thereof, shall never be occupied, used or resided on by any person not of the white or Caucasian race, except in the capacity of a servant or

domestic employed theron as such by a white Caucasian owner, tenant or occupant.

The effectiveness of a house deed that contained a racial covenant was limited, however. If a white family sold a property to an African American, it was difficult (although not impossible) for a neighbor to establish standing in court to reverse the sale and have the black family evicted, because the covenant was a contract between the present and previous owner. If the contract was violated, the original owner, not a neighbor, was the directly injured party. The subdivision developer who initially inserted the clause in the deed might have had standing, but in most cases once he had sold each of the homes, he no longer had much interest in who the subsequent buyers might be.

So increasingly in the twentieth century, racial covenants took the form of a contract among all owners in a neighborhood. Under these conditions, a neighbor could sue if an African American family made a purchase. Sometimes owners created such contracts and persuaded all or most of their neighbors to sign. But this was also not fully satisfactory, because anyone who didn't sign might sell to an African American with little fear of being successfully sued.

To get around this problem, many subdivision developers created a community association before putting homes up for initial sale, and they made membership in it a condition of purchase. Association bylaws usually included a whites-only clause. In the 1920s, this tactic gained national prominence when developer J. C. Nichols constructed the Country Club District in Kansas City, which included 6,000 homes, 160 apartment buildings, and 35,000 residents. Nichols required each purchaser to join the district's association. Not only did its rules prohibit sales or rentals to black families, but this racial exclusion policy could not be modified without the assent of owners of a majority of the development's acreage. Nichols's developments were a racial model for the rest of Kansas City, which was soon covered by such agreements.

In the Northeast the pattern established in Brookline was pervasive. Around suburban New York City, for example, a survey of 300 developments built between 1935 and 1947 in Queens, Nassau, and

Westchester Counties found that 56 percent had racially restrictive covenants. Of the larger subdivisions (those with seventy-five or more units), 85 percent had them.

It was also the case in midwestern metropolises. By 1943, an estimated 175 Chicago neighborhood associations were enforcing deeds that barred sales or rentals to African Americans. By 1947, half of the city's residential area outside its African American areas had such deed restrictions. In Detroit from 1943 to 1965, white homeowners, real estate agents, or developers organized 192 associations to preserve racial exclusion.

And so it was, too, in the Great Plains. The Oklahoma Supreme Court in 1942 not only voided an African American's purchase of a property that was restricted by a racial covenant; it charged him for all court costs and attorney's fees, including those incurred by the white seller.

Cities and their suburbs in the West were also blanketed by racial covenants. Between 1935 and 1944 W. E. Boeing, the founder of Boeing Aircraft, developed suburbs north of Seattle. During this period and after World War II, the South Seattle Land Company, the Puget Mill Company, and others constructed more suburbs. These builders all wrote racially restrictive language into their deeds. The result was a city whose African American population was encircled by all-white suburbs. Boeing's property deeds stated, for example, "No property in said addition shall at any time be sold, conveyed, rented, or leased in whole or in part to any person or persons not of the White or Caucasian race." An African American domestic servant, however, was permitted to be an occupant. Within Seattle itself, numerous neighborhood associations sponsoring racial covenants were also formed during the first half of the twentieth century.

In Oakland, California, DeWitt Buckingham was a respected African American physician who had been a captain in the Army Medical Corps during World War II. After the war he established a medical practice serving the city's African American community, and in 1945, a white friend purchased and then resold a home to him in Claremont, a Berkeley neighborhood where many University of California professors and administrators lived. When the identity of the true buyer became known, the Claremont Improvement Club, a neighborhood association that controlled a covenant restricting the area to those of "pure Caucasian blood," sued. A state court ordered Dr. Buckingham to vacate the residence.*

In Los Angeles from 1937 to 1948, more than one hundred lawsuits sought to enforce restrictions by having African Americans evicted from their homes. In a 1947 case, an African American man was jailed for refusing to move out of a house he'd purchased in violation of a covenant.

The Westwood neighborhood, bordering the Los Angeles campus of the University of California, was segregated by such methods. In 1939, George Brown, later a congressman but then a nineteen-year-old UCLA student, was president of a cooperative housing association seeking a property. None was available to a group that refused to exclude African Americans. The association, however, went ahead and purchased a piece of property with a racial covenant that had the usual exception for live-in domestic servants. Brown's cooperative included a rule that each student must contribute five hours a week of cleaning, cooking, and shopping, so the student group obtained a legal opinion that each member of the cooperative was actually a domestic servant, and an African American student was then able to join. However, this gimmick did nothing to desegregate Westwood generally.

# II

GOVERNMENT AT all levels became involved in promoting and enforcing the restrictive covenants. Throughout the nation, courts ordered African Americans evicted from homes they had purchased. State supreme courts upheld the practice when it was challenged—in Alabama, California, Colorado, Kansas, Kentucky, Louisiana,

---

* The court order was under appeal when, in 1948, the Supreme Court forbade state court enforcement of restrictive covenants, so the Claremont Improvement Club was unable, in the end, to evict Dr. Buckingham.

Maryland, Michigan, Missouri, New York, North Carolina, West Virginia, and Wisconsin. In the many hundreds of such cases, judges endorsed the view that restrictive covenants did not violate the Constitution because they were private agreements.

Local governments aggressively promoted such covenants, undermining any notion that they were purely private instruments. For example, following the 1917 *Buchanan* decision, the mayor of Baltimore organized an official "Committee on Segregation," led by the city's chief legal officer. One of the committee's activities was to organize and support neighborhood associations that would adopt such agreements. In 1943, Culver City, an all-white suburb of Los Angeles, convened a meeting of its air raid wardens—their job was to make sure families turned off lights in the evening or installed blackout curtains to avoid helping Japanese bombers find targets. The city attorney instructed the assembled wardens that when they went door to door, they should also circulate documents in which homeowners promised not to sell or rent to African Americans. The wardens were told to focus especially on owners who were not already parties to long-term covenants.

The most powerful endorsement, however, came not from states or municipalities but from the federal government. In 1926, the same year that the U.S. Supreme Court upheld exclusionary zoning, it also upheld restrictive covenants, finding that they were voluntary private contracts, not state action. With this decision to rely upon, successive presidential administrations embraced covenants as a means of segregating the nation.

At President Hoover's 1931 conference on homeownership, Harland Bartholomew's committee on planning subdivisions recommended that all new neighborhoods should have "appropriate restrictions." To define "appropriate," the Bartholomew report referred conference participants to an earlier document, a 1928 review of deeds showing that thirty-eight of forty recently constructed developments barred sale to or occupancy by African Americans. The review observed that racial exclusion clauses were "in rather general use in the vicinity of the larger eastern and northern cities which have experienced an influx of colored people in recent years."

These prohibitions, it explained, benefited both the developer (by making his project more desirable to prospective buyers) and the owner (by protecting his property from "the deteriorating influence of undesirable neighbors"). The 1928 review assured planners that the racial clauses were legal because they required only private action in which the government was not involved.

What is remarkable about this assurance was its acknowledgment that any governmental involvement in segregation would violate the Constitution. There was evidently some defensiveness about the recent Supreme Court opinion that "private" racial deed language was constitutionally permissible. This may explain why the Bartholomew report recommended racial exclusion only obliquely, by referring conference participants to the 1928 report without itself repeating the recommendation verbatim. But this indirection could not mask that the federal government took a step toward involvement when the conference report adopted a recommendation that "appropriate" rules for new subdivisions included racial exclusion. It remained, however, for the Franklin D. Roosevelt administration to turn this recommendation into a requirement.

## III

FROM THE FHA's beginning, its appraisers not only gave high ratings to mortgage applications if there were no African Americans living in or nearby the neighborhood but also lowered their risk estimates for individual properties with restrictive deed language. The agency's earliest underwriting manuals recommended such ratings where "[p]rotection against some adverse influences is obtained by the existence and enforcement of proper zoning regulations and appropriate deed restrictions," and added that "[i]mportant among adverse influences . . . are infiltration of inharmonious racial or nationality groups."

The manual explained that if a home was covered by an exclusionary zoning ordinance—for example, one that permitted only single-family units to be constructed nearby—it would probably deserve a high rating, but such an ordinance itself was inadequate because it could not prevent middle-class African Americans from buying houses in the neighborhood. So the FHA recommended that deeds to properties for which it issued mortgage insurance should include an explicit prohibition of resale to African Americans. The 1936 manual summarized instructions to appraisers like this:

> 284 (2). Carefully compiled zoning regulations are the most effective because they not only exercise control over the subject property but also over the surrounding area. However, they are seldom complete enough to assure a homogeneous and harmonious neighborhood.

> 284 (3). Recorded deed restrictions should strengthen and supplement zoning ordinances. . . . Recommended restrictions include . . . [p]rohibition of the occupancy of properties except by the race for which they are intended [and a]ppropriate provisions for enforcement.

By "appropriate provisions for enforcement," the FHA meant the right of neighbors to seek a court order for the eviction of an African American purchaser or renter.

In developments with FHA production financing for builders, the agency recommended—and in many cases, demanded—that developers who received the construction loans it sponsored include racially restrictive covenants in their subdivisions' property deeds. When the federal government commissioned David Bohannon to build the all-white Rollingwood subdivision outside Richmond, California, it not only barred him from selling to African Americans but required that he include a racial exclusion in the deed of each property. When FHA racial policy made it necessary for Wallace Stegner's Peninsula Housing Association to disband its integrated housing cooperative, the private developer who purchased the Ladera property received FHA approval for a bank loan that obliged him to include restrictive covenants in his sales. When the St. Louis developer Charles Vatterott procured FHA-sponsored financing for his St. Ann suburb, he had to include language in the deeds stating that "no lot or portion of a lot or building erected thereon shall be sold, leased, rented or occupied by any other than those of the Caucasian race." And when the agency authorized production loans for the construction of Levittown, its standards included a racial covenant in each house deed.

In the FHA's finance program, a production builder who gained preapproval for loans frequently inserted language in property deeds with preambles such as "Whereas the Federal Housing Administration requires that the existing mortgages on the said premises be subject and subordinated to the said restrictions . . ." And when the VA began to guarantee mortgages after World War II, it also recommended and frequently demanded that properties with VA mortgages have racial covenants in their deeds.

# IV

THEN THE Supreme Court issued a ruling that was as much of an upheaval for housing policy as *Brown v. Board of Education* would be, six years later, for education. In 1948 the Court repudiated its 1926 endorsement of restrictive covenants and acknowledged that enforcement by state courts was unconstitutional. It was one thing, the Court ruled in *Shelley v. Kraemer*, for private individuals to discriminate. But deeds that barred sales to African Americans could be effective only if state courts enforced them by ordering black families to vacate homes purchased in white neighborhoods. Racial covenants' power depended upon the collaboration of the judicial system and as such violated the Fourteenth Amendment, which prohibits state governments from participating in segregation.

The Court, in a companion case decided on the same day, also banned the use of federal courts to enforce covenants in federal territory like Washington, D.C. A logical consequence of this decision was that if complicity in racial discrimination by federal courts constituted *de jure* segregation, then surely discrimination by executive branch agencies, like the FHA, also did so. Nonetheless, the federal government responded to *Shelley* and its federal companion case by attempting to undermine the Supreme Court decisions.

As would happen later with *Brown*, the response to the Court's ruling was massive resistance. But in the case of *Shelley*, the resistance came not so much from states as from federal agencies.

Two weeks after the Court announced its decision, FHA commissioner Franklin D. Richards stated that the *Shelley* decision would "in no way affect the programs of this agency," which would make "no change in our basic concepts or procedures." Richards added that it was not "the policy of the Government to require private individuals to give up their right to dispose of their property as they [see] fit, as a condition of receiving the benefits of the National Housing Act." Six months later, when Thurgood Marshall, then the NAACP legal counsel (and later a Supreme Court justice), challenged the FHA policy of requiring restrictive covenants in deeds of the massive Levittown development, Richards responded, "I find nothing in the [*Shelley* decision] to indicate that in the absence of statutory authority the government, or any agency thereof, is authorized to withdraw its normal protection and benefits from persons who have executed but do not seek judicial enforcement of such covenants."

A year after the *Shelley* decision, Berchmans Fitzpatrick, the chief counsel of the FHA's parent organization, the Housing and Home Finance Agency, revealed the contempt of federal officials for the ruling. Explaining that owners in a particular neighborhood would no longer be deemed ineligible for FHA insurance on the basis of inhabitants' race, he stated that henceforth "there must be some concrete, objective set of standards on which a writing down because of race is permitted." Fitzpatrick did not explain what objective standards could possibly justify denying mortgage insurance "because of race," but he was doubtlessly referring to the FHA's conviction that property values invariably declined if African American families lived nearby.

FHA field staff understood perfectly what Fitzpatrick had in mind. In 1948, a group of families had formed a cooperative to build and occupy sixty homes in Lombard, Illinois, a suburb about twenty miles west of Chicago. Like the cooperative that Wallace Stegner had helped lead in California, the Lombard group was racially inclusive, counting two African American families among its members. As it did when beseeched by Stegner and his colleagues, the FHA refused to insure mortgages for the cooperative because of its refusal to bar nonwhites. William J. Lockwood, the assistant commissioner of the FHA, wrote to the cooperative that the agency could not insure the project because "infiltration [of Negroes] will be unacceptable to the local real estate market." As Thurgood Marshall pointed out in a memo to President Truman, allowing local real estate markets to trump constitutional rights was no different from racial zoning ordinances found unconstitutional twenty years earlier, in which a vote of residents on a block could determine whether black families could move in.

In 1949, after the Supreme Court's *Shelley* decision, the leaders of the Lombard cooperative tried to persuade the FHA to reconsider. They met with the chief of the Chicago area FHA office and with the agency's chief underwriter for that region. The leaders protested that the federal government was creating the kind of segregation that *Shelley* was intended to prevent. The officials responded that they had "no responsibility for a social policy," that they were "just a business organization" that could consider only "the cold facts and the elements of risk," and that "an interracial community was a bad risk" that the FHA could not insure.

On December 2, 1949, a year and a half after the *Shelley* decision, U.S. solicitor general Philip Perlman announced that the FHA could no longer insure mortgages with restrictive covenants. But he said the new policy would apply only to those executed after February 15, 1950—two and half months after his announcement and nearly two years after the Supreme Court's ruling. This delay could only have been designed to permit property owners to hurry, before the deadline, to record restrictions where they hadn't previously existed. The new rules, the solicitor general stated, would "not [a]ffect mortgage insurance already in force and will apply only to properties where the covenant in question and the insured mortgage are recorded after the [two-and-half-month delay]." Upon hearing the solicitor general's announcement, the FHA executive board announced that it would ignore it, resolving that "it should be made entirely clear that violation [of the new ban on insuring mortgages with restrictive covenants] would not invalidate insurance."

The day after Perlman's announcement, FHA commissioner Richards sent a memo to all field offices emphasizing that they should continue to insure properties with new restrictive covenants that were not recorded with counties but were, as he put it, "gentlemen's agreements" and that the new policy would not apply to any FHA commitments for insurance that had already been made nor to properties where applications were pending. Then, to emphasize how much the agency opposed the spirit of the new rules, Richards's memo added that the agency "will not attempt to control any owner in determining what tenants he shall have or to whom he shall sell his property." Officials' disdain for the Supreme Court's ruling was apparent. An article in *The New York Times* reporting on the memo was headlined, "No Change Viewed in Work of F.H.A."

When in February 1950, the FHA began its lackluster compliance with *Shelley*, it continued to insure properties with covenants that were not explicitly racial. Instead, these agreements were designed to evade the Court's intent by requiring neighbors or a community board to approve any sale. Another year and a half later, an assistant FHA commissioner stated that "it was not the purpose of these Rules to forbid segregation or to deny the benefits of the National Housing Act to persons who might be unwilling to disregard race, color, or creed in the selection of their purchasers or tenants."

When Solicitor General Perlman made his 1949 announcement, unnamed "FHA officers" told *The New York Times* that the agency would go beyond the *Shelley* decision and not insure developers who, even without restrictive covenants, refused to sell or rent to African Americans. This was plainly untrue, as the agency continued to finance developments (Westlake in Daly City, California, is one example) through the 1950s that excluded African American purchasers. Only in 1962, when President John F. Kennedy issued an executive order prohibiting the use of federal funds to support racial discrimination in housing, did the FHA cease financing subdivision developments whose builders openly refused to sell to black buyers.

DECLARATION OF RESTRICTIONS OF

HENRY DOELGER BUILDER, INC.

The undersigned, HENRY DOELGER BUILDER, INC., a corporation, being the owner of those certain lands in Daly City, San Mateo County, State of California, described as follows, to wit:...

being desirous of making and maintaining said property as a desirable residential neighborhood, does, in consideration of that object and all its mutual promises, covenants, agree that for the term beginning on the date hereof and ending January 1, 1975, at which time said covenants shall be automatically extended for successive periods of 10 years, unless by vote of the majority of the then owners of the lots subject thereto, it is agreed to change or abandon said covenants in whole or in part, said lots and each and all of them thereof, shall be subject to the following restrictions and covenants and limitations, to wit:...

(a) The real property above described, or any portion thereof, shall never be occupied, used or resided on by any person not of the white or Caucasian race, except in the capacity of a servant or domestic employed thereon as such by a white Caucasian owner, tenant or occupant.

If any owner of any lot or plot in said tract sells, conveys,, leases, or rents his property to a person not of the Caucasian race the owner of the eight lots situated most closely to the lot so sold, conveyed, leased, or rented, regardless of any intervening streets or ways, shall have a cause of action for damages against such owner so selling, conveying, leasing or renting his property. Inasmuch as it would be impracticable or extremely difficult to fix and ascertain the actual damages suffered by such neighboring owners, it shall be conclusively presumed that the amount of damage sustained by each such neighboring owner is the sum of Two Thousand Dollars ($2,000.00) for each and every sale, conveyance, leasing or rental to a person not of the Caucasian race.

*After the Supreme Court prohibited enforcement of restrictive covenants, the FHA continued to subsidize projects that penalized sellers of homes to African Americans. In Westlake, Daly City, California, the total fine, $16,000, was greater than the typical home sale price.*

Although the 1948 *Shelley* ruling forbade courts from ordering evictions, parties to restrictive covenants continued for another five years to bring suits for damages against fellow signatories who violated their pacts, and two state supreme courts upheld the propriety of such damage awards. One was the Supreme Court of Missouri, the state where the *Shelley* case originated. The court took the position that neighbors of a homeowner who violated a restrictive covenant could sue the seller for damages, even though they could no longer obtain a court order evicting the purchaser. The other was the Oklahoma Supreme Court, which went a step further, finding that *Shelley* did not preclude neighbors from suing both seller and purchaser for engaging in a conspiracy to diminish a community's property values. In this Oklahoma suit, the complaining white owners alleged that "it is well known generally . . . that the purchase, rental, or leasing of real property by [African Americans] will always cause the remainder of the property in the same block to decrease in value at least from fifty to seventy-five percent."

In some cases, the FHA continued to insure developments with racially explicit covenants that provided for violators to pay exorbitant damages rather than cancel sales and evict African American residents. In the case of the subdivision in Westlake, the first homes were sold in 1949 for about $10,000. By 1955 the typical price was about $15,000. The covenant provided for damages of $2,000 to each of the eight closest neighbors, a prohibitive amount that exceeded the value of the property itself.

In 1953, the Supreme Court ended this circumvention of *Shelley*. It ruled that the Fourteenth Amendment precluded state courts not only from evicting African Americans from homes purchased in defiance of a restrictive covenant but also from adjudicating suits to recover damages from property owners who made such sales. Still, the Court refused to declare that such private contracts were unlawful or even that county clerks should be prohibited from accepting deeds that included them.

It took another nineteen years before a federal appeals court ruled that the covenants themselves violated the Fair Housing Act and that recording deeds with such clauses would constitute state action in violation of the Fourteenth Amendment. As the court observed, such provisions, even if they lacked power, still would make black purchasers reluctant to buy into white neighborhoods if the recorded deeds gave implicit recognition of the racial prohibition and gave an official imprimatur to the message that the purchasers should not live where they were not wanted. Since the 1950s, new restrictive covenants have rarely been recorded, but in most states old ones, though without legal authority, can be difficult to remove from deeds without great legal expense.

The Supreme Court decision in *Shelley v. Kraemer*, banning court enforcement of restrictive covenants, had been unanimous, 6–0. Three of the nine justices excused themselves from participating because their objectivity might have been challenged—there were racial restrictions covering the homes in which they lived.

*Chicago, 1970. When federal policy denied mortgages to African Americans, they had to buy houses on the installment plan, which led to numerous evictions.*

# 6

--------------------------------

# WHITE FLIGHT

Along with the real estate industry and state courts, the FHA justified its racial policies—both its appraisal standards and its restrictive covenant recommendations—by claiming that a purchase by an African American in a white neighborhood, or the presence of African Americans in or near such a neighborhood, would cause the value of the white-owned properties to decline. This, in turn, would increase the FHA's own losses, because white property owners in the neighborhood would be more likely to default on their mortgages. In the three decades during which it administered this policy, however, the agency never provided or obtained evidence to support its claim that integration undermined property values.

The best it could apparently do was a 1939 report by Homer Hoyt, the FHA's principal housing economist, that set out principles of "sound public and private housing and home financing policy." Hoyt explained that racial segregation must be an obvious necessity because it was a worldwide phenomenon. His only support for this assertion was an observation that in

China enclaves of American missionaries and European colonial officials lived separately from Chinese neighborhoods. On this basis, he concluded that "where members of different races live together . . . racial mixtures tend to have a depressing effect on land values."

# I

STATISTICAL EVIDENCE contradicted the FHA's assumption that the presence of African Americans caused the property values of whites to fall. Often racial integration caused property values to increase. With government policy excluding working- and middle-class African Americans from most suburbs, their desire to escape dense urban conditions spurred their demand for single-family or duplex homes on the outskirts of urban ghettos nationwide. Because these middle-class families had few other housing alternatives, they were willing to pay prices far above fair market values. In short, the FHA policy of denying African Americans access to most neighborhoods itself created conditions that prevented property values from falling when African Americans did appear.

In an unusual 1942 decision, the federal appeals court for the District of Columbia refused to uphold a restrictive covenant because the clause undermined its own purpose, which was to protect property values. Enforcement, the court said, would depress property values by excluding African Americans who were willing to pay higher prices than whites. In 1948 an FHA official published a report asserting that "the infiltration of Negro owner-occupants has tended to appreciate property values and neighborhood stability." A 1952 study of sales in San Francisco compared prices in racially changing neighborhoods with those in a control group of racially stable neighborhoods. Published in the *Appraisal Journal*, a periodical with which housing practitioners, including FHA officials, would have been familiar, it concluded that "[t]hese results do not show that any deterioration in market prices occurred following changes in the racial pattern." Indeed, the study confirmed that because African Americans were willing to pay more than whites for similar housing, property values in neighborhoods where African Americans could purchase increased more often than they declined. Ignoring these studies' conclusions, the FHA continued its racial policy for at least another decade.

## II

IN ONE respect, however, the FHA's theories about property values could become self-fulfilling. An African American influx could reduce a neighborhood's home prices as a direct result of FHA policy. The inability of African American families to obtain mortgages for suburban dwellings created opportunities for speculators and real estate agents to collude in blockbusting. Practiced across the country as it had been in East Palo Alto, blockbusting was a scheme in which speculators bought properties in borderline black-white areas; rented or sold them to African American families at above-market prices; persuaded white families residing in these areas that their neighborhoods were turning into African American slums and that values would soon fall precipitously; and then purchased the panicked whites' homes for less than their worth.

Blockbusters' tactics included hiring African American women to push carriages with their babies through white neighborhoods, hiring African American men to drive cars with radios blasting through white neighborhoods, paying African American men to accompany agents knocking on doors to see if homes were for sale, or making random telephone calls to residents of white neighborhoods and asking to speak to someone with a stereotypically African American name like "Johnnie Mae." Speculators also took out real estate advertisements in African American newspapers, even if the featured properties were not for sale. The ads' purpose was to attract potential African American buyers to walk around white areas that were targeted for blockbusting. In a 1962 *Saturday Evening Post* article, an agent (using the pseudonym "Norris Vitchek") claimed to have arranged house burglaries in white communities to scare neighbors into believing that their communities were becoming unsafe.

Real estate firms then sold their newly acquired properties at inflated prices to African Americans, expanding their residential boundaries. Because most black families could not qualify for mortgages under FHA and bank policies, the agents often sold these homes on installment plans, similar to the one Charles Vatterott developed in De Porres, in which no equity accumulated from down or monthly payments. Known as contract sales, these agreements usually provided that ownership would transfer to purchasers after fifteen or twenty years, but if a single monthly payment was late, the speculator could evict the would-be owner, who had accumulated no equity. The inflated sale prices made it all the more likely that payment would not be on time. Owner-speculators could then resell these homes to new contract buyers.

The full cycle went like this: when a neighborhood first integrated, property values increased because of African Americans' need to pay higher prices for homes than whites. But then property values fell once speculators had panicked enough white homeowners into selling at deep discounts.

Falling sale prices in neighborhoods where blockbusters created white panic was deemed as proof by the FHA that property values would decline if African Americans moved in. But if the agency had not adopted a discriminatory and unconstitutional racial policy, African Americans would have been able, like whites, to locate throughout metropolitan areas rather than attempting to establish presence in only a few blockbusted communities, and speculators would not have been able to prey on white fears that their neighborhoods would soon turn from all white to all black.

## III

THE FHA's redlining necessitated the contract sale system for black homeowners unable to obtain conventional mortgages, and this created the conditions for neighborhood deterioration. Mark Satter was a Chicago attorney who in the early 1960s represented contract buyers facing eviction; mostly he was unsuccessful. His daughter Beryl, now a professor of history at Rutgers University, described the conditions he encountered in her memoir, *Family Properties*, and summarized them like this:

> Because black contract buyers knew how easily they could lose their homes, they struggled to make their inflated monthly payments. Husbands and wives both worked double shifts. They neglected basic maintenance. They subdivided their apartments, crammed in extra tenants and, when possible, charged their tenants hefty rents. . . . White people observed that their new black neighbors overcrowded and neglected their properties. Overcrowded neighborhoods meant overcrowded schools; in Chicago, officials responded by "double-shifting" the students (half attending in the morning, half in the afternoon). Children were deprived of a full day of schooling and left to fend for themselves in the after-school hours. These conditions helped fuel the rise of gangs, which in turn terrorized shop owners and residents alike.
>
> In the end, whites fled these neighborhoods, not only because of the influx of black families, but also because they were upset about overcrowding, decaying schools and crime. . . . But black contract buyers did not have the option of leaving a declining neighborhood before their properties were paid for in full—if they did, they would lose everything they'd invested in that property to date. Whites could leave—blacks had to stay.

This contract arrangement was widespread not only in Chicago but in Baltimore, Cincinnati, Detroit, Washington, D.C., and

*In the Lawndale neighborhood of Chicago, community opposition to evictions of contract buyers was so strong that sheriffs were often needed to prevent owners and neighbors from carrying belongings back in.*

probably elsewhere. In Mark Satter's time, approximately 85 percent of all property purchased by African Americans in Chicago had been sold to them on contract. When the neighborhood where he worked, Lawndale on the city's West Side, was changing from predominantly white to predominantly black, more than half of the residences had been bought on contract.

Although banks and savings and loan associations typically refused to issue mortgages to ordinary homeowners in African American or in integrated neighborhoods, the same institutions issued mortgages to blockbusters in those neighborhoods, all with the approval of federal bank regulators who failed their constitutional responsibilities. State real estate regulators also defaulted on their obligations when they licensed real estate brokers who engaged in blockbusting. Instead, regulators looked the other way when real estate boards expelled brokers who sold to African Americans in stable white neighborhoods.

Blockbusting, the subsequent loss of home values when speculators caused panic, the subsequent deterioration of neighborhood quality when African Americans were forced to pay excessive prices for housing, the resulting identification of African Americans with slum conditions, and the resulting white flight to escape the possibility of those conditions all had their bases in federal government policy. Blockbusting could work only because the FHA made certain that African Americans had few alternative neighborhoods where they could purchase homes at fair market values.

*Denver, 1961. When a few African Americans moved to a middle-class white neighborhood, speculators panicked white homeowners into selling at a deep discount.*

# 7

## IRS SUPPORT AND
## COMPLIANT REGULATORS

A S PUBLIC HOUSING packed African Americans into urban
projects, and federal loan insurance subsidized white families to disperse into single-family suburban homes, other racial
policies of federal, state, and local governments contributed to,
and reinforced, the segregation of metropolitan areas. One was
the willingness of the Internal Revenue Service (IRS) to grant tax-
exempt status to churches, hospitals, universities, neighborhood
associations, and other groups that promoted residential segregation. Another was the complicity of regulatory agencies in the discriminatory actions of the insurance companies and banks they
supervised.

*The Color of Law* does not argue that merely because government regulates a private business, the firm's activities become state
action and, if discriminatory, constitute *de jure* segregation. Such a
claim would eliminate the distinction between the public and private
spheres and be inimical to a free democratic society. But because of
slavery's legacy, the Constitution gives African Americans a special degree of protection. The three constitutional amendments—
the Thirteenth, Fourteenth, and Fifteenth—adopted after the Civil

War were specifically intended to ensure that African Americans had equal status. When government regulation is so intrusive that it blesses systematic racial exclusion, regulators violate their constitutional responsibilities and contribute to *de jure* segregation.

Real estate brokers don't become government agents simply by dint of their state licensure. But when state real estate commissions licensed members of local and national real estate boards whose published codes of ethics mandated discrimination, acts to establish *de jure* segregation were committed. Similarly, universities, churches, and other nonprofit institutions cannot be considered state actors simply by dint of their tax exemptions. But we have a right to expect the IRS to have been especially vigilant and to have withheld tax-exempt status when the promotion of segregation by nonprofit institutions was blatant, explicit, and influential.

# I

THE IRS has always had an obligation to withhold tax favoritism from discriminatory organizations, but it almost never acted to do so. Its regulations specifically authorize charitable deductions for organizations that "eliminate prejudice and discrimination" and "defend human and civil rights secured by law." The IRS leadership recognized this in 1967 when the agency exercised its authority to withhold the tax exemption of a recreational facility that excluded African Americans. Yet until 1970, sixteen years after *Brown v. Board of Education*, the IRS granted tax exemptions to private whites-only academies that had been established throughout the South to evade the ruling. It rejected the exemptions only in response to a court injunction won by civil rights groups.

In 1976, the IRS denied the tax exemption of Bob Jones University because the school would not allow interracial dating by its students. The university mounted a court challenge to the IRS action, and when the case reached the Supreme Court the Reagan administration refused to defend the agency. So the Supreme Court appointed an outside lawyer, William T. Coleman, Jr., to make the argument that the government itself should have presented. Coleman's brief asserted: "Indeed, if [the charitable organization provision of the IRS code] were construed to permit tax exemptions for racially discriminatory schools, the provision would be unconstitutional under the Fifth Amendment. The Government has an affirmative constitutional duty to steer clear of providing significant aid to such schools."

In its widely noticed 1983 decision, the Court upheld the IRS decision and concluded that "an institution seeking tax-exempt status must serve a public purpose and not be contrary to established public policy." It did not adopt Coleman's constitutional argument to make its case, but neither did the Court reject it. In his opinion, Chief Justice Warren Burger wrote that many of those who submitted briefs in the case, including Coleman, "argue that denial of tax-exempt status to racially discriminatory schools is independently required by the equal protection component of the Fifth Amendment. In light of our resolution of this litigation, we do not reach that issue." But Coleman's argument was solid, and it implicitly condemned the decades-long passivity of the IRS by confronting how its tax-exemption policy strengthened residential segregation. Support for a ban on interracial dating certainly offended the Constitution, but its national policy significance was trivial in comparison to the IRS's silence when nonprofit institutions promoted restrictive covenants or engaged in other activities to prevent African Americans from moving into white neighborhoods.

Churches, synagogues, and their clergy frequently led such efforts. *Shelley v. Kraemer*, the 1948 Supreme Court ruling that ended court enforcement of restrictive covenants, offers a conspicuous illustration. The case stemmed from objections of white St. Louis homeowners, Louis and Fern Kraemer, to the purchase of a house in their neighborhood by African Americans, J.D. and Ethel Shelley. The area had been covered by a restrictive covenant organized by a white owners' group, the Marcus Avenue Improvement Association, which was sponsored by the Cote Brilliante Presbyterian Church. Trustees of the church provided funds from the church treasury to finance the Kraemers' lawsuit to have the African American family evicted. Another nearby church, the Waggoner Place Methodist Episcopal Church South, was also a signatory to the restrictive covenant; its pastor had defended the clause in a 1942 legal case arising from the purchase of a nearby house by Scovel Richardson, a distinguished attorney who later became one of the first African Americans nationwide appointed to the federal judiciary.

Such church involvement and leadership were commonplace in property owners' associations that were organized to maintain neighborhood segregation. In North Philadelphia in 1942, a priest spearheaded a campaign to prevent African Americans from living in the neighborhood. The same year a priest in a Polish American parish in Buffalo, New York, directed the campaign to deny public housing for African American war workers, stalling a proposed project for two years. Just south of the city, 600 units in the federally managed project for whites went vacant, while African American war workers could not find adequate housing.

In Los Angeles, the Reverend W. Clarence Wright, pastor of the fashionable Wilshire Presbyterian Church, led efforts to keep the Wilshire District all white. He personally sued to evict an African American war veteran who had moved into the restricted area in 1947. Wright lost the case, one of the few times before *Shelley* in which a state court held covenants to be unconstitutional. In a widely publicized ruling, the judge said that there was "no more reprehensible un-American activity than to attempt to deprive persons of their own homes on a 'master race' theory." Yet the IRS took no notice; Reverend Wright's activities didn't threaten his church's tax subsidy.

The violent resistance to the Sojourner Truth public housing project for African American families in Detroit was organized by a homeowners association headquartered in St. Louis the King Catholic Church whose pastor, the Reverend Constantine Dzink, represented the association in appeals to the United States Housing Authority to cancel the project. The "construction of a low-cost housing project in the vicinity . . . for the colored people . . .

would mean utter ruin for many people who have mortgaged their homes to the FHA, and not only that, but it would jeopardize the safety of many of our white girls," Reverend Dzink wrote, adding this warning: "It is the sentiment of all people residing within the vicinity to object against this project in order to stop race riots in the future."

On Chicago's South Side, signatures on a 1928 restrictive covenant were obtained in door-to-door solicitations by the priest of St. Anselm Catholic Church, the rabbi of Congregation Beth Jacob, and the executive director of the area's property owners association. Trinity Congregational Church was also party to the agreement. In 1946, the Congregational Church of Park Manor sponsored a local improvement association's efforts to cancel an African American physician's home purchase in the previously all-white neighborhood.

On Chicago's Near North Side, a restrictive covenant was executed in 1937 by tax-exempt religious institutions, including the Moody Bible Institute, the Louisville Presbyterian Theological Seminary, and the Board of Foreign Missions of the Methodist Episcopal Church. Other nonprofit organizations also participated, including the Newberry Library and the Academy of Fine Arts.

Tax-exempt colleges and universities, some religious-affiliated and some not, also were active in promoting segregation. In Whittier, a Los Angeles suburb, the Quaker-affiliated Whittier College participated in a restrictive covenant covering its neighborhood.

The University of Chicago organized and guided property owners' associations that were devoted to preventing black families from moving nearby. The university not only subsidized the associations but from 1933 to 1947 spent $100,000 on legal services to defend covenants and evict African Americans who had arrived in its neighborhood. When criticized for these activities, University of Chicago president Robert Maynard Hutchins wrote in 1937 that the university "must endeavor to stabilize its neighborhood as an area in which its students and faculty will be content to live," and that therefore the university had the "right to invoke and defend" restrictive covenants in its surrounding areas.

## II

INSURANCE COMPANIES also participated in segregation. They have large reserve funds to invest, and because they are heavily regulated, state policy makers are frequently involved in plans for any housing projects that insurers propose.

In 1938, when Frederick Ecker, president of the Metropolitan Life Insurance Company, wanted to build the 12,000-unit Parkchester apartments in New York City, he could not proceed without an amendment to the state's insurance code, permitting insurers to invest in low-rent housing. The state legislature adopted the amendment, fully aware that it was authorizing a project from which African Americans would be excluded.

After Parkchester was completed in 1942, Metropolitan Life embarked on a new project, the 9,000-unit Stuyvesant Town housing complex on the east side of Manhattan. For the development, New York City condemned and cleared eighteen square city blocks and transferred the property to the insurance company. The city also granted Metropolitan Life a twenty-five-year tax abatement, whose value meant that far more public than private money was invested in the project. The subsidies were granted despite Metropolitan Life's announcement that, like Parkchester, the project would be for "white people only." Ecker advised the New York City Board of Estimate that "Negroes and whites don't mix. If we brought them into this development . . . it would depress all of the surrounding property." Because of the project's refusal to accept African Americans, the board was divided whether to allow it to proceed. It eventually paired its approval with an ordinance forbidding racial segregation in any subsequent developments for which the city had to engage in "slum clearance." In response to public protests against its policy of excluding African Americans from Stuyvesant Town, Metropolitan Life built the Riverton Houses, a smaller development for African Americans in Harlem. Abiding by the new ordinance, the project was open to whites, but in practice it rented almost exclusively to African American families.

In 1947, a New York State court rejected a challenge to Stuyvesant Town's racial exclusion policy. The decision was upheld on appeal in 1949; the U.S. Supreme Court declined review. The following year, the New York State legislature enacted a statute prohibiting racial discrimination in any housing that received state aid in the form of a tax exemption, sale of land below cost, or land obtained through condemnation. That same year, Metropolitan Life finally agreed to lease "some" apartments in Stuyvesant Town to "qualified Negro tenants." But by then, the development was filled. New York City's rent control laws, by which existing tenants pay significantly less than market-rate rents, helped to ensure that turnover would be slow. Rapidly rising rents in apartments that had been vacated made the development increasingly unaffordable to middle-income families. These conditions combined to make the initial segregation of Stuyvesant Town nearly permanent. By the 2010 census, only 4 percent of Stuyvesant Town residents were African American, in a New York metropolitan area that was 15 percent African American.

As in so many other instances, the low-income neighborhood that the city razed to make way for Stuyvesant Town had been integrated and stable. About 40 percent of those evicted were African American or Puerto Rican, and many of them had no alternative but to move to racially isolated communities elsewhere in the city and beyond. Although New York ceased to allow future discrimination in publicly subsidized projects, it made no effort to remediate the segregation it had created.

# III

EVEN WHEN mortgage loans were not insured by the FHA or the VA, banks and savings (thrift) institutions pursued discriminatory policies. Banks and thrifts, however, are private institutions. Can it fairly be said that these discriminatory lending activities contributed to *de jure* segregation? I think so.

Government deposit insurance programs underwrite bank and thrift institution profits; in return, there is extensive oversight of lending practices. Examiners from the Federal Reserve, the Comptroller of the Currency, the Federal Deposit Insurance Corporation (FDIC), and the Office of Thrift Supervision all have regularly reviewed loan applications and other financial records of bank and savings and loan offices to ensure that lending practices were sound. Banks and thrifts were able to refuse service to African Americans only because, until recently, federal and state regulators chose to allow it.

The Federal Home Loan Bank Board, for example, chartered, insured, and regulated savings and loan associations from the early years of the New Deal but did not oppose the denial of mortgages to African Americans until 1961. It did not enforce the new race-blind policy, however—perhaps because it was in conflict with the board's insistence that mortgage eligibility account for "economic" factors. Like the FHA, it claimed that judging African Americans to be poor credit risks because they were black was not a racial judgment but an economic one. As a result, its staff failed to remedy the industry's consistent support for segregation.

In 1961 the U.S. Commission on Civil Rights challenged regulators about their complicity in banks' redlining practices. Ray M. Gidney, then Comptroller of the Currency (responsible for chartering, supervising, regulating, and examining national banks), responded, "Our office does not maintain any policy regarding racial discrimination in the making of real estate loans by national banks." FDIC chairman Erle Cocke asserted that it was appropriate for banks under his supervision to deny loans to African Americans because whites' property values might fall if they had black neighbors. And Federal Reserve Board chairman William McChesney Martin stated, "[N]either the Federal Reserve nor any other bank supervisory agency has—or should have—authority to compel officers and directors of any bank to make any loan against their judgment." Martin's view was that federal regulators should only prohibit the approval of unsound loans, not require the nondiscriminatory approval of sound loans. If a black family was denied a loan because of race, Martin asserted, "the forces of competition" would ensure that another bank would come forward to make the loan. With his regulatory authority over all banks that were members of the Federal Reserve System, and with all such banks engaging in similar discriminatory practices, Martin surely knew (or should have known) that his claim was false.

When regulated businesses engage in systematic racial discrimination, when government regulation is intense, and when regulators openly endorse the racial discrimination carried out by the sector they are supervising, then in those cases the regulators ignore the civil rights they are sworn to uphold and contribute to *de jure* discrimination. As the Supreme Court once said, referring to banks chartered by the federal government: "National banks are instrumentalities of the federal government, created for a public purpose."

## IV

Racially discriminatory government activities did not end fifty years ago. On the contrary, some have continued into the twenty-first century. One of the more troubling has been the regulatory tolerance of banks' "reverse redlining"—excessive marketing of exploitative loans in African American communities. This was an important cause of the 2008 financial collapse because these loans, called subprime mortgages, were bound to go into default. When they did, lower-middle-class African American neighborhoods were devastated, and their residents, with their homes foreclosed, were forced back into lower-income areas. In the early 2000s, reverse redlining was tolerated, sometimes winked at, by bank regulators.

Banks, thrift institutions, and mortgage companies designed subprime loans for borrowers who had a higher risk of default, and they charged higher interest payments to subprime borrowers to compensate for that risk. In itself, this was a legitimate practice. But federally regulated banks and other lenders created many subprime loans with onerous conditions that were designed to make repayment difficult. These mortgages had high closing costs and prepayment penalties and low initial "teaser" interest rates that skyrocketed after borrowers were locked in. Some subprime loans also had negative amortization—requirements for initial monthly payments that were lower than needed to cover interest costs, with the difference then added to the outstanding principal.

Borrowers should have been more careful before accepting loans they could not understand or reasonably repay, but they were victims of a market that was not transparent—in some cases deliberately not so. For example, mortgage broker compensation systems included incentives to pressure borrowers into accepting subprime mortgages, without the brokers disclosing the consequences. Brokers received bonuses, in effect kickbacks (called "yield spread premiums," or YSPs), if they made loans with interest rates higher than those recommended by their banks on formal rate sheets for borrowers with similar characteristics. Regulators and banks that purchased these mortgages from marketers did not require brokers to disclose to borrowers what these rate sheets specified. The 2010 Dodd-Frank financial reform and consumer protection act banned YSPs. It took another year for the Federal Reserve to issue a rule implementing the ban, but borrowers who were deceived as a result of the kickback system are without recourse. Nothing, however, would have prevented the Federal Reserve from banning the practice years earlier.

Brokers and loan officers manipulated borrowers by convincing them they could take advantage of perpetually rising equity to refinance their loans before the teaser rates expired and take cash out of the increased equity (with a share left as profit for the lending institution). But frequently these mortgages were promoted and sold to African Americans who lived in distressed neighborhoods where little or no gain in equity could be expected—even before the housing bubble burst. In these areas where property values would be unlikely to appreciate, the scheme could not possibly work as promised, even if the nationwide housing boom continued.

These discriminatory practices were widespread throughout the industry at least since the late 1990s, with little state or federal regulatory response. Data on lending disparities suggest that the discrimination was based on race, not on economic status. Among homeowners who had refinanced in 2000 as the subprime bubble was expanding, lower-income African Americans were more than twice as likely as lower-income whites to have subprime loans, and

*Before the 2008 burst of a housing bubble, lenders targeted African American and Hispanic homeowners for the marketing of subprime refinance loans. When the economy collapsed, many homes went into foreclosure, devastating entire neighborhoods—like this block of boarded-up homes on Chicago's Southwest Side.*

higher-income African Americans were about three times as likely as higher-income whites to have subprime loans. The most extreme case occurred in Buffalo, New York, where three-quarters of all refinance loans to African Americans were subprime. In Chicago, borrowers in predominantly African American census tracts were four times as likely to have subprime loans as borrowers in predominantly white census tracts.

In 2000, 41 percent of all borrowers with subprime loans would have qualified for conventional financing with lower rates, a figure that increased to 61 percent in 2006. By then, African American mortgage recipients had subprime loans at three times the rate of white borrowers. Higher-income African Americans had subprime mortgages at four times the rate of higher-income whites. Even though its own survey in 2005 revealed a similar racial discrepancy, the Federal Reserve did not take action. By failing to curb discrimination that its own data disclosed, the Federal Reserve violated African Americans' legal and constitutional rights.

In 2010, the Justice Department agreed that "[t]he more segregated a community of color is, the more likely it is that homeowners will face foreclosure because the lenders who peddled the most toxic loans targeted those communities." Settling a lawsuit against the Countrywide mortgage company (later a subsidiary of the Bank of America), Secretary of Housing and Urban Development Shaun Donovan remarked that because of Countrywide's and other lenders' practices, "[f]rom Jamaica, Queens, New York, to Oakland, California, strong, middle-class African American neighborhoods saw nearly two decades of gains reversed in a matter of not years— but months." For those dispossessed after foreclosures, there has been greater homelessness, more doubling up with relatives, and more apartment rental in less stable neighborhoods where poor and minority families are more tightly concentrated.

In its legal action against Countrywide, the government alleged that the statistical relationship between race and mortgage terms was so extreme that top bank officials must have been aware of the racial motivation. And if top bank officials were aware, so too must have been the government regulators. Indeed, the Justice Department got involved only because Countrywide modified its government charter in 2007 so that the Office of Thrift Supervision assumed responsibility for its regulation from the Federal Reserve Board. The office noticed the racially tinged statistics and referred the lender to the Department of Justice for prosecution. The discriminatory practices had continued for years under the Federal Reserve's supervision.

Several cities sued banks because of the enormous devastation that the foreclosure crisis imposed on African Americans. A case that the City of Memphis brought against Wells Fargo Bank was supported by affidavits of bank employees stating that they referred to subprime loans as "ghetto loans." Bank supervisors instructed their marketing staffs to target solicitation to heavily African American zip codes, because residents there "weren't savvy enough" to know they were being exploited. A sales group sought out elderly African Americans, believing they were particularly susceptible to pressure to take out high-cost loans.

A similar suit by the City of Baltimore presented evidence that Wells Fargo established a unit staffed exclusively by African Americans whom supervisors instructed to visit black churches to market subprime loans. The bank had no similar practice of marketing such loans through white institutions.

In 2008 the City of Cleveland sued a large group of subprime lenders, including Citicorp, the Bank of America, Wells Fargo, and others. The lawsuit alleged that the institutions should not have marketed any subprime loans in Cleveland's depressed black neighborhoods because the lenders knew that high poverty and unemployment rates and flat property values in those communities would preclude borrowers from capturing sufficient appreciation to afford the higher adjustable rates they faced, once the initial low "teaser" rates expired.

Cleveland's suit argued that the banks should be held liable for the harm they created, including loss of tax revenues and an increase in drug dealing and other crime in neighborhoods with many foreclosed and abandoned buildings. The city charged that the financial firms had created a public nuisance. A federal court dismissed the suit, concluding that because mortgage lending is so heavily regulated by the federal and state governments, "there is no question that the subprime lending that occurred in Cleveland was conduct which 'the law sanctions.'"

The consequences of racially targeted subprime lending continue to accumulate. As the housing bubble collapsed, African American homeownership rates fell much more than white rates. Families no longer qualify for conventional mortgages if they previously defaulted when they were unable to make exorbitant loan payments; for these families, the contract buying system of the 1960s is now making its return. Some of the same firms that exploited African Americans in the subprime crisis are now reselling foreclosed properties to low- and moderate-income households at high interest rates, with high down payments, with no equity accumulated until the contract period has ended, and with eviction possible after a single missed payment.

By failing to ensure that banks fulfilled the public purposes for which they were chartered, regulators shared responsibility for reverse redlining of African American communities. When federal and state regulatory agencies chartered banks and thrift institutions whose unhidden policy was racial discrimination, the agencies themselves defaulted on their constitutional obligations.

*Miami, 1966. Mayor Chuck Hall sends the first wrecking ball into homes of African Americans near downtown, fulfilling the city's plan to relocate them to a distant ghetto.*

# 8

## LOCAL TACTICS

WHEN FRANK STEVENSON and his carpoolers needed housing near the new Ford plant, FHA- and VA-insured subdivisions were rapidly filling the area between Milpitas and the African
American communities of Richmond and Oakland. The most
active developer was David Bohannon, who had built the whites-
only Rollingwood subdivision just outside Richmond in 1943. The
following year, he created the massive whites-only San Lorenzo
Village about five miles south of the Oakland border. With more
than 5,000 units and 17,000 residents, San Lorenzo Village was the
nation's largest wartime government-insured project, intended for
workers at naval shipyards and support factories. Like the homes
in Rollingwood, each house included a bedroom with a separate
entrance, so the owner could rent it to another war worker.

The development was financed by a seven-million-dollar FHA-
authorized loan from the Bank of America and the American Trust
Company. As was the case with other FHA developments, houses
were sold at relatively low prices so as to be within reach of war
workers, and the deeds included restrictive covenants to prevent
future resales to African Americans. Within easy commuting dis-

tance of Milpitas, San Lorenzo Village was an ideal location for Ford workers. Sales brochures in the early to mid-1950s, when Ford workers would have been seeking housing in the area, assured prospective buyers that the village was "a safe investment" because "farsighted protective restrictions . . . permanently safeguard your investment."

# I

IN 1955, Bohannon began developing Sunnyhills, a project in Milpitas itself. After Western Pacific announced plans to create its new industrial zone, other builders had also obtained FHA guarantees to construct whites-only, single-family subdivisions in the area. One, Milford Village, a development of 1,500 units on unincorporated land just outside the town boundaries, was guaranteed by the VA and required little or no down payment for veterans and low monthly payments.

When it became apparent that no existing Milpitas-area development would sell or rent to black workers, the American Friends Service Committee (AFSC), a Quaker group committed to racial integration, offered to assist Ben Gross—the chair of the Ford plant's union housing committee—by finding a developer who would agree to build an interracial subdivision. The AFSC had an existing campaign to press (unsuccessfully) Richmond to desegregate its public housing and find adequate, integrated residences for its African American population being displaced by the demolition of federal war projects. The group also operated a settlement house in North Richmond with after-school tutoring, dances and other youth recreational opportunities, a well-baby clinic for mothers, a day care program for children of working parents, a small playground for toddlers, and a meeting room for community organizations. Ford workers were involved in all these activities.

The rapid growth of the Milpitas area had resulted in some overbuilding, and several new subdivisions had unsold units that were affordable to Ford workers. Despite this excess inventory, the AFSC was unsuccessful in persuading any existing developer to sell to African Americans.

The first builder recruited by the AFSC selected a plot in an unincorporated area south of Mountain View, a Santa Clara County community about ten miles west of Milpitas and accessible to other growing industrial areas in Silicon Valley. The AFSC, however, could not find a financial institution in the San Francisco Bay or San Jose areas willing to provide funds for a development that would permit sales to African Americans. After a few months, an AFSC official flew to New York to meet with a Quaker vice-president of the Metropolitan Life Insurance Company who, despite his skepticism about the feasibility of integrated suburban development, agreed to issue a loan for initial construction. Only as a result of this Quaker connection was the AFSC able to obtain a financial commitment. It may also have helped that Metropolitan Life was a bit chastened by the reversal of its racial segregation policy by New York city and state legislative bodies.

But when the builder's intent to sell both to blacks and whites became known, the Santa Clara Board of Supervisors rezoned the site from residential to industrial use. When he found a second plot, Mountain View officials told him that they would never grant the necessary approvals. He next identified a third tract of land in another town near the Ford plant; when officials discovered that the project would not be segregated, the town adopted a new zoning law increasing the minimum lot size from 6,000 to 8,000 square feet, making the project unfeasible for working-class buyers. After he attempted to develop a fourth site on which he had an option, the seller of the land canceled the option upon learning that the project would be integrated. At that point, the builder gave up.

Ben Gross then recruited another builder who proposed to the union that he create two projects, one integrated and the other all white. Because white buyers would be directed to the all-white project, it was apparent that the plan for a nominally integrated project would result in an all-black one. The builder proposed to construct the white project in a suburban area and the integrated one in a less desirable environment—a plot sandwiched between the Ford plant and two tracts zoned for heavy industry.

Workers at Ford, members of the United Auto Workers (UAW), were divided over whether to accept this proposal, and at the next local union election, candidates who opposed the two-project concept challenged those who were in favor. It was a difficult decision, because the union was faced with choosing between segregated housing and no new housing for any union members, black or white. It was a dilemma similar to the one confronted by Hubert Humphrey and other congressional liberals when they attempted to enact President Truman's housing proposal. But the union decided differently from the congressional liberals. Although the membership was overwhelmingly white, the union adopted a policy that it would support only developers who would commit to integrated housing.

A San Jose businessman in the meatpacking business, with no previous experience as a developer, obtained a tract adjoining David Bohannon's all-white Sunnyhills project and proposed an all-black development. When the UAW and AFSC became aware of these plans, they persuaded the developer to construct an integrated project instead, and the union promised to promote the project to its white as well as to its African American members. For six months, the businessman sought financing, but every bank or thrift institution he approached, knowing that FHA backing would be unavailable, either refused to lend money for a project that was open to African Americans or agreed to lend only if he paid higher interest, a premium for integration ranging from an additional 5½ percent to an additional 9 percent. Such a payment would have greatly increased project costs and made the houses unaffordable to union members. The businessman advised the UAW that he would have to drop his plans. The union was able to persuade him to continue only by promising that the union itself would take responsibility for finding a lender. UAW and AFSC representatives again went to New York to ask Metropolitan Life to provide construction financing, which the insurance company agreed to do.

In January 1955, more than a year after Ford notified its Richmond workers that their jobs were going to Milpitas, and only a month and a half before the scheduled transfer of automobile assembly, the UAW was able to advise its black members in Richmond that a nondiscriminatory housing development, called Agua Caliente, was going to be available in the Milpitas area. By this time, many white workers had already found housing in racially restricted Santa Clara County neighborhoods.

David Bohannon's company, however, remained fiercely opposed to an integrated project adjoining Sunnyhills, and after a San Francisco newspaper article revealed the plan to establish "the first subdivision in the Bay Area where Negro families will be sold homes without discrimination," the company began to pressure the newly formed Milpitas City Council to prevent the construction of Agua Caliente by denying it access to sewer lines.

The sanitary district for Milpitas, whose chair was a member of the Santa Clara County board of supervisors and whose other members were the Milpitas mayor and a Milpitas city councilman, had advised the Agua Caliente builder that its fee for sewer access would be one hundred dollars an acre, based on the project's anticipated use of about 3 percent of the sewer line's capacity. The union and its builder estimated project costs and set sale prices using this figure; Metropolitan Life had extended its financing based on it. Under pressure from David Bohannon's company, the sanitary district board held an emergency meeting and adopted an ordinance that increased the sewer connection fee by more than ten times the hundred-dollar figure.

The new charge caused the builder to suspend work. He attempted unsuccessfully to negotiate a compromise with the sanitary district and the Bohannon organization, whose representatives acknowledged that the purpose of the ordinance was to prevent minorities from living close to Sunnyhills. The mayor of Milpitas, however, denied that his motive in voting to increase the sewer fee was discriminatory but added that he did not think it would be a great loss if the subdivision never got developed because, he asserted, the Ford workers' tract would depress property values in Milpitas. A real estate agent himself, the mayor claimed that Negroes inquiring about housing had told him that they did not want to go where they weren't wanted. He was only deferring to these customers' wishes, he said, in declining to show them properties in the city.

Problems persisted even after the UAW's builder indicated he would proceed with the Agua Caliente project, despite the higher sewer connection fees. The Bohannon group next filed suit to prevent the project from using a drainage ditch alongside its tract. This was purely a nuisance suit because the drainage ditch belonged to the county, not to Bohannon. The UAW then mounted a public campaign against the Sunnyhills project. Not only did union members refrain from purchasing the houses, but they flooded open houses to disrupt sales to white buyers. Meanwhile the UAW and the AFSC contacted California attorney general Edmund C. (Pat) Brown, who sent an assistant to Milpitas to investigate the sewer fee controversy. Brown promised help "in overcoming any racial discrimination by governmental units which might be disclosed."

The Agua Caliente builder could no longer sustain the delays; nor could he afford the legal bills that would be incurred if he persisted. The Bohannon company, perhaps influenced by the attorney general's implicit threat, also tired of the fight. The union's boycott had been responsible, or partly responsible, for the company's being stuck with finished but unsold homes. In November 1955, both the Agua Caliente builder and Bohannon sold out to a new developer recruited by the UAW, making the sewer connection controversy moot, and a combined project was finally constructed.

The combined development took the name of the original Bohannon project, Sunnyhills. California banks and thrift institutions continued to refuse, without an exorbitant interest rate surcharge, to issue individual mortgages, without FHA insurance, to borrowers living in an integrated project. At first the UAW's own pension fund offered to guarantee the African American workers' loan repayments. Eventually the FHA agreed to guarantee mortgages with a favorable rate only if the subdivision were converted to a cooperative, in which the owners would possess shares of the overall project rather than their individual houses. The union and its member-buyers agreed, and on this basis twenty of the project's first 500 units were sold to African American families.

By this time, however, the Milpitas Ford plant had been operational for nearly a year, and almost all white workers who wanted to move to the area had done so. The delays, legal fees, and financing problems had raised the cost of the combined Sunnyhills project to a level that was unaffordable to all but the most highly skilled and highly paid Ford workers. Many of the African American workers had become so discouraged about housing opportunities in the Milpitas area that, like Frank Stevenson, they had formed carpools to share the hundred-mile daily round trip from Richmond. As a last alternative, the UAW and other area unions pressed for a public authority to create rental housing, but the idea was met with strong resistance from the local finance and real estate industry—the local association of savings and loan institutions called it "dangerous to our American way of life"—and the county refused to act.

In the ensuing years, African American residence in Milpitas continued to be confined to Sunnyhills and a relatively undesirable project, built in the 1960s between two freeways and a heavily trafficked main shopping thoroughfare. The Ford plant closed in 1984. Milpitas is no longer all white—it now has many Hispanic and Asian families—but the effects of its earlier segregation remain visible: African Americans make up only 2 percent of the population.

As the Milpitas area developed, other plants transferred there from the Oakland-Richmond corridor. One was a Trailmobile factory that relocated from Berkeley in 1955. Soon after, the plant manager announced a change in hiring policy: the company would accept only new workers who lived in the vicinity, and they, of course, were almost exclusively white. Black workers, he said, attempting to commute from the Oakland area, were too likely to have car accidents from the long drives, leading to excessive absenteeism. Before Trailmobile moved from Berkeley, its workforce was 16 percent African American. By 1967 it had dropped to 6 percent, mostly carryovers from before the new hiring policy was adopted.

## II

THE MILPITAS story illustrates the extraordinary creativity that government officials at all levels displayed when they were motivated to prevent the movement of African Americans into white neighborhoods. It wasn't only the large-scale federal programs of public housing and mortgage finance that created *de jure* segregation. Hundreds, if not thousands of smaller acts of government contributed. They included petty actions like denial of access to public utilities; determining, once African Americans wanted to build, that their property was, after all, needed for parkland; or discovering that a road leading to African American homes was "private." They included routing interstate highways to create racial boundaries or to shift the residential placement of African American families. And they included choosing school sites to force families to move to segregated neighborhoods if they wanted education for their children.

Taken in isolation, we can easily dismiss such devices as aberrations. But when we consider them as a whole, we can see that they were part of a national system by which state and local government supplemented federal efforts to maintain the status of African Americans as a lower caste, with housing segregation preserving the badges and incidents of slavery.

## III

DEVICES LIKE those that Milpitas and surrounding towns employed to exclude African Americans were common segregation tactics throughout the country after World War II. In numerous instances, local governments condemned or rezoned property to prevent African Americans from residing there.

For example, in 1954 a University of Pennsylvania professor and his wife purchased a site in Swarthmore, a town just outside Philadelphia, where they planned to develop a tract of twenty-eight middle-class homes to be sold to both African Americans and whites. The couple's intent was to prove that "families of differing races, colors, and religions can live together in harmony." The Swarthmore Property Owners' Association petitioned the borough council that it did not want the town to become "a laboratory" for social experiments. The council reacted by refusing to consider the housing plan without a certified engineer's drawing, an expensive condition that it had not imposed on other developments.

After the couple submitted the drawing, the council made a series of objections, none of which it had made when considering other recent projects: It blocked the construction of a private drive leading to some of the homes, and it required a costly new sewer system. The professor and his wife forged ahead, scaling back their plans to avoid the need for a private drive. Adjoining property owners then asserted that the project could not proceed because the main road accessing the property was also private, notwithstanding that the borough had made public improvements to the road in the past without anyone raising similar issues. When the neighbors sued to halt the project on these grounds, borough officials supported the neighbors and did not intervene. With no prospect that such impediments would ever end, the professor and his wife abandoned the project.

A similar situation developed in Deerfield, Illinois, a white suburb of Chicago. In 1959 a developer purchased two tracts of vacant land and proposed to subdivide and build fifty-one houses on them, with a plan to sell ten to African Americans. He specifically chose Deerfield for the project because it was far from an existing African American community; he hoped it would be less likely to attract the attention of real estate speculators who could spur panic selling and white flight. Without knowing that the developer intended an integrated project, the village approved his plans, and water, sewer, and street improvements proceeded. Work had begun on two model homes when village officials discovered his intention.

Almost immediately speculators did arrive and attempt to create fear among village residents by offering to purchase their properties for as little as half of fair market values. A citizens committee was organized, and 600 protesters marched on a town board meeting being held in a school gymnasium. By a show of hands, the crowd vowed its uncompromising rejection of integration. The police were unable or unwilling to prevent the model homes from being vandalized. A survey of Deerfield residents found that opposition to the development ran nearly eight to one.

The day after the survey results were announced, the village's park district announced it would condemn the land. The idea was not new. Several months earlier, voters had rejected a proposal that the district take these properties, but now they overwhelmingly approved a bond issue for that purpose. A federal court held that the park district's exploitation of community hostility to integration was not unlawful because the district was not itself racially motivated; it had unsuccessfully attempted to get voter approval before the likelihood of African American buyers had arisen. The court concluded that voters cannot be compelled to express nonracial motives at the ballot box. By this logic, though, a democratic vote could insulate any racially discriminatory action from legal challenge. The Bill of Rights and Civil War amendments are designed to restrict popular majorities in just this way.

## IV

AT THE time, condemning a proposed African American residence for park purposes was a useful device for whites-only communities because, as a Missouri appeals court ruled, also in 1959, the judicial system could not inquire as to the motives for a condemnation, provided the purpose of the condemnation was public, which a park surely was. In the Missouri case, an African American couple had attempted to build a home in the white St. Louis suburb of Creve Coeur. Again, permits had been approved and work had begun when the town discovered that the purchasers were African American. A hastily organized citizens committee then raised contributions to purchase the property. White property owner groups frequently attempted this ploy when faced with integration: in Lorraine Hansberry's 1959 play, *A Raisin in the Sun,* an owners' group in a white Chicago community attempts a similar buyout of African American neighbors. As in the Hansberry drama, the Creve Coeur couple refused the offer. The city then condemned the property for recreational use.

Condemnations of property and manipulations of zoning designations to prevent African Americans from building occurred almost routinely in the 1950s and 1960s. But one case caught national attention. In 1969, a Methodist church-sponsored nonprofit organization proposed to construct a federally subsidized, racially integrated complex for moderate- and low-income families in Black Jack, an all-white suburb in unincorporated St. Louis County. In response, voters in Black Jack incorporated their community and adopted a zoning ordinance that prohibited future development of more than three homes per acre. This made development of new moderate-income housing impossible, although such modest units already existed within the new city boundaries. Several African Americans in St. Louis City sued. They claimed they had been unable to find decent homes outside the ghetto and therefore had little access to jobs that were increasingly suburban. The incident attracted national attention, and the Nixon administration deliberated for many months about whether to file its own suit to enjoin the zoning ordinance.

Eventually it did, and a federal appeals court ordered Black Jack to permit the pro-integration group to proceed. The court observed that hostility to the development was "repeatedly expressed in racial terms by persons whom the District Court found to be leaders of the incorporation movement, by individuals circulating petitions, and by zoning commissioners themselves." The court continued: "Racial criticism [of the proposed development] was made and cheered at public meetings. The uncontradicted evidence indicates that, at all levels of opposition, race played a significant role, both in the drive to incorporate and the decision to rezone."

Citing similar cases from elsewhere in the country, the court concluded that Black Jack's actions were "but one more factor confining blacks to low-income housing in the center city, confirming the inexorable process whereby the St. Louis metropolitan area becomes one that has the racial shape of a donut, with the Negroes in the hole and with mostly Whites occupying the ring." The court further noted that Black Jack's actions were exacerbating residential segregation that was "in large measure the result of deliberate racial discrimination in the housing market by the real estate industry *and by agencies of the federal, state, and local governments.*" This is *de jure* segregation.

The Methodist organization, however, did not win its legal victory until 1974, five years after it had first proposed the integrated project. By then, financing was no longer available, interest rates had climbed, and the federal government had become less supportive of subsidizing integrated housing. The lawyers for the church group said that, despite the court ruling, "no developer in his or her right mind" would proceed with the project in the face of such hostility. It was never built. "Justice delayed is justice denied" was the frequent experience of African Americans having to fight legal battles to obtain housing in white neighborhoods.

## V

WHILE MANY *de jure* segregation policies aimed to keep African Americans far from white residential areas, public officials also shifted African American populations away from downtown business districts so that white commuters, shoppers, and business elites would not be exposed to black people.

"Slum clearance" was the way to accomplish this. By the mid-twentieth century, "slums" and "blight" were widely understood euphemisms for African American neighborhoods. Once government had succeeded in preventing black families from joining their white peers in the suburbs, and in concentrating them within a few urban districts, these communities were indeed blighted. In many cases, slum clearance could have been a good idea. Where low-income African Americans were living in squalor, plans to demolish substandard structures and provide new, decent homes in integrated neighborhoods would have been appropriate. But mostly policy makers contemplated no such relocation. Instead, slum clearance reinforced the spatial segregation of African Americans as well as their impoverishment. This, in turn, led to further segregation because the more impoverished African Americans became, the less welcome they were in middle-class communities.

One slum clearance tool was the construction of the federal interstate highway system. In many cases, state and local governments, with federal acquiescence, designed interstate highway routes to destroy urban African American communities. Highway planners did not hide their racial motivations.*

The story of such highway planning begins in 1938, when the federal government first considered aid for interstate highways. Secretary of Agriculture (and subsequently Vice President) Henry Wallace proposed to President Roosevelt that highways routed through cities could also accomplish "the elimination of unsightly and unsanitary districts." Over the next two decades, the linkage

---

* "Urban renewal" programs, to clear slums not only for highways but for hospitals, universities, middle-class housing, and offices, operated similarly. That "urban renewal means Negro removal" was a frequent twentieth century slogan of civil rights groups protesting such displacement.

between highway construction and removal of American Americans was a frequent theme of those who stood to profit from a federal road-building program. They found that an effective way to argue a case for highway spending was to stress the capacity of road construction to make business districts and their environs white. Mayors and other urban political leaders joined in, seizing on highway construction as a way to overcome the constitutional prohibition on zoning African Americans away from white neighborhoods near downtowns.

In 1943, the American Concrete Institute urged the construction of urban expressways for "the elimination of slums and blighted areas." In 1949, the American Road Builders Association wrote to President Truman that if interstates were properly routed through metropolitan areas, they could "contribute in a substantial manner to the elimination of slum and deteriorated areas." An important influence on national legislation and administration of the highway system was the Urban Land Institute, whose 1957 newsletter recommended that city governments survey the "extent to which blighted areas may provide suitable highway routes." By 1962 the Highway Research Board boasted that interstate highways were "eating out slums" and "reclaiming blighted areas."

Alfred Johnson, the executive director of the American Association of State Highway Officials, was the lobbyist most deeply involved with the congressional committee that wrote the 1956 Highway Act. He later recalled that "some city officials expressed the view in the mid-1950s that the urban Interstates would give them a good opportunity to get rid of the local 'niggertown.'" His expectation did not go unfulfilled.

Hamtramck, Michigan, for example, was an overwhelmingly Polish enclave surrounded by Detroit. The city's 1959 master plan called for a "program of population loss," understood to refer to its small number of African American residents. In 1962, with federal urban renewal funds, the city began to demolish African American neighborhoods. The first project cleared land for expansion of a Chrysler automobile manufacturing plant. Then, federal dollars were used to raze more homes to make way for the Chrysler Expressway (I-75) leading to the plant. In advance, the U.S. Commission on Civil Rights had warned that the expressway would displace about 4,000 families, 87 percent of whom were African American.

Twelve years later, a federal appeals court concluded that HUD officials knew that the highway would disproportionately destroy African American homes and make no provision for assisting them in finding new lodgings: "The record supports a finding that HUD must have known of the discriminatory practices which pervaded the private housing market [in Hamtramck] and *the indications of overt prejudice among some of the persons involved in carrying out the urban renewal projects of the City.*" The court-ordered remedy was construction of new housing in the city only for those families who had been displaced, who could still be found, and who had indicated to interviewers that they would be willing to return to Hamtramck. Because the litigation had dragged on, their number was a small share of those who had suffered harm, most of whom had no choice but to move into the Detroit ghetto.

Federal interstate highways buttressed segregation in cities across the country. In 1956, the Florida State Road Department routed I-95 to do what Miami's unconstitutional zoning ordinance had intended but failed to accomplish two decades earlier: clear African Americans from an area adjacent to downtown. An alternative route utilizing an abandoned railway right of way was rejected, although it would have resulted in little population removal. When the highway was eventually completed in the mid-1960s, it had reduced a community of 40,000 African Americans to 8,000.

In Camden, New Jersey, an interstate highway destroyed some 3,000 low-income housing units from 1963 to 1967. A report by the New Jersey State Attorney General's office concluded: "It is obvious from a glance at the . . . transit plans that an attempt is being made to eliminate the Negro and Puerto Rican ghetto areas by . . . building highways that benefit white suburbanites, facilitating their movement from the suburbs to work and back."

*After Miami-Dade mayor Chuck Hall sent the first wrecking ball to destroy an African American neighborhood, buildings were demolished to make way for I-95, as children look on.*

In Los Angeles, routing of the Santa Monica Freeway in 1954 destroyed the city's most prosperous black middle-class area, Sugar Hill. In an all-too-familiar series of events, when the first African American—an insurance company executive—arrived there in 1938, neighborhood association leaders suggested to him that he would be happier if he lived elsewhere. When the executive failed to act on that advice, the group proposed to buy the property from him but then could not raise the funds. By 1945, a few middle-class African Americans had settled in Sugar Hill, and the association went to court to apply its restrictive covenant and have them evicted. But anticipating the U.S. Supreme Court's *Shelley* ruling by three years, a state judge ruled that enforcement of the covenant would violate the Fourteenth Amendment. After more African Americans bought houses in the area, the Los Angeles City Council rezoned the neighborhood for rentals, over the protests of affluent African Americans who already lived in Sugar Hill. More lower-income black families then moved in. The routing of the Santa Monica Freeway through Sugar Hill succeeded in demolishing the black community where other efforts had failed. African American leaders pleaded that the freeway be shifted slightly north, but the city engineer dismissed their concerns, assuring them that they would have up to five years to find new housing before properties were seized.

In few of these cases did federal or local agencies provide assistance to displaced African Americans in finding adequate and safe new housing. When enacted into law in 1956, the interstate highway program did not impose even a nominal obligation on federal or state governments to assist those whose residences were being demolished. Although the House version of the bill permitted (but did not require) payment of moving costs to tenants in demolished homes, the Eisenhower administration objected. Council of Economic Advisors chairman Arthur Burns warned that compensation would "run up costs" of the highway program, predicting that the system would evict nearly 100,000 people a year as it grew. The Senate then removed language permitting such payments from the final legislation. In 1965, the federal government began to require that new housing be provided for those forced to relocate by future interstate highway construction, but by then the interstate system was nearly complete.

# VI

IN SOUTHERN and border states and in some northern cities where explicit school segregation was practiced before the Supreme Court's 1954 *Brown* decision, authorities developed another tactic to impose residential segregation where it would not otherwise exist: placing the only schools that served African American children in designated African American neighborhoods and providing no transportation for black students who lived elsewhere. African American families who wanted their children to be educated had no choice but to find new housing in the newly segregated areas.

When in 1928 Austin, Texas, adopted its master plan that proposed a single African American neighborhood on the Eastside, the document explicitly lamented the *Buchanan* ruling. It noted that "there has been considerable talk in Austin, as well as other cities, in regard to the race segregation problem. This problem cannot be solved legally under any zoning law known to us at present. Practically all attempts at such have proven unconstitutional."

Unable to legislate explicit segregation, the master plan proposed creating an "incentive to draw the negro population to this [Eastside] area." The incentive was to relocate segregated schools and other public services for African Americans to Austin's Eastside. These actions were effective, and soon almost all African Americans in Austin had moved east. For example, in 1930, the integrated neighborhood of Wheatsville had an African American population of 16 percent. In 1932, its segregated school for African American pupils was shut down, and by 1950 the community's African American population was 1 percent.

The city closed other schools and parks for African Americans outside the Eastside area that had been designated for their residence. Additional inducements for African Americans to consolidate were created by the construction on the Eastside of a new segregated library, a new park, and an improved segregated high school. Then, in 1938, the segregation of the African American population in the area was further reinforced when the planning commission chose it as the location for Rosewood Courts, the all-black public housing project that had been won for Austin by Congressman Lyndon Johnson, while he also won a companion project for whites close to downtown.

Once African Americans had been pushed into the Eastside, municipal services in the neighborhood declined. Streets, for example, were more likely to be unpaved than in other parts of the city; sewers were poorly maintained and often clogged; and bus routes that served the Eastside were suspended during the summer, because the same routes served the University of Texas and were not needed for students when the university was on break. Zoning rules to preserve neighborhoods' residential characters were not enforced on the Eastside, leading to the establishment of industrial facilities in the area.

Although the strategic placement of schools to designate racial zones was a tactic primarily available to southern cities with codified school segregation, the device was occasionally employed in the North as well. In the 1920s, Indianapolis used its school siting policy to pursue the goal of residential segregation. The school board shifted the academically prestigious and all-white high school to an exclusive white community, far from the city's racial boundary. This left the former high school in an area near the border between the city's black and white neighborhoods, but the board refused to designate it for use by African Americans; rather, it constructed a new high school for African American students near a glue factory and city dump, far from white areas.

The case of Raleigh and surrounding Wake County, North Carolina, is particularly noteworthy because, in recent years, advocates of school integration have praised the county for its program of busing children to make its schools more diverse. Barred by the Supreme Court from explicitly integrating schools by race, the district—which includes the city of Raleigh and its suburbs—has bused low-income children from the south and east sides of the county to middle-class neighborhoods in the north and west. As it happens, children in the southeast are mostly black, while those in the northwest are mostly white. The segregated design that the busing was designed to overcome was no accident. It was created, in part, by racially motivated school siting decisions in the early twentieth century.

Karen Benjamin, a historian at St. Xavier College in Chicago, has uncovered records that reveal how school placement decisions helped force the segregation of Raleigh as well as of Houston and Atlanta. In Raleigh in the early twentieth century, neighborhoods of black and white concentration were scattered across the city. They included two relatively prosperous African American neighborhoods, Idlewild and College Park, on what was then the city's northeast side. These middle-class communities of owner-occupied single-family homes no longer exist because in the 1920s the school board decided to transfer all schools for black students to the far southeastern section of the city, where planners hoped to isolate Raleigh's African Americans. (Making matters worse, when the board provided Idlewild's and College Park's middle-class residents with a new school, it put the campus next to the city dump and a rock quarry filled with stagnant water.) At the same time, it established the newest and most well-equipped schools for white students in far northwestern neighborhoods. In some cases, these areas were still largely undeveloped, where real estate interests hoped to attract white families.

There was nothing hidden about the racial context of these school-site decisions, and they generated considerable debate. An editorial in the moderate *Raleigh Times* said:

> The negroes making protest are of the best element of the race in Raleigh. Many of them live in the northeastern section already occupied by a numerous, growing population of negro citizens, the majority of whom are owners of their own homes. They have built up with who knows what sacrifice a self-respecting and steadily improving community. . . . It is a

fact well-known that the northeastern negro section was due largely to the desire of better class negroes to escape the very Rock Quarry locality in which it is suggested the new school will take place.

In Atlanta, the school board also helped to segregate a city that previously had some mixed-race housing. Before World War I, mostly black and white blocks were interspersed in central city neighborhoods. After the war, however, city planners determined that future city growth would be rigidly segregated. Even though courts had struck down an explicit Atlanta racial zoning ordinance in 1924, the segregation maps guided school closure and construction decisions by the Atlanta School Board for the next two decades.

Gradually, schools for whites were closed if they were in zones designated for future African American residence, and schools for African Americans were closed if they were in zones reserved for whites. New schools for white students were built in the developing white suburbs, which forced white families to move to these communities if their children were to have access to the most up-to-date schools. As with white families, black families who did not already live in their racially designated area were forced to find new housing if they wanted their children to attend a modern school.

In 1919, when the policy was developing but still not fully formal, the school board converted the Ashby Street School on the west side in a planned ghetto area, from a school for whites to one for African Americans. The minutes of a school board meeting report the adoption of a motion that white families may be given one year to keep their children in the school, "to allow the white residents of that section to sell their homes, it being understood that the school [would be] turned over to the negroes at the close of the year."

Two high schools for white students in a racially mixed downtown area were closed and moved to the northern suburbs, while the city's first high school for black students was constructed far west of downtown, in a still relatively undeveloped area but one intended for African Americans. The Atlanta School Board commissioned a study by two Columbia University experts, who recommended placing a new junior high school for whites in a densely populated neighborhood northwest of the central city area where elementary school overcrowding was most severe. Because this area was racially mixed (and designated for future African American residence), the board rejected the consultants' recommendation and instead constructed a new white junior high school across the railroad tracks in the far northern suburbs, forcing white families to cease living in an integrated community if they wished their adolescent children to be educated.

In Houston, in the 1920s the city plan commission also drew up a map designating "Race Restriction Areas." Seeing that a Georgia court had rejected Atlanta's zoning ordinance, Houston never formally adopted the map. But as in Atlanta, the school board used it as a guide. At the beginning of the twentieth century, many Houston neighborhoods were integrated; substantial numbers of African American and white children lived in each of the city's six wards. Each ward had a school for African American children that was near, and in some cases on the same block as, the school for whites. Over one-fourth of African American children lived in a school attendance district that was at least 70 percent white. The city plan, however, foresaw developing the west side of Houston for exclusive white residence while pushing African Americans out of the west side and into developing ghettos in the south and northeast.

To accomplish this, in the 1920s and '30s the school board built, on the west side, new schools with advanced facilities for whites; it set up, on the far south side, a modern high school for African Americans, to induce middle-class black families to move there. The city also established a new Houston Negro Hospital near the new high school as a further incentive for African Americans to relocate. The school board closed an elementary school for African American pupils on the west side and built better-equipped schools for them in the working-class neighborhoods of the northeast. While building relatively expensive schools for African Americans on the south and northeast sides, the school board appropriated little money for improvements at schools for African American pupils in the west. Similarly, white schools in the area designated for African Americans were closed or allowed to deteriorate. Each time the board made a decision about schools for African American pupils, a chief consideration was avoiding "proximity to white districts." Professor Benjamin concludes that Houston's "school building programs were the key to preserving school segregation long after the *Brown* decision declared it unconstitutional."

*Levittown, Pennsylvania, 1954. A crowd mobilizes before proceeding to harass the first African American family to move into the all-white development.*

# 9

## STATE-SANCTIONED VIOLENCE

I N 1952, WILBUR GARY, a building contractor, was living with his family in one of Richmond, California's, public housing projects. He was an African American navy war veteran, a former shipyard worker, and vice-commander of his American Legion post. The Gary family needed to find a new residence—their apartment complex was slated for demolition because the federal Lanham Act had required government projects for war workers to be temporary. A fellow navy veteran, Lieutenant Commander Sidney Hogan, was moving out of Rollingwood, the suburb just outside Richmond built during World War II with an FHA requirement that the suburb be covered with restrictive covenants. Four years earlier, though, the Supreme Court had ruled that covenants were not enforceable, so Hogan sold his property to Wilbur Gary and his wife.

Nonetheless, the Rollingwood Improvement Association, a homeowners group, insisted that its covenants gave it the right to evict African Americans. The NAACP came to the family's aid and dared the group to try to enforce the covenant. The neighbors then attempted to buy back the Gary house for nearly 15 percent more than the Garys had paid. They refused the offer.

Soon after the Garys arrived, a mob of about 300 whites gathered outside their house, shouting epithets, hurling bricks (one crashed through the front window), and burning a cross on the lawn. For several days, police and county sheriff deputies refused to step in, so the NAACP found it necessary to organize its own guards. A Communist Party–affiliated civil rights group also provided help. The journalist Jessica Mitford, in her book *A Fine Old Conflict*, described her participation in the group's efforts, which included escorting Mrs. Gary and the children to work and school and patrolling nearby streets to alert the Garys to mobs that might be gathering.

Meanwhile, the NAACP pressed California governor Earl Warren, Attorney General Brown, and the local district attorney to step in. They eventually did so, ordering the city police and county sheriff to provide the family with protection. Still, the protests and harassment continued for another month, with continued pleas from Wilbur Gary and civil rights groups for the police to intervene. No arrests, however, were made. The sheriff claimed that he did not have enough manpower to prevent the violence. Yet a single arrest is probably all that would have been required to persuade the mob to withdraw.

# I

AT ABOUT the same time, the Levitt company began to build its second large development, this one in Bucks County, Pennsylvania, a suburb of Philadelphia. Built post-*Shelley*, the Pennsylvania project did not have restrictive covenants, but the FHA continued to support Levitt and other developers only if they refused to sell to African Americans. Robert Mereday, the African American trucker who had delivered material to Levitt's Long Island project, won another contract with the company to deliver sheetrock to the Bucks County site. He settled his family in an African American neighborhood in nearby Bristol. His son, Robert Jr., attended Bristol High School, graduating in 1955. He had a girlfriend there, Shirley Wilson, and he recalls that the Wilson family had attempted to move to Levittown but was rebuffed by the Levitt company despite the negative publicity that the Wilsons' rejection had generated.

I mention the "flap" (the term Robert Mereday, Jr., uses in recalling the Wilson incident) because such instances were more commonplace than historians can document, and they must have had a profound effect on the awareness within the African American community of how their housing options were limited. It is remarkable that African American families continued to make the attempt to break into white suburban life—as they did at the Levittown in Bucks County.

By the late 1950s, white homeowners wanting to leave that development realized that it would be to their benefit to sell to African Americans who, because they were desperate for housing, would pay more than whites. So it happened that in 1957 an African American veteran, Bill Myers, and his wife Daisy, found a Levittown homeowner willing to sell.

Like many Levittown residents, Myers had served in World War II. He was discharged as a staff sergeant and held a steady job as a lab technician in the engineering department of a factory in nearby Trenton, New Jersey. Daisy Myers was a college graduate, and Bill Myers was taking courses toward a degree in electrical engineering. When no bank would provide a mortgage because the Myers family was black, a New York City philanthropist offered to give them a private mortgage, and Bill and Daisy Myers, with their three children, occupied their new home.

A few days later, the U.S. Post Office mail carrier, a federal government employee performing his official duties, noticed that he was delivering mail to an African American family. As he made his rounds, he shouted, "Niggers have moved into Levittown!" As many as 600 white demonstrators assembled in front of the house and pelted the family and its house with rocks. Some rented a unit next door to the Myerses and set up a clubhouse from which the Confederate flag flew and music blared all night. Police arrived but were ineffective. When Mr. Myers requested around-the-clock protection, the police chief told him that the department couldn't afford it. The town commissioners accused the state police of "meddling" because troopers were dispatched when the police failed to end the harassment. It was a needless worry; the state troopers also declined to perform their duty.

For two months law enforcement stood by as rocks were thrown, crosses were burned, the Ku Klux Klan symbol was painted on the wall of the clubhouse next door, and the home of a family that had supported the Myerses was vandalized. Some policemen, assigned to protect the African American family, stood with the mob, joking and encouraging its participants. One sergeant was demoted to patrolman because he objected to orders he had been given not to interfere with the rioters.

The district attorney approached Bill Myers and offered to purchase his property for a price substantially above what he had paid. Even though riot leaders were well known, for several weeks the police made no attempt to arrest them or to shut down the clubhouse. The federal government did not discipline or reprimand the mail carrier. Eventually, the Pennsylvania attorney general prosecuted some of the rioters for harassment and obtained an injunction against its continuation. But Bill and Daisy Myers, feeling constantly under threat, lasted only another four years; in 1961, they sold their Levittown home and returned to the African American neighborhood in York, Pennsylvania, where they had previously lived.

Does the failure of police to protect the Gary and Myers families constitute government-sponsored, *de jure* segregation? When police officers stood by without preventing the intimidation these families endured, were the African American families' constitutional rights violated, or were they victims of rogue police officers for whom the state was not responsible? Certainly, we cannot hold the government accountable for every action of racially biased police officers. Yet if these officers' superiors were aware of racially discriminatory activities conducted under color of law, as they surely were, and either encouraged these activities or took inadequate steps to restrain them, then these were no longer merely rogue actions but expressed state policy that violated the Fourteenth Amendment's guarantees of due process and equal protection.

If we apply that standard to police behavior in Rollingwood and in Levittown, we must conclude that law enforcement officers conspired to violate the civil rights of the Garys and of the Myerses and that this unremedied conspiracy of government authorities contributed to *de jure* segregation of the communities for whose welfare they were responsible.

## II

WHAT THE Gary and the Myers families experienced was not an aberration. During much of the twentieth century, police tolerance and promotion of cross burnings, vandalism, arson, and other violent acts to maintain residential segregation was systematic and nationwide.

The attacks on African American pioneers, sanctioned by elected officials and law enforcement officers, could not have been attributable to whites' discomfort with a lower social class of neighbors. Wilbur and Borece Gary and Bill and Daisy Myers were solidly middle class. Because more affluent communities were closed to them, the African Americans who were victimized by such mob action often had higher occupational and social status than the white neighbors who assaulted them. This circumstance belies the oft-repeated claim that resistance to integration has been based on fears of deteriorating neighborhood quality. Indeed, when African Americans did succeed in moving to previously white neighborhoods, they frequently were "on their best behavior," giving no cause, or pretext, for complaint, taking pains to make certain that their homes and lawns were better cared for than others on their blocks.

Events in Chicago were only slightly more pervasive than elsewhere. Although most frequent in the post–World War II period, state-sanctioned violence to prevent integration began at the turn of the twentieth century, during the beginnings of the Jim Crow era.

In 1897, white property owners in Chicago's Woodlawn neighborhood "declared war" on African Americans, driving all African

American families from the area with threats of violence, unimpeded by public authority. A decade later in Hyde Park, adjacent to Woodlawn, the Hyde Park Improvement Protective Club organized boycotts of merchants who sold to African Americans and offered to buy out the homes of African Americans who lived in the area. If these tactics were unsuccessful, whites engaged in vandalism, throwing rocks through African Americans' windows. The leader of the club was a prominent attorney, and the club published a newsletter promoting segregation, so it would not have been difficult for authorities to interfere with the conspiracy, but no measures were undertaken.

From 1917 to 1921, when the Chicago ghetto was first being rigidly defined, there were fifty-eight firebombings of homes in white border areas to which African Americans had moved, with no arrests or prosecutions—despite the deaths of two African American residents. In one case, explosives were lobbed at the home of Richard B. Harrison, a well-known black Shakespearean actor who had purchased a house in a white neighborhood. The bombs were thrown from a vacant and locked apartment in a building next door. The police did not make a serious attempt to find the perpetrator, failing even to question the building's occupants, although few possible conspirators could have had access to the apartment.

Nearly thirty of the fifty-eight firebombings were concentrated in a six-month period in the spring of 1919, leading up to one of the nation's worst race riots, set off when a white youth stoned an African American swimmer who had drifted toward a public beach area, generally understood to be for whites' use only. The swimmer drowned, and policemen at the scene refused to arrest the attacker. Subsequent battles between whites and blacks left thirty-eight dead (twenty-three of whom were African American) and poisoned race relations in Chicago for years afterward.

Interracial violence continued unabated. In the first five years after World War II, 357 reported "incidents" were directed against African Americans attempting to rent or buy in Chicago's racial border areas. From mid-1944 to mid-1946, there were forty-six attacks on the homes of African Americans in white communities adjacent to Chicago's overcrowded black neighborhoods; of these, twenty-nine were arson-bombings, resulting in at least three deaths. In the first ten months of 1947 alone, twenty-six arson-bombings occurred, without an arrest.

In 1951, Harvey Clark, an African American Chicago bus driver and air force veteran, rented an apartment in all-white Cicero, a Chicago suburb. At first, the police forcefully attempted to prevent him, his wife Johnnetta, and two small children from occupying the apartment. They threatened him with arrest and worse if the family did not depart. "Get out of Cicero," the police chief told the real estate agent who rented the apartment, adding, "Don't come back . . . or you'll get a bullet through you." When Harvey Clark got a court injunction ordering the police to cease interfering with his occupancy and "to afford him full protection from any attempt to so restrain him," the police ignored it, making no effort, for example, to impede a group of teenagers who were pelting the apartment's windows with stones. When the Clarks refused to leave, a mob of about 4,000 rioted, raiding the apartment, destroying the fixtures, and throwing the family's belongings out the window onto the lawn where they were set ablaze. The officers present arrested no one. *Time* magazine reported that the police "acted like ushers politely handling the overflow at a football stadium."

Governor Adlai Stevenson mobilized the National Guard to restore order. Although 118 rioters were arrested, a Cook County grand jury did not indict a single one. The grand jury, however, did indict Harvey Clark, his real estate agent, his NAACP attorney, and the white landlady who rented the apartment to him as well as her attorney on charges of inciting a riot and conspiring to lower property values. Thirty-six years later, when an African American family again attempted to live in Cicero, it was met with firebombs and rifle shots. Nobody was convicted of these attacks, either. Cicero's council president boasted after the clash that "[t]he area is well-secured."

In 1953, the Chicago Housing Authority leased apartments to African American families for the first time in its Trumbull Park project in the all-white South Deering neighborhood. Ten years of sporadic mob violence ensued. The African American families required police protection during the entire period. As many as 1200 policemen were deployed to guard African American families on the day a group of them moved in, but little was done to end the attacks by arresting and prosecuting the perpetrators. A neighborhood association, the South Deering Improvement Association, led the violence, but its officers were not charged with any crime. A few bomb throwers were arrested but only after police had passively watched them launch their bombs. They faced only minor charges. An observer concluded that "sympathy for the white rioters on the part of the average policeman . . . [was] extreme." Addressing a South Deering Improvement Association meeting, the chief of the Chicago Park District Police commiserated with his audience that "it is unfortunate the colored people chose to come out here." The mob's attacks were successful. The Chicago Housing Authority fired Elizabeth Wood, its executive director who had authorized the leasing of apartments in previously all-white projects to African Americans.*

In 1964, a white civil rights activist in Bridgeport, Chicago mayor Richard J. Daley's all-white neighborhood, rented an apartment to African American college students. A mob gathered and pelted the apartment with rocks. Police entered the apartment, removed the students' belongings, and told them when they returned from school that they had been evicted.

Events in Detroit and its suburbs were similar. During the immediate postwar period, the city saw more than 200 acts of intimidation and violence to deter African Americans from moving to predominantly white neighborhoods. Such an epidemic was possible because police could be counted on to stand by, making no effort to stop, much less to prevent, the assaults. In 1968, an official of the Michigan Civil Rights Commission reported that "our expe-

---

* Wood had been pressing the Chicago Housing Authority board to abandon its practice of segregation. The CHA's purported reason for firing Wood was that, without authorization, she had disclosed to the press her futile efforts to persuade the CHA to follow its stated nondiscrimination policy.

rience has been that nearly all attempts by black families to move to Detroit's suburbs have been met with harassment."

In the Philadelphia area, the attacks encountered by the Myers family were not unusual. In the first six months of 1955, 213 violent incidents ensured that most African Americans remained in the North Philadelphia ghetto. Some incidents involved move-in violence like that experienced by the Myerses; others involved white teenagers defending what they considered a neighborhood boundary that African Americans should not cross. Although in some cases perpetrators might have been difficult to identify, it is improbable that police were incapable of finding a sufficient number to prevent repetitive conflict.

In the Los Angeles area, cross burnings, dynamite bombings, rocks thrown through windows, graffiti, and other acts of vandalism, as well as numerous phone threats, greeted African Americans who found housing in neighborhoods just outside their existing areas of concentration. In 1945, an entire family—father, mother, and two children—was killed when its new home in an all-white neighborhood was blown up. Of the more than one hundred incidents of move-in bombings and vandalism that occurred in Los Angeles between 1950 and 1965, only one led to an arrest and prosecution—and that was because the California attorney general took over the case after local police and prosecutors claimed they were unable to find anyone to charge.

Although the 1968 Fair Housing Act made violence to prevent neighborhood integration a federal crime and the Department of Justice prosecuted several cases, frequent attacks on African Americans attempting to leave predominantly black areas continued into the 1980s. The Southern Poverty Law Center found that in 1985–86, only about one-quarter of these incidents were prosecuted, but the share in which charges were brought grew rapidly from 1985 to 1990, up to 75 percent. That such an increase in the rate of prosecution was possible suggests how tolerant of such crimes police and prosecutors had previously been. Still, the center documented 130 cases of move-in violence in 1989 alone.

During the mid-twentieth century, local police and the FBI went to extraordinary lengths to infiltrate and disrupt liberal and left-wing political groups as well as organized crime syndicates. That they did not act similarly in the case of a nationwide terror campaign against African Americans who integrated previously white communities should be deemed, at the least, complicity in the violence. Had perpetrators been held to account in even a few well-publicized cases, many thousands of others might have been prevented.

Nor can the failure to control mob assaults be blamed on police officers who acted without explicit authorization of their superiors. In recent years we have seen several examples of the choices that confront public officials in analogous situations. When a police officer has killed or beaten an African American man with apparent racial motivation, we now expect that the officer's superiors will fire him (or her) or, if there is doubt about whether a citizen's civil rights were violated, will suspend the officer, pending an investigation. If superiors fail to take such measures, we expect still higher authorities to intervene. If they do not, we can reasonably assume that the police officer's approach fit within the bounds of what his or her superiors consider appropriate response and reflect governmental policy.

# III

IN 1954, Andrew Wade—an African American electrical contractor and Korean War navy veteran—wanted to purchase a house in a middle-class African American neighborhood of Louisville, Kentucky, but couldn't find anything suitable. A friend and prominent left-wing activist, Carl Braden, suggested he look at a white middle-class community instead; Braden and his wife, Anne, then agreed to buy a house for Andrew Wade and his wife, Charlotte. The Wades found a property in Shively, an all-white suburb, which the Bradens bought, signing over the deed.

When the Wades and their child were moving in, a crowd gathered in front, and a cross was burned on an empty lot next door. On the first evening the family spent at home, a rock crashed through its front window with a message tied to it, "Nigger Get Out," and later

*Top: Charlotte, Rosemary, and Andrew Wade, after rocks were hurled through the windows of their Shively, Kentucky, home in 1954. Bottom: A policeman inspects damage after the Wades' house was dynamited.*

that night, ten rifle shots were fired through the glass of its kitchen door. Under the watch of a police guard, demonstrations continued for a month until the house was dynamited. The police guard said he saw nothing. There was one arrest following the Wades' moving in: of Andrew Wade and a friend for "breach of the peace," because Mr. Wade had failed to notify the police that the friend would be visiting. The police chief was familiar enough with the bombers to warn Carl Braden that the people responsible for blowing up the Wade property were targeting the Braden home next.

Although the chief acknowledged that both the dynamiter and the cross burners had confessed, the perpetrators were not indicted. Instead, a grand jury indicted Carl and Anne Braden, along with four others whom the jury accused of conspiring to stir up racial conflict by selling the house to African Americans. The formal charge was "sedition." Charges against the others were dropped, but Carl Braden was sentenced to fifteen years in prison (he eventually won release on appeal), and the Wades went back to Louisville's African American area.

Such violence in Kentucky did not end in the 1950s. In 1985, Robert and Martha Marshall bought a home in Sylvania, another suburb of Louisville that had remained exclusively white. Their house was firebombed on the night they moved in. A month later, a second arson attack destroyed the house, a few hours before a Ku Klux Klan meeting at which a speaker boasted that no African Americans would be permitted to live in Sylvania. The Marshall family then sued a county police officer who had been identified as a member of the Klan. The officer testified that about half of the forty Klan members known to him were also in the police department and that his superiors condoned officers' Klan membership, as long as the information did not become public.*

---

* Two perpetrators, one of whom was the brother-in-law of the Klan member at whose house a Klan rally was held, were convicted of committing the initial firebombing, but no arrests were made of those responsible for the later, more serious arson attack. It can be presumed that if a police department in which twenty officers were Klan members wanted to identify the perpetrators, it could have done so.

Many years ago I read *The Wall Between*, Anne Braden's memoir that describes how she and her husband were prosecuted by the state of Kentucky for helping Andrew Wade attempt to live in a white neighborhood. I remembered that account when, in 2007, the U.S. Supreme Court prohibited the Louisville school district from carrying out a racial integration plan, on the ground that the segregation of Louisville is "a product not of state action but of private choices."

State-sponsored violence was a means, along with many others, by which all levels of government maintained segregation in Louisville and elsewhere. The Wades and Marshalls were only two middle-class families confronted with hostile state power when they tried to cross the residential color line. How many other middle-class African Americans in Louisville were intimidated from attempting to live in neighborhoods of their own choosing after hearing of the Wade and Marshall experiences? Did the next generation imbibe a fear of integration from their parents? How long do the memories of such events last? How long do they continue to intimidate?

*Sausalito, California, 1943. Joseph James (front, at table, second from the right) organized the refusal of black shipyard workers to pay dues to a segregated and powerless union auxiliary.*

# 10

## SUPPRESSED INCOMES

A COMMON EXPLANATION FOR *de facto* segregation is that most black families could not afford to live in predominantly white middle-class communities and still are unable to do so. African American isolation, the argument goes, reflects their low incomes, not *de jure* segregation. Racial segregation will persist until more African Americans improve their educations and then are able to earn enough to move out of high-poverty neighborhoods.

The explanation at first seems valid. But we cannot understand the income and wealth gap that persists between African Americans and whites without examining governmental policies that purposely kept black incomes low throughout most of the twentieth century. Once government implemented these policies, economic differences became self-perpetuating. It is not impossible, but it is rare for Americans, black or white, to have a higher rank in the national income distribution than their parents. Everyone's standard of living may grow from generation to generation, but an individual's relative income—how it compares to the incomes of others in the present generation—is remarkably similar to how his or her parents' incomes compared to others in their generation.

So an account of *de jure* residential segregation has to include not only how public policy geographically separated African Americans from whites but also how federal and state labor market policies, with undisguised racial intent, depressed African American wages. In addition, some and perhaps many local governments taxed African Americans more heavily than whites. The effects of these government actions were compounded because neighborhood segregation itself imposed higher expenses on African American than on white families, even if their wages and tax rates had been identical. The result: smaller disposable incomes and fewer savings for black families, denying them the opportunity to accumulate wealth and contributing to make housing in middle-class communities unaffordable.

If government purposely depressed the incomes of African Americans, with the result that they were priced out of mainstream housing markets, then these economic policies are also important parts of the architecture of *de jure* segregation.

# I

UNTIL LONG after emancipation from slavery, most African Americans were denied access to free labor markets and were unable to save from wages. This denial of access was another badge of slavery that Congress was duty bound to eliminate, not to perpetuate.

Following the Civil War, and intensifying after Reconstruction, a sharecropping system of indentured servitude perpetuated aspects of the slave system. After food and other living costs were deducted from their earnings, sharecroppers typically owed plantation owners more than their wages due. Local sheriffs enforced this peonage, preventing sharecroppers from seeking work elsewhere, by arresting, assaulting, or murdering those who attempted to leave, or by condoning violence perpetrated by owners.

In many instances, African Americans were arrested for petty and phony offenses (like vagrancy if they came to town when off work), and when they were unable to pay fines and court fees, wardens sometimes sold prisoners to plantations, mines, and factories. Douglas Blackmon, in his book *Slavery by Another Name*, estimates that from the end of Reconstruction until World War II, the number enslaved in this way exceeded 100,000. Mines operated by U.S. Steel alone used tens of thousands of imprisoned African Americans. The practice ebbed during World War II, but it wasn't until 1951 that Congress fulfilled its Thirteenth Amendment obligation and explicitly outlawed the practice.

Some African Americans managed to escape to the North early in the twentieth century, yet others were forcibly prevented or intimidated from doing so. But during World War I, when immigration of unskilled Europeans was sharply curtailed, northern manufacturers sent recruiters south. They frequently traveled in disguise, pretending, for example, to be insurance salesmen, to avoid capture by sheriffs. During this time, more than 600,000 African Americans left the South, mostly to seek work in the North and Midwest. Historians call this the First Great Migration.

World War II then spurred the Second Great Migration, from 1940 to 1970, when more than four million African Americans made the journey. Thus most African Americans could not begin to accumulate capital for home purchases until fairly recently, well after European immigrant groups were able to participate in the wage economy. And when African Americans who left the South entered a northern labor market, federal, state, and local governments collaborated with private employers to ensure that they were paid less and treated worse than whites.

## II

IN THE 1930s, President Franklin D. Roosevelt could assemble the congressional majorities he needed to adopt New Deal legislation only by including southern Democrats, who were fiercely committed to white supremacy. In consequence, Social Security, minimum wage protection, and the recognition of labor unions all excluded from coverage occupations in which African Americans predominated: agriculture and domestic service. State and local governments behaved similarly. When, for example, in the mid-1930s St. Louis constructed a segregated hospital for African American patients, a contractor hired a single black tile setter; white union members protested, and the city fired the contractor and announced it would no longer use any firm that employed African American labor.

The Tennessee Valley Authority (TVA) segregated its workers on the job as well as in housing. At construction projects, African Americans were assigned to work separately, but only if enough were needed at particular sites to make up full crews. If not, then African Americans were denied work entirely. No African Americans were permitted to be promoted to foreman or other supervisory roles in the TVA. The first national New Deal program, the Federal Emergency Relief Administration, adopted in 1933, disproportionately spent its funds on unemployed whites, frequently refused to permit African Americans to take any but the least skilled jobs, and even in those, paid them less than the officially stipulated wage.

Similar policies later prevailed under the National Recovery Administration (NRA), another New Deal agency established in Roosevelt's first year. It established industry-by-industry minimum wages, maximum hours, and product prices. Codes routinely withheld benefits from African Americans that white workers enjoyed. In addition to agriculture and domestic service, the NRA did not cover subindustries and even individual factory types in which African Americans predominated. Canning, citrus packing, and cotton ginning were industrial, not agricultural jobs, but workers were usually African American, and so they were denied the NRA's wage and hours standards. The NRA took account of the lower cost of living in the South by setting lower wages in that region. In Delaware, 90 percent of fertilizer manufacturing workers were African American; thus fertilizer plants were classified as "southern," while other factories in the state that hired whites were classified as "northern," so higher minimum wages applied.

The first industrial code that the administration negotiated with business leaders in 1933 increased minimum wages in the cotton textile industry, resulting in price increases through the production chain, including retail clothing. But the agreement bypassed jobs in which African Americans predominated: cleaners, outside crews, and yardmen. Of the 14,000 African Americans in the industry, 10,000 held one of these job classifications. The NAACP complained, "For these workers the NRA meant increases of from 10 to 40 per cent in the cost of everything they had to buy, without a single penny in increased wages."

The Civilian Conservation Corps (CCC) not only segregated residential camps but allowed local policies that did not permit African Americans to enroll or restricted them to menial jobs in which they could not develop the higher skills that the corps was meant to provide. Florida announced that it would not accept African Americans, while Texas officials declared that "this work is for whites only." Many other states had long waiting lists of eligible African Americans because localities refused to allow the CCC to establish camps to lodge them. Where the army set up segregated camps, it did not permit African Americans to lead the units, assigning white commanders instead. CCC sites usually had educational programs, but army officers often refused to hire black teachers, leaving "educational adviser" positions vacant.

African American corps members were also rarely allowed to upgrade to better-paying jobs like machine operators or clerks, even if they'd had experience as civilians. The painter Jacob Lawrence worked as a youth at Breeze Hill, a segregated camp for African Americans about seventy miles northwest of New York City, where 1,400 young men shoveled mud for a flood control project. Not one could be promoted to a higher classification.

My father-in-law told how, in a white CCC camp, he claimed to know how to type (although his skills were minimal), then quickly learned to do so after persuading a supervisor to give him a clerk's job. He was then able to send a few dollars back to his parents, helping to keep them and his younger brothers and sister from losing their home. African American youths who already knew how to type (or were equally capable of faking it) had no such opportunities. Anecdotes like these, multiplied tens of thousands of times, help to explain the different African American and white economic conditions during the Depression and afterward.

# III

IN 1935, President Roosevelt signed the National Labor Relations Act, granting unions at construction sites and factories the right to bargain with management if the unions were supported by a majority of workers. Labor organizations that gained this official certification could negotiate contracts that covered all of a firm's employees. The original bill, proposed by Senator Robert Wagner of New York, had prohibited government certification of unions that did not grant African Americans membership and workplace rights. The American Federation of Labor (AFL) lobbied Wagner to remove the clause, and he did so. The enactment of the Wagner Act was accomplished with the knowledge that it sanctioned an unconstitutional policy of legally empowering unions that refused to admit African Americans. For at least the next thirty years, the government protected the bargaining rights of unions that denied African Americans the privileges of membership or that segregated them into janitorial and other lower-paid jobs.

In some cases, newly certified unions used their collective bargaining rights to force companies to fire African Americans who had been employed before unionization, and the National Labor Relations Board (NLRB), the agency delegated to administer the act, did nothing in response. In New York, for example, the NLRB-certified Building Service Employees Union forced Manhattan hotels, restaurants, and offices to fire African American elevator operators and restaurant workers and then give the jobs to whites.

# IV

THE GOVERNMENT'S participation in blocking African Americans' wage-earning opportunities had its most devastating effect during World War II, when black workers migrated to centers of war production in search of jobs. The Roosevelt administration required factories to convert from civilian to military production. The army and navy effectively operated shipbuilding yards, munitions makers, and aircraft and tank manufacturers. Yet federal agencies both tolerated and supported joint management-union policies that kept African Americans from doing any but the most poorly paid tasks in defense plants.

Events in the San Francisco Bay Area, where Allen and Frank Stevenson sought work during the war, were typical. The region was the largest center of war-related shipbuilding in the nation. The Marine Laborers Union, which had seven members in 1941, grew to more than 30,000 during the next few years. The Steamfitters union membership soared from 400 to 17,000. Unions like these had NLRB-certified agreements that companies could not hire without a union referral, and the unions would not refer African Americans.

From 1941 to 1943, the Henry J. Kaiser Company built four shipyards in Richmond with a capacity for 115,000 jobs. It could not recruit enough white men for all of them, so it began to take on white women. By 1944, women made up 27 percent of Kaiser's Richmond workforce. Then, with the supply of white women also exhausted, Kaiser sent agents to the South to seek African American men. By war's end, still short of workers, defense industries opened some industrial jobs to African American women, who were previously employed only as janitors, cafeteria workers, and restroom attendants.

After four years of fierce conflict with union activists, Ford Motor finally recognized the UAW as its workers' representative in 1941. Faced with a labor shortage that threatened its military contracts, the company hired African Americans like Frank Stevenson. Initially, Ford would not permit them to work in the higher-paid paint department, or as foremen, electricians, or in other skilled crafts, but as the union got stronger, activists like Ben Gross pressed Ford to open more classifications to African Americans.

The UAW was part of the new, more egalitarian Congress of Industrial Organizations. Shipyard workers, however, were mostly represented by the more conservative AFL. So while the Stevenson brothers became full-fledged union members, AFL unions mostly would not permit African Americans to join. There were a few exceptions—90 percent of the Shipyard Laborers union was African American because it represented workers in the lowest-paid occupations, like unskilled maintenance, in which whites were rarely found. But the largest union in the industry, the International Brotherhood of Boilermakers, Iron Shipbuilders and Helpers of America (representing about 70 percent of all shipyard workers) had signed a 1940 contract with Kaiser and other shipbuilders providing that only union members could work. The Boilermakers' constitution prohibited African Americans from enrolling. Under its NLRB-certified contract, the Kaiser Company could recruit nonmembers only if the union lists had been exhausted. But before going on the job, these hires had to join the union.

Unable to supply enough white workers, but unwilling to admit African Americans, the Boilermakers established segregated auxiliary union chapters. In 1943, their first year of operation, the auxiliaries placed 10,000 African Americans in shipyards and other industries where the Boilermakers controlled jobs. Auxiliary members had to pay dues to the white local but were not permitted to file grievances or vote in union elections. They received fringe benefits worth about half what white members received. The union did not assist black workers in advancing to better-paid jobs, and African Americans could not promote to foreman if the role involved supervising whites. Even if fully qualified African Americans performed skilled work, the shipyards classified and paid them as trainees. One Kaiser worker went to a civil rights meeting in protest of these policies; the company fired him for attending.

The NAACP filed an NLRB complaint regarding these practices; the agency criticized the Boilermakers' policy but maintained its certification of the whites-only union. At least twenty-nine other national unions either excluded African Americans entirely or restricted them to second-class auxiliaries.

In the postwar years, some unions began to desegregate voluntarily, but federal agencies continued to recognize segregated unions within the government itself until 1962, when President Kennedy banned the practice. Nonetheless, the Post Office's National Association of Letter Carriers did not permit African Americans to join in some areas until the 1970s. African American mailmen could not file grievances to protest mistreatment and instead had to join a catchall organization for African Americans, the National Alliance of Postal Employees, a union mostly serving truck drivers, sorters, and miscellaneous lower-paid job categories. The alliance, one member later recalled, "didn't have the clout with the [local] postmaster the way the Letter Carriers did," so African Americans were less likely to receive promotions, consideration of vacation time preferences, and other job rights.

The construction trades continued to exclude African Americans during the home and highway construction booms of the postwar years, so black workers did not share with whites the substantial income gains that blue collar workers realized in the two big wage growth periods of the mid-twentieth century—war production and subsequent suburbanization. African Americans were neither permitted to live in the new suburbs nor, for the most part, to boost their incomes by participating in suburban construction.

In 1964 the NLRB finally refused to certify whites-only unions. Although the policy was now changed, the agency offered African Americans no remedy for decades of income suppression that flowed from its unconstitutional embrace of segregation. Still another decade passed before African Americans were admitted to most AFL craft unions, but seniority rules meant it would take many more years for them to achieve incomes in these trades that were comparable to whites'. Racial income inequality by then was firmly established, and suburban segregation was mostly complete.

## V

IN 1941, A. Philip Randolph, national president of the Pullman car porters' union, organized a civil rights march on Washington to demand that President Roosevelt ban the segregation and exclusion of African Americans in defense industries. The president stalled for months, trying to convince civil rights leaders to call off the march, but less than a week before it was scheduled, he persuaded Randolph to cancel the demonstration in return for an executive order prohibiting racial discrimination by unions and management in government-controlled war industries. While some firms complied, the new policy was toothless.

*First Lady Eleanor Roosevelt supported civil rights leader A. Philip Randolph's demand that war industries be required to hire black workers. She was his emissary to her husband, but also her husband's emissary to Randolph, urging him to call off the threatened June 1941 march on Washington.*

The order created a Fair Employment Practices Committee (FEPC) that could recommend cancellation of defense contracts in cases of persistent discrimination, but at the West Coast FEPC office, for example, no such recommendation was ever made. The

FEPC had jurisdiction over any firm that was related to the war effort, such as nonmilitary hospitals that might be called upon to treat wounded soldiers. Yet the San Francisco FEPC director was unable to get San Francisco's medical centers to admit African American physicians.

President Roosevelt ensured the agency's weakness by naming Mark Ethridge, publisher of the *Louisville Courier-Journal*, as the committee's first chairman. In a speech following his appointment, Ethridge praised segregation in defense plants. A public uproar forced his resignation, but he remained as an FEPC member, stating that nondiscrimination was a federal order "in the Nazi dictator pattern," and not even "the mechanized armies of the earth, Allied or Axis . . . could now force the Southern white people to give up the principle of social segregation" in war industries.*

FEPC accomplishments were small. On one occasion, two skilled African American steamfitters in the Richmond shipyards filed a complaint with the committee over their relegation to the auxiliary local; the union agreed to create an exception for these two, provided that its policy covering all others would be unchanged. On another occasion, an African American was refused work at the Bethlehem Shipbuilding Company in San Francisco because the Machinists Union would not admit African Americans to membership; the FEPC called the union leaders to a hearing, but they ignored the invitation and no further action was taken.

Like cities nationwide, San Francisco practiced discrimination in public employment and in its public utilities, such as telephone

---

* Thirteen years later, Mark Ethridge was still publisher of his Louisville newspaper when Andrew Wade attempted to occupy the home he had bought from Carl and Anne Braden. As violence flared at the Wade residence, the *Courier-Journal* published an editorial urging the mob to use "proper legal procedures" to evict the Wades, even though these events occurred six years after the Supreme Court had found that no such legal procedures were permissible. Ethridge's editorial stated, "The real fault of judgment, in our opinion, lies with Mr. and Mrs. Carl Braden. . . . [Their white neighbors] are entirely within their rights . . . in protesting the purchase of property in their subdivision by Negroes . . . [and] there is no use denying that the value of their property will decrease as a result of the sale."

*Joseph James, leader of African American shipyard workers in the San Francisco Bay Area, singing the national anthem at a launching in 1943. Yet his union denied him the chance for promotion, and he received few fringe benefits.*

companies, which at the time were very heavily regulated because they had local monopolies. Pacific Telephone and Telegraph, one of the region's largest firms, did not have a single black operator; it hired African Americans only as janitors or for similar low-level work, and it even refused an FEPC request that it issue a state-

ment saying it would comply with the president's nondiscrimination order. The city's streetcar system refused to hire African
Americans until 1942. Maya Angelou, who lied about her age to
get a conductor's job as a teenager, was one of the first. Indicat-
ing the considerable availability of qualified African American
workers in the Bay Area, within two years of the new policy there
were 700 black platform operators when there had been none at
the beginning of the war.

In 1943 at the Marinship yard in Sausalito, where workers' dormitories had been unintentionally integrated after recruits arrived too
rapidly to be separated by race, half of the African American workers
refused to pay dues to the segregated branch of the Boilermakers. The
union then demanded that Marinship dismiss the delinquent African
Americans, and the shipyard complied. The California attorney general and the navy admiral in charge of the area's shipbuilding pressed
the workers to abandon their protest and rejoin the segregated auxiliary, but when they refused, the officials urged Marinship, without
success, to cancel the layoffs.

At an FEPC hearing, the union argued that it was in full compliance with the president's order because no African American
was denied work if he paid his dues, the same requirement that
applied to whites. The FEPC rejected this claim but suspended
the ruling pending a company appeal. The black Marinship workers then sued, but a federal judge concluded that the workers had
no relevant rights under the "federal constitution or any federal
statutes."

The African Americans then took their case to California state
courts, where a judge suspended the firings, pending a company
appeal. Eventually, in 1945, the California Supreme Court upheld
the order, stating in unprecedented language that racial discrimination is "contrary to the public policy of the United States and this
state." The Boilermakers complied with the decisions, but they had
come too late. At the time of the California Supreme Court ruling,
25,000 African Americans worked in area shipyards, but the war
was ending. Eight months later, the number had dropped to 12,000,

and in another nine months, the shipyards shut down and virtually all its employees were laid off.

The FEPC was similarly ineffective elsewhere. Lockheed and North American Aviation in Los Angeles and Boeing in Seattle only hired African Americans as janitors; when labor shortages forced these defense contractors to open other categories, the companies denied equal compensation and job rights to the black workers. In Kansas City, Standard Steel responded to the FEPC by saying, "We have not had a Negro working in twenty-five years and do

*"We Fight for the Right to Work as well as Die for Victory for the United Nations."* In 1942, demonstrators protest the refusal of the St. Louis Small Arms Ammunition Plant to hire black workers.

not plan to start now." In St. Louis, the Small Arms Ammunition Plant employed 40,000 workers at the height of World War II and initially refused to hire African Americans. It responded to civil rights demonstrations by setting up a segregated production line for black workers and agreed to include them on an integrated line only when the war was winding down and most workers were laid off.

Noncompliance with the president's nondiscrimination order did not affect companies' federal contracts, partly because the Roosevelt administration's enthusiasm for racial equality, while genuine, was lukewarm. More important was the president's conviction, hard to dispute, that every other objective had to be subordinated to winning the war. But even granting this premise, the unconstitutional treatment of African Americans called for remediation, if not during the war, then afterward, yet the federal government's complicity in the suppression of African American labor rights and opportunities was never addressed, not then and not since.

A government-backed dual labor market continued after the war's end. In 1944, the G.I. Bill was adopted to support returning servicemen. The VA not only denied African Americans the mortgage subsidies to which they were entitled but frequently restricted education and training to lower-level jobs for African Americans who were qualified to acquire greater skills. In some cases, local benefit administrators refused to process applications to four-year colleges for African Americans, directing them to vocational schools instead. Servicemen with dishonorable discharges were ineligible for benefits under the G.I. Bill, and African American soldiers disproportionately received dishonorable discharges—some for protesting segregation in army towns.*

---

* At the end of World War II, dishonorable discharges were issued to African American soldiers at nearly twice the rate of white soldiers. In 1944 Jackie Robinson was arrested and tried in a general court-martial when he was an army lieutenant stationed at Fort Hood, Texas. His crime was refusing to move to the segregated section of a bus. Robinson, who three years later would be the first African American to play major league baseball, was already nationally known as an athlete, and the army might have feared arousing unrest in the African American community if he were convicted. Also, during his trial, the army finally prohibited segregation on buses that transported soldiers. Probably for both of these reasons, he was not convicted. Had Robinson been dishonorably discharged, the Brooklyn Dodgers would undoubtedly have refused to hire him, and the trajectory of civil rights in the twentieth century would have been retarded, at least.

# VI

IN THE mid-twentieth century, job seekers depended on state employment offices for referrals to vacancies and training programs. As a war measure in 1942, these agencies were put under the control of a federal organization, the U.S. Employment Service, which generally refused to enroll African Americans in training for skilled work. Its instructions to local offices advised that if a company failed to specify a racial exclusion in its request for workers, the office should solicit one, assuming that the firm might have overlooked the opportunity to state it.

These practices continued after the war, when placement and training services were returned to state control. In 1948, for example, 45 percent of all job orders placed with the Michigan State Employment Service were for whites only, despite a severe labor shortage during much of the postwar period; although African Americans were available, many jobs went unfilled. Michigan did not adopt a Fair Employment Practices law until 1955, and even then it was poorly enforced.

A 1960s executive order covering contractors on federally funded construction projects prohibited racial discrimination and required affirmative action to recruit African Americans. Yet when a new central post office was authorized for Oakland, California (on land cleared by displacing more than 300 families, mostly African American), not a single black plumber, operating engineer, sheet metal worker, ironworker, electrician, or steamfitter was hired for its construction. When the Bay Area Rapid Transit subway system (BART) was built in 1967, not a single African American skilled worker was hired to work on it. The Office of Federal Contract Compliance blamed the unions, all certified by the NLRB, for not admitting black members. The BART general manager allowed that although BART was "committed to equal opportunity," it was unwilling to insist on nondiscrimination because that might provoke a union work stoppage and "[o]ur prime responsibility to the public . . . is to deliver the system . . . as nearly on time as we possibly can." Although federal regulations provided for termination of a contractor for failing to comply with the nondiscrimination order, no penalty was imposed.

Even today African Americans continue to have lesser rights in NLRB-certified unions. In 2015, New York City's sheet metal workers union began paying thirteen million dollars in compensation to African Americans who, although union members, received fewer job assignments than whites from 1991 to 2006. Ongoing litigation over similar discrimination by NLRB-certified unions that also participate in government contracts involves Chicago pipefitters, Philadelphia operating engineers, and New York City ironworkers. For many African American workers, the discrimination meant that, unlike white unionists, they were never able to afford housing in integrated middle-class communities.

# VII

AFRICAN AMERICANS could save less from their wages because in some (perhaps many) cities, discriminatory property assessments left them with less disposable income than whites with similar earnings. A homeowner's property tax is calculated by taking the property's assessed value, usually set by a county tax assessor, and multiplying it by the tax rate set by a municipal government agency (city, county, school district, water district, fire district, etc.). The total tax rate is the sum of rates set by each of these public entities. Each one sets its property tax rate by dividing its total budgeted expenditures—how much it expects to spend in the coming year—by the total assessed value of all properties in its jurisdiction.

Assessed values do not have to be the same as market values, but a fair and nondiscriminatory system requires that all properties be assessed at the same percentage of their market values. Whether a tax assessor says that assessed values should be 20 percent of market values, or 200 percent of market values, homeowners pay the same dollar amount of tax after the calculations are completed. If the city's total assessed value is high, dividing it into the budget will yield a low rate. If the city's total assessed value is low, dividing it into the same budget will yield a high rate. A low rate multiplied by a high value will yield the same tax revenue as a high rate multiplied by a low value.

But an assessor can undermine tax fairness by using different percentages of market value in different communities. By doing this in the mid-twentieth century, city and county governments extracted excessive taxes from African Americans. These governments did so by overassessing properties in black neighborhoods and underassessing them in white ones. Although assessors may have had a bias that led them to assess houses of lower-income families of any race at a higher percentage of their market values than houses of affluent families of any race, this alone cannot explain the differences. A 1979 study of Chicago assessments, for example, included a statistical analysis demonstrating that the chances of these differences being attributable to social-class bias alone were less than one in a hundred.

Homeowners have no way of knowing about the underassessments in other neighborhoods. African Americans felt that their property taxes were excessive but typically could not identify the cause. This made racial discrimination by assessors especially pernicious.

Taxpayers have a natural tendency to be pleased when the assessor gives a high value to their property. It makes them feel wealthier, increasing their equity on paper. But what an assessor says about property value can't affect the potential sale price of a home; higher assessed values only mean that tax payments will be higher if other properties are not overassessed in the same way. Whether some neighborhoods are overassessed and others underassessed is difficult to study. It requires painstaking property-by-property comparisons of assessed value and market value. Since it is impossible to know with certainty what the market value might be of a property that has not recently been sold, studies can't be terribly precise. Nonetheless, studies of Albany, Boston, Buffalo, Chicago, Fort Worth, and Norfolk have documented the higher effective property tax burdens borne by African Americans.

An investigation of 1962 assessment practices in Boston, for example, found that assessed values in the African American community of Roxbury were 68 percent of market values, while assessed values in the nearby white middle-class community of West Roxbury were 41 percent of market values. The researchers could not find a nonracial explanation for the difference.

Seventeen years later, an analysis of Chicago assessments found the most underassessed neighborhood to be Bridgeport, the all-white home of Mayor Richard J. Daley, where resistance to African Americans was among the most violent in the nation. Bridgeport assessed values were about 50 percent lower than the legally prescribed ratio of assessed-to-market value; in the nearby African American North Lawndale neighborhood, they were about 200 percent higher than the legally prescribed ratio.

In a 1973 study of ten large U.S. cities, the federal Department of Housing and Urban Development (HUD) found a systematic pattern of overassessment in low-income African American neighborhoods, with corresponding underassessment in white middle-class neighborhoods. The study revealed that in Baltimore, the property tax burden in the white middle-class community of Guilford, near Johns Hopkins University, was one-ninth that of African American East Baltimore. In Philadelphia the burden in white middle-class South Philadelphia was one-sixth that of African American Lower North Philadelphia. In Chicago the burden in white middle-class Norwood was one-half that of African American Woodlawn. The report provoked no action by the U.S. Department of Justice. Considering all these studies, the differences are too stark and consistent to make benign explanations likely.

The higher property taxes paid by African American owners—and through their landlords, by African American renters—contributed to the deterioration of their neighborhoods. After taxes, families had fewer funds left for maintenance, and some were forced to take in boarders or extended family members to pay their property taxes.

In Chicago, excessive taxation also led to loss of homes by African Americans because speculators were permitted to pay off delinquent tax liabilities and then seize the properties, evict the owners, and then resell the houses at enormous profit. Because African

Americans' property taxes were often higher relative to market value, black families were more likely to be delinquent in tax payments and more likely to be prey for speculators who could seize their houses after paying off the taxes due. There are no contemporary studies of assessed-to-market value ratios by community and by race, so we cannot say whether discriminatory tax assessments persist to the present time, and if so, in which communities. In cities like Baltimore and Cleveland, however, African Americans are still more likely than whites to lose homes through tax-lien repossessions.

Costs of segregation attributable to discriminatory assessment practices, suffered by an unknown number of African Americans, are not trivial. This was not simply a result of vague and ill-defined "structural racism" but a direct consequence of county assessors' contempt for their Fourteenth Amendment responsibilities, another expression of *de jure* segregation.

# VIII

THE CREATION of racial ghettos was self-perpetuating: residence in a community where economic disadvantage is concentrated itself depresses disposable income, which makes departure more difficult. Restricting African Americans' housing supply led to higher rents and home prices in black neighborhoods than for similar accommodations in predominantly white ones. If African Americans had access to housing throughout metropolitan areas, supply and demand balances would have kept their rents and home prices at reasonable levels. Without access, landlords and sellers were free to take advantage of the greater demand, relative to supply, for African American housing.

This exploitation persisted throughout the twentieth century and was well understood by economists and social welfare experts. African Americans, of course, understood it as well. In his autobiography Langston Hughes described how, when his family lived in Cleveland in the 1910s, landlords could get as much as three times the rent from African Americans that they could get from whites, because so few homes were available to black families outside a few integrated urban neighborhoods. Landlords, Hughes remembered, subdivided apartments designed for a single family into five or six units, and still African Americans' incomes had to be disproportionately devoted to rent. Four decades later little had changed. In its 1947 brief to the Supreme Court in *Shelley v. Kraemer*, the U.S. government cited half a dozen studies, each of which demonstrated that "[c]olored people are forced to pay higher rents and housing costs by the semi-monopoly which segregation fosters." In 1954, the FHA estimated that African Americans were overcrowded at more than four times the rate of whites and were doubled up at three times the rate of whites because of the excessive rents they were forced to pay.

A Chicago Department of Public Welfare report in the mid-1920s stated that African Americans were charged about 20 percent more in rent than whites for similar dwellings. It also observed that in neighborhoods undergoing racial change, rents increased by 50 to 225 percent when African Americans occupied apartments that formerly housed whites. The limited supply of housing open to African Americans gave property owners in black neighborhoods the opportunity to make exorbitant profits.

A 1946 national magazine article described a Chicago building where the landlord had divided a 540-square-foot storefront into six cubicles, each housing a family. He had similarly subdivided the second story. Total monthly rent was as great as that generated by a luxury apartment on Chicago's "Gold Coast" along Lake Michigan. The article recounted another case where rents were so high that thirty-eight people lived in a six-room apartment, sleeping in three shifts. In 1947, after a Chicago landlord converted his property from white to black tenancy, a fire killed ten African American tenants. The inquest revealed that a white tenant who had been paying fifteen dollars a month was evicted so that the landlord could charge a black family sixty dollars for the same apartment. Such exploitation was possible only because public policy denied African Americans opportunities to participate in the city's white housing market.

Other urban housing markets were similarly distorted. A 1923 Philadelphia survey found that as the First Great Migration proceeded, nearly twice as many African American as white tenants had faced rent hikes the previous year; the average increase for African Americans was 18 percent, for whites 12 percent. In 1938, African Americans' median rent in Manhattan was as much as 50 percent greater than the median for whites, although African Americans had lower incomes.

These inequities were exacerbated during World War II and its aftermath, when the Office of Price Administration froze rents nationwide. Without violating regulations, landlords subdivided apartments in already-crowded urban areas and then charged more. These higher costs accumulated throughout the twentieth century, making it more difficult for African Americans, even with stable employment, to save. Reduced savings made it less likely they could afford even modest down payments for houses in middle-class neighborhoods—were such homes made available to them.

# IX

THE RICHMOND, California, Ford plant had a sister facility in Edgewater, New Jersey, on the Hudson River just south of the George Washington Bridge. The same technological factors that made the Richmond plant obsolete in the 1950s affected the Edgewater plant. Locked in by the river on one side and the Palisades cliffs on the other, the facility had no room to expand to serve a growing customer base in the postwar boom. New highways made it no longer necessary for the plant to have its own deepwater port, so its inefficient elevator system was a needless burden.

When Ford shifted the Richmond plant to Milpitas in 1955, it also moved the Edgewater plant to the suburb of Mahwah, about twenty-five miles to the northwest. The Edgewater workforce, older and mostly white, was able to commute to the new plant without great difficulty from homes in the Edgewater area. But as these workers retired, their jobs were taken by younger African Americans who lived in Newark and New York City. With zoning ordinances that, like many in the country, may well have had a racial intent, Mahwah and surrounding towns prohibited the construction of housing that would be affordable to working-class families. In Mahwah, for example, the minimum lot size for house construction was a full acre. Because many of the new African American workers were unable to find housing for sale near the Mahwah plant, they drove sixty to seventy miles each way or depended on carpools and lengthy bus rides. Some rented single small apartments in nearby towns, returning to their families on weekends.

African American autoworkers who commuted from distant urban neighborhoods incurred annual costs attributable to the travel of $1,000 to $1,500 each in 1970, or about 10 percent of their annual gross incomes, far more than if they had lived in Mahwah or its vicinity. The African American autoworkers' incomes were also depressed because the excessive travel contributed to job losses when workers were fired for absenteeism that was partly attributable to transportation obstacles. Ford executives complained of high turnover, and later, when they closed the Mahwah plant and reopened it in Mexico, high absenteeism was a factor executives cited in explaining the decision. This was not a problem unique to workers in Mahwah. Nationwide, African Americans had disposable incomes that were lower than those of the whites with whom they worked, because of higher commuting costs from segregated neighborhoods to jobs that were now found in the suburbs.

It is certainly true that one cause of segregation today is the inability of many African Americans to afford to live in middle-class communities. But segregation itself has had a high cost for African Americans, exacerbating their inability to save to purchase suburban homes. Income differences are only a superficial way to understand why we remain segregated. Racial policy in which government was inextricably involved created income disparities that ensure residential segregation, continuing to this day.

*St. Louis, 1947. To construct its Gateway Arch, the city demolished a downtown African American neighborhood, displacing residents to new black areas like Ferguson.*

# 11

## LOOKING FORWARD, LOOKING BACK

Fᴿᴏᴍ 1957 ᴛᴏ 1968, Congress adopted civil rights laws prohibiting second-class citizenship for African Americans in public accommodations and transportation, voting, and employment. Although not without challenges, these laws were effective. Ending segregation in housing, however, is much more complicated. Prohibiting discrimination in voting and restaurants mostly requires modifying future behavior. But ending *de jure* segregation of housing requires undoing past actions that may seem irreversible.

President Kennedy's 1962 executive order attempted to end the financing of residential segregation by federal agencies. In 1966, President Lyndon Johnson pushed to have a housing discrimination bill passed, but in a rare legislative defeat, the Senate killed his proposal. Two years later, civil rights advocates tried again, and this time the Senate eked out by the narrowest of margins a Fair Housing Act that prohibited private discrimination in housing sales and rentals; shortly after, pressured by national emotion following the assassination of Martin Luther King, Jr., in April 1968, the House of Representatives enacted the law. For the first time since 1883, when the Supreme Court rejected the Civil Rights Act's ban on housing discrimination, government endorsed the rights of African Americans to reside wherever they chose and could afford.

This law is now a half-century old. You might think that fifty years would be long enough to erase the effects of government promotion of and support for segregation. But the public policies of yesterday still shape the racial landscape of today.

Where other civil rights laws have fallen short, the failures have been in implementation and enforcement, not in concept. Their design was straightforward. If African Americans were permitted to vote freely, their political power would be no different from that of others. If discrimination were prohibited in hiring, it would take some years for African Americans to gain comparable seniority, but once they did so, their workplace status would no longer be inferior. Once we prohibited segregation in hotels and restaurants, patrons of any race could be served. Likewise, if segregation was abolished on buses and trains, passengers of both races could sit in any empty seat the next day. The past had no structural legacy—we could use the same buses and trains, and no gargantuan social engineering was needed to make the transition to integration.

Ending school segregation was much harder, but how to achieve it was clear: districts could revise local school attendance boundaries so that children of either race could attend their neighborhood schools, and districts could upgrade the lower-quality schools that African Americans had attended, so that all facilities would be equal. Certainly there was massive resistance after 1954, when the Supreme Court ordered the dismantling of separate black and white school systems, yet in principle school desegregation in most locales was easy. And if achieving it the next day was politically difficult, the time required should have been a matter of years, not decades. Unlike desegregating housing, desegregating schools required not undoing the discrimination that previous generations received but only practicing integration going forward.*

---

* Whether African Americans were entitled to compensation for having received inferior and unconstitutional educations prior to 1954 is an important issue but not the subject of this book.

As it has turned out, schools are more segregated today than they were forty years ago, but this is mostly because the neighborhoods in which schools are located are so segregated. In 1970, the typical African American student attended a school in which 32 percent of the students were white. By 2010, this exposure had fallen to 29 percent. It is because of neighborhood segregation that African American students are more segregated in schools in states like New York and Illinois than they are anywhere else. Throughout the country, not just in the South, busing of school-children was almost the only tool available to create integrated schools—because few children lived near enough to opposite-race peers for any other approach to be feasible. Were housing segregation not pervasive, school desegregation would have been more successful.

Yet unlike the progress we anticipated from other civil rights laws, we shouldn't have expected much to happen from a Fair Housing Act that allowed African Americans now to resettle in a white suburb. Moving from an urban apartment to a suburban home is incomparably more difficult than registering to vote, applying for a job, changing seats on a bus, sitting down in a restaurant, or even attending a neighborhood school.

Residential segregation is hard to undo for several reasons:

- Parents' economic status is commonly replicated in the next generation, so once government prevented African Americans from fully participating in the mid-twentieth-century free labor market, depressed incomes became, for many, a multigenerational trait.

- The value of white working- and middle-class families' suburban housing appreciated substantially over the years, resulting in vast wealth differences between whites and blacks that helped to define permanently our racial living arrangements. Because parents can bequeath assets to their children, the racial wealth gap is even more persistent down through the generations than income differences.

- We waited too long to try to undo it. By the time labor market discrimination abated sufficiently for substantial numbers
  of African Americans to reach for the middle class, homes
  outside urban black neighborhoods had mostly become unaffordable for working- and lower-middle-class families.

- Once segregation was established, seemingly race-neutral policies reinforced it to make remedies even more difficult. Perhaps
  most pernicious has been the federal tax code's mortgage interest deduction, which increased the subsidies to higher-income
  suburban homeowners while providing no corresponding
  tax benefit for renters. Because *de jure* policies of segregation
  ensured that whites would more likely be owners and African
  Americans more likely be renters, the tax code contributes to
  making African Americans and whites less equal, despite the
  code's purportedly nonracial provisions.

- Contemporary federal, state, and local programs have reinforced residential segregation rather than diminished it. Federal subsidies for low-income families' housing have been
  used mainly to support those families' ability to rent apartments in minority areas where economic opportunity is
  scarce, not in integrated neighborhoods. Likewise developers
  of low-income housing have used federal tax credits mostly to
  construct apartments in already-segregated neighborhoods.
  Even half a century after government ceased to promote segregation explicitly, it continues to promote it implicitly, every
  year making remedial action more difficult.

# I

FROM THE end of World War II until about 1973, the real wages
and family incomes of all working- and middle-class Americans
grew rapidly, nearly doubling. African Americans, however, experienced the biggest growth toward the end of that period. In the

1960s, the income gap between them and white workers narrowed somewhat. The incomes of African American janitors and white production workers grew at the same pace, and the gap between them didn't much narrow, but more African Americans, who previously would have been employed only as janitors, were hired as production workers, and they made gradual progress into better jobs in the skilled trades, at least in unionized industry. African Americans remained mostly excluded, however, from highly paid blue-collar occupations—the construction trades, for example. In most government jobs (teaching, the federal civil service, state and municipal government) but not in all, African Americans made progress: they were hired in city sanitation departments, for example, but rarely as firefighters. Overall, African American incomes didn't take off until the 1960s, when suburbanization was mostly complete.

From 1973 until the present, real wages of working- and middle-class Americans of all races and ethnicities have been mostly stagnant. For those with only high school educations, or perhaps some college, real earnings declined, as production workers with unionized factory jobs were laid off and found employment in service occupations where the absence of unions meant wages would be much lower.*

Just as the incomes of all working-class Americans, white and black, began to stagnate, single-family home prices began to soar. From 1973 to 1980, the African American median wage fell by one percent, while the average American house price grew by 43 percent. In the next decade wages of African American workers fell by

---

* In addition to de-unionization of the less-skilled workforce, the decline in the real (inflation-adjusted) minimum wage has also contributed. We tend to romanticize this economic history, saying that good factory jobs have been replaced by bad service jobs. But in truth, there is nothing better about banging hubcaps onto cars on a moving assembly line than about serving hamburgers in a fast food restaurant or changing bed linens in a hotel. The difference between these types of jobs is mainly that industrial jobs were frequently unionized and service jobs are not. Service jobs might even be a more secure source of stable income if they were unionized and protected by an adequate minimum wage standard. An automobile assembly plant can move overseas, but a hotel or fast food restaurant cannot.

another percent, while the average house price increased yet another 8 percent.

By the time the federal government decided finally to allow African Americans into the suburbs, the window of opportunity for an integrated nation had mostly closed. In 1948, for example, Levittown homes sold for about $8,000, or about $75,000 in today's dollars. Now, properties in Levittown without major remodeling (i.e., one-bath houses) sell for $350,000 and up. White working-class families who bought those homes in 1948 have gained, over three generations, more than $200,000 in wealth.

Most African American families—who were denied the opportunity to buy into Levittown or into the thousands of subdivisions like it across the country—remained renters, often in depressed neighborhoods, and gained no equity. Others bought into less desirable neighborhoods. Vince Mereday, who helped build Levittown but was prohibited from living there, bought a home in the nearby, almost all-black suburb of Lakeview. It remains 74 percent African American today. His relatives can't say precisely what he paid for his Lakeview house in 1948, but with Levittown being the least expensive, best bargain of the time, it was probably no less than the $75,000 he would have paid in Levittown. Although white suburban borrowers could obtain VA mortgages with no down payments, Vince Mereday could not because he was African American. He would have had to make a down payment, probably about 20 percent, or $15,000.

One-bath homes in Lakeview currently sell for $90,000 to $120,000. At most, the Mereday family gained $45,000 in equity appreciation over three generations, perhaps 20 percent of the wealth gained by white veterans in Levittown. Making matters worse, it was lower-middle-class African American communities like Lakeview that mortgage brokers targeted for subprime lending during the pre-2008 housing bubble, leaving many more African American families subject to default and foreclosure than economically similar white families.

Seventy years ago, many working- and lower-middle-class African American families could have afforded suburban single-family homes that cost about $75,000 (in today's currency) with no down payment. Millions of whites did so. But working- and lower-middle-class African American families cannot now buy homes for $350,000 and more with down payments of 20 percent, or $70,000.

The Fair Housing Act of 1968 prohibited future discrimination, but it was not primarily discrimination (although this still contributed) that kept African Americans out of most white suburbs after the law was passed. It was primarily unaffordability. The right that was unconstitutionally denied to African Americans in the late 1940s cannot be restored by passing a Fair Housing law that tells their descendants they can now buy homes in the suburbs, if only they can afford it. The advantage that FHA and VA loans gave the white lower-middle class in the 1940s and '50s has become permanent.

## II

THE REDUCTION of discriminatory barriers in the labor market that began in the mid-twentieth century did not translate easily into African Americans' upward mobility. Movement from lower ranks to the middle class in the national income distribution has always been difficult for all Americans. This reality challenges a fantasy we share: that children born into low-income families can themselves escape that status through hard work, responsibility, education, ambition, and a little luck. That myth is becoming less prevalent today, as more Americans become aware of how sticky our social-class positions are.

Imagine that we lined up all American families in order of their incomes from highest to lowest and then divided that line into five equal groups. In discussions of mobility, it is usual to call the richest fifth the top (or fifth) quintile, the next richest fifth the fourth quintile, and so on. If we were fully an equal-opportunity society (and no society is), children whose parents have incomes in the bottom quintile of the income distribution would have equal chances of having incomes as adults anywhere in that distribution. In other words, of children in the bottom quintile, one fifth would remain, as adults, in that bottom quintile. Another fifth would have incomes in the fourth quintile; another fifth would have climbed to the middle, or third quintile (we can call this the "middle class"); another fifth would rise to the second quintile; and another fifth would land in the top quintile, having the highest incomes.

In fact, however, the United States has less mobility than many other industrialized societies. Of American children born to parents whose incomes were in the bottom income quintile, almost half (43 percent) remain trapped in the bottom quintile as adults. Only 30 percent of children born to parents in the lowest-earning quintile make it to the middle quintile or higher.

African Americans have even less mobility. For those born to parents in the bottom income quintile, over half (53 percent) remain there as adults, and only a quarter (26 percent) make it to the middle quintile or higher. Considering the disadvantages that low-income African Americans have had as a result of segregation—poor access to jobs and to schools where they can excel—it's surprising that their mobility, compared to that of other Americans, isn't even lower. Two explanations come to mind. One is that many African Americans heed the warning that they have to be twice as good to succeed and exhibit more than average hard work, responsibility, and ambition to supplement a little luck. The other is that our affirmative action programs have been moderately successful. Probably some of both are involved.

## III

MEDIAN WHITE family income is now about $60,000, while median black family income is about $37,000—about 60 percent as much. You might expect that the ratio of black to white household wealth would be similar. But median white household wealth (assets minus liabilities) is about $134,000, while median black household wealth is about $11,000—less than 10 percent as much. Not all of this enormous difference is attributable to the government's racial housing policy, but a good portion of it certainly is.

Equity that families have in their homes is the main source of wealth for middle-class Americans. African American families today, whose parents and grandparents were denied participation in the equity-accumulating boom of the 1950s and 1960s, have great difficulty catching up now. As with income, there is little mobility by wealth in America. In fact, intergenerational wealth mobility is even less than intergenerational income mobility.

An equal opportunity society with respect to wealth would operate similarly to an equal opportunity society with respect to income. No matter how wealthy your parents, you would have an equal chance, as an adult, of ending up anywhere in the national wealth distribution. But nearly half (41 percent) of children born to parents in the least wealthy fifth of American families remain in that lowest quintile as adults. Another 25 percent make it to the next-lowest wealth quintile, meaning that only one-third of children born to the least wealthy American families make it as high as the middle quintile in wealth.

As is true with income, African Americans are also less mobile in wealth than whites. Fewer than one-fourth of African American adults whose parents were in the bottom wealth quintile make it to the middle wealth quintile. Nearly twice as many (42 percent) white adults whose parents were in the lowest wealth quintile make it that far. Since African Americans were mostly prevented by government racial policy from owning single-family homes in the suburbs, it is not surprising that this would be so.

This difference becomes especially significant in that white families are more often able to borrow from their home equity, if necessary, to weather medical emergencies, send their children to college, retire without becoming dependent on those children, aid family members experiencing hard times, or endure brief periods of joblessness without fear of losing a home or going hungry. If none of these emergencies consume their savings or home equity, families can bequeath wealth to the next generation.

In 1989, the most recent year for which such data are available,

6 percent of black households inherited wealth from the previous generation. Of those who inherited wealth, the average inheritance was $42,000. Four times as many white households—24 percent—inherited wealth, and the average inheritance was $145,000. In that year 18 percent of black households received cash gifts from parents who were still living, in an average amount of $800. About the same share of white households received such gifts, but the average amount—$2,800—was much greater. This, too, is the consequence of government's twentieth-century racial policy in housing and income.

# IV

ONE REASON low-income African Americans are less upwardly mobile than low-income whites is that low-income African Americans are more likely to be stuck for multiple generations in poor neighborhoods. Patrick Sharkey, a New York University sociologist, analyzed data on race and neighborhood conditions and reported his findings in a 2013 book, *Stuck in Place*. He defines a poor neighborhood as one where 20 percent of families have incomes below the poverty line. In 2016, the poverty line was about $21,000 for a family of three. In a neighborhood where 20 percent of families have incomes below poverty, many more families are likely to have incomes just above it. Notwithstanding the government's official poverty line, most of us would consider families to be poor if they had incomes that were below twice that line, $42,000 for a family of three. The federal government itself considers schoolchildren whose family incomes are nearly twice (185 percent) the poverty line to be too poor to pay for their own lunches without a subsidy. Families like theirs are also unable to move to middle-class neighborhoods, either by saving for down payments or by renting apartments at market rates. So Sharkey is reasonable when he considers such neighborhoods to be "poor."

He finds that young African Americans (from thirteen to

twenty-eight years old) are now ten times as likely to live in poor neighborhoods as young whites—66 percent of African Americans, compared to 6 percent of whites. He finds that 67 percent of African American families hailing from the poorest quarter of neighborhoods a generation ago continue to live in such neighborhoods today. But only 40 percent of white families who lived in the poorest quarter of neighborhoods a generation ago still do so.

Forty-eight percent of African American families, at all income levels, have lived in poor neighborhoods over at least two generations, compared to 7 percent of white families. If a child grows up in a poor neighborhood, moving up and out to a middle-class area is typical for whites but an aberration for African Americans. Neighborhood poverty is thus more multigenerational for African Americans and more episodic for whites.

The consequences of being exposed to neighborhood poverty are greater than the consequences of being poor itself. Children who grow up in poor neighborhoods have few adult role models who have been educationally and occupationally successful. Their ability to do well in school is compromised from stress that can result from exposure to violence. They have few, if any, summer job opportunities. Libraries and bookstores are less accessible. There are fewer primary care physicians. Fresh food is harder to get. Airborne pollutants are more present, leading to greater school absence from respiratory illness. The concentration of many disadvantaged children in the same classroom deprives each child of the special attention needed to be successful. All these challenges are added to those from which poor children suffer in any neighborhood—instability and stress resulting from parental unemployment, fewer literacy experiences when parents are poorly educated, more overcrowded living arrangements that offer few quiet corners to study, and less adequate health care, all of which contribute to worse average school performance and, as a result, less occupational success as adults.

Certainly some children overcome these difficulties. But the average child living in a poor household is less likely to escape poverty as an adult, and the average child living in a poor household in a poor neighborhood is even less likely to do so. The cycle can be broken only by a policy as aggressive as that which created ghettos of concentrated poverty in the first place.

## V

BECAUSE AMERICANS vary greatly in their economic and social circumstances, any government program will affect different Americans differently even if, on its face, the program treats all alike. A sales tax, for example, applies equally to all but will be more of a burden to lower-income consumers than to higher-income ones. The legal jargon for this is that it has a "disparate impact" on different groups. In a society where everyone's situation is different, disparate impacts are unavoidable, but we can try to minimize them—in the case of a sales tax, by exempting grocery purchases.

Once *de jure* segregation was established, African Americans and whites were not affected similarly by subsequent race-neutral policies. The Fair Housing Act prohibits housing programs whose disparate impact on African Americans reinforces their segregation, unless the programs have a legitimate purpose that cannot be accomplished otherwise. But the Fair Housing Act does not prevent disparate impacts from other, nonhousing programs that build on preexisting residential patterns. Unlike the activities that comprise *de jure* segregation, these programs need not have the intent of harming African Americans (although sometimes they may) but they do harm nonetheless. Several seemingly "race-neutral" programs have reinforced the disadvantages of African Americans that were initially created by race-conscious housing policy.

Along with the mortgage interest deduction, another policy that on its face is race-neutral but has a discriminatory effect is our national transportation system. We have invested heavily in highways to connect commuters to their downtown offices but comparatively little in buses, subways, and light rail to put suburban jobs within reach of urban African Americans and to reduce their isolation from the broader community. Although in many cases urban spurs of the interstate highway system were unconstitutionally routed to clear African Americans away from white neighborhoods and businesses, that was not the system's primary purpose, and the decision to invest limited transportation funds in highways rather than subways and buses has had a disparate impact on African Americans.

Transportation policies that affected the African American population in Baltimore illustrate those followed throughout the country. Over four decades, successive proposals for rail lines or even a highway to connect African American neighborhoods to better opportunities have been scuttled because finances were short and building expressways to serve suburbanites was a higher priority. Isolating African Americans was not the stated purpose of Maryland's transportation decisions, though there also may have been some racial motivation. In 1975, when Maryland proposed a rail line to connect suburban Anne Arundel County and downtown Baltimore, white suburbanites pressed their political leaders to oppose the plan, which they did. A review by Johns Hopkins University researchers concluded that the residents believed that the rail line "would enable poor, inner-city blacks to travel to the suburbs, steal residents' T.V.s and then return to their ghettos." Maryland's state transportation secretary stated that his office "would not force a transit line on an area that clearly does not want it," failing to explain how he balanced the desires of a white suburban area "that clearly does not want it" with the desires of urban African Americans who needed it.

Forty years later little had changed. In 2015, Maryland's governor canceled a proposed rail link to Baltimore's west-side black neighborhood, saying the funds were needed for highway improvements. The NAACP Legal Defense Fund then filed a complaint with the U.S. Department of Transportation, claiming that Maryland's priority for highways over mass transit had a disparate impact on African Americans. The case was still pending when the Obama administration left office.

# VI

ACTIONS OF government in housing cannot be neutral about segregation. They will either exacerbate or reverse it. Without taking care to do otherwise, exacerbation is more likely. The federal government now operates two large programs to address the housing crisis faced by the poor and near-poor, most of whom, in many metropolitan areas, are African American. Without an intent to do so, each program has been implemented in a manner that deepens racial segregation. One, the Low-Income Housing Tax Credit, subsidizes developers whose multiunit projects are available to low-income families. The other, Housing Choice Vouchers (popularly known as "Section 8"), subsidizes families' rental payments so they can lease housing that they would not otherwise be able to afford.

In the tax credit program, communities can veto developers' proposals, something that officials in middle-class areas don't hesitate to do. Many policy makers urge developers to build in already segregated neighborhoods in the hope (usually a vain one) that their projects will revitalize deteriorating areas. Developers themselves also prefer to use tax credits in low-income neighborhoods because land is cheaper, it is easier to market new apartments to renters in the immediate vicinity, and there is less political opposition to additional housing for minorities and lower-income families. These conditions ensure that tax credit projects will have a disparate impact on African Americans, reinforcing neighborhood segregation. An analysis of all tax credit units nationwide, completed through 2005, found that about three-fourths were placed in neighborhoods where poverty rates were at least 20 percent.

In the Section 8 program, landlords in most states and cities can legally refuse to rent to tenants who use housing vouchers, although a few jurisdictions prohibit such discrimination. The voucher amount is usually too small to allow for rentals in middle-class areas. A family that receives a voucher may find that the only way to take advantage of it is to move to a neighborhood even more segregated than the one where they were already living. As a result, few families with children who used Section 8 vouchers rented apartments in low-poverty neighborhoods in 2010, while over half rented in neighborhoods where the poverty rate was 20 percent or more, including some who rented where poverty was extreme—40 percent or more. Where vouchers are used to rent suburban apartments, these apartments are frequently in segregated enclaves within otherwise middle-class suburbs.

In 2008, the Inclusive Communities Project (ICP), a Dallas civil rights group, sued the state of Texas, claiming that the operation of the tax credit program had a disparate impact on African Americans, violating the Fair Housing Act. In the city of Dallas, 85 percent of all tax credit units for families were in census tracts where at least 70 percent of residents were minority. The ICP had been attempting to promote racial integration in the Dallas area by helping African American families with Section 8 vouchers find affordable apartments in predominantly white neighborhoods, but it was impeded because so many of the tax-subsidized family housing developments approved by the State of Texas were in heavily minority and low-income areas.

In June 2015, the Supreme Court ruled in the ICP case that the disproportionate placement of subsidized housing in neighborhoods that had been segregated by past government policy could violate the Fair Housing Act, even if the placement was not intended to intensify segregation. But the opinion, written by Justice Anthony Kennedy, also allowed that placing subsidized units to support the revitalization of deteriorating neighborhoods could also be legitimate. So it is not evident how much of a nationwide push toward desegregation will result from the ICP case.

Gentrification of private housing in urban areas, redevelopment projects, and highway routing have forced low-income and minority families to search for new accommodations in a few inner-ring suburbs that are in transition from white to major-

ity minority. When the tax credit and Section 8 programs subsidize the movement of low-income families into such suburbs,
and not into predominantly middle-class ones, they contribute
to segregation. Ferguson, Missouri, outside of St. Louis, is such
a place. When the Section 8 and tax credit programs failed to
offer opportunities to settle throughout the St. Louis metropolitan area, they contributed to Ferguson's transformation from an
integrated to a predominantly minority and increasingly low-
income community.

*As public housing towers like Pruitt-Igoe in St. Louis were
taken down in the early 1970s and their sites redeveloped,
residents were forced into other segregated neighborhoods.*

Civil rights advocates and local housing officials face a difficult conundrum. The ongoing income stagnation of working-class
families and the growing distance between job opportunities and
affordable housing makes the need for subsidized housing more
pronounced. Government officials can satisfy more of that need by

using scarce Section 8 funds and supporting tax credit developments in segregated neighborhoods where rents and land are cheaper and where white middle-class voters place fewer hurdles in the way. In the long run, however, African Americans will be harmed more by the perpetuation of segregation than by continued overcrowding and inadequate living space. Neither is a good alternative, but short-term gains may not be worth the long-term costs.

*Plano, Texas, 2016. Attorney Elizabeth Julian (left) success-
fully sued HUD and Dallas over intentional discrimination.
A settlement enabled Bernestine Williams (right) to move to
this middle-class integrated neighborhood, where she raised
two college-bound children.*

# 12

## CONSIDERING FIXES

A S A NATION, we have paid an enormous price for avoiding
an obligation to remedy the unconstitutional segregation we
have allowed to fester.

African Americans, of course, suffer from our evasion. But so,
too, does the nation as a whole, as do whites in particular. Many of
our serious national problems either originate with residential segregation or have become intractable because of it. We have greater
political and social conflict because we must add unfamiliarity with
fellow citizens of different racial backgrounds to the challenges we
confront in resolving legitimate disagreements about public issues.
Racial polarization stemming from our separateness has corrupted
our politics, permitting leaders who ignore the interests of white
working-class voters to mobilize them with racial appeals. Whites
may support political candidates who pander to their sense of racial
entitlement while advocating policies that perpetuate the inferior
economic opportunities that some whites may face. Interracial
political alliances become more difficult to organize when whites
develop overly intolerant judgments of the unfortunate—from a

need to justify their own acceptance of segregation that so obviously conflicts with both their civic ideals and their religious ones.

The existence of black ghettos is a visible reminder of our inequalities and history, a reminder whose implications are so uncomfortable that we find ways to avoid them. Whites can develop a dysfunctional cynicism from living in a society that proclaims values of justice while maintaining racial inequalities that belie those values.

It is not only the distribution of our national wealth that suffers from racial isolation but also our productivity in generating that wealth. Organizations work better if members are comfortable with colleagues' cultural assumptions that may give rise to different perspectives. Social psychologists have found that segregation can give whites an unrealistic belief in their own superiority, leading to poorer performance if they feel less need to challenge themselves. Experiments show that when we are in teams with others from similar backgrounds, we tend to go along with the popular view rather than think for ourselves, resulting in less creative groups more prone to make errors.

## I

As for children, segregation is not healthy for either whites or African Americans. In segregated schools, neither can gain experience navigating the diverse environments in which, as adults, they will have to make their way.

For low-income African American children, the social and economic disadvantages with which they frequently come to school make higher achievement more difficult. Consider just one example, asthma, an affliction from which African American children suffer at nearly twice the rate of white children—probably because African Americans live in or near residential-industrial neighborhoods with more dust, pollutants, and vermin. Asthmatic children are more likely to awaken at night wheezing and, if they come to school after an episode, can be drowsy and less able to pay attention. A child who has more frequent absences—from poor health, unreliable transportation, having to stay home to care for younger siblings, or family instability—will have less opportunity to benefit from instruction.

Not all students with these disadvantages perform poorly. A few with asthma achieve at higher levels than typical children without this and similar disadvantages. But on average, a student with problems like these, stemming from life in segregated neighborhoods, performs more poorly.

If such a child attends school where few others have these handicaps—a mostly middle-class school—a teacher can devote special attention and help so that the child can accomplish more than he or she would otherwise. But if most students in a classroom share these impediments, teachers cannot devote special attention to each one. In that case, curriculum becomes remedial, and too much time is taken from instruction for discipline. High average achievement is almost impossible to realize in a low-income, segregated school, embedded in a segregated neighborhood. Many children in it could do much better in an integrated school, leading to their stronger and more likely positive contributions to society later, as adults.

The false sense of superiority that segregation fosters in whites contributes to their rejection of policies to integrate American society. The lower achievement of African American children that results from life in a segregated neighborhood adds another impediment to those children's ability to merge into middle-class workplaces. In these ways, segregation perpetuates itself, and its continued existence makes it ever harder to reverse.

## II

REMEDIES THAT can undo nearly a century of *de jure* residential segregation will have to be both complex and imprecise. After so much time, we can no longer provide adequate justice to the descendants of those whose constitutional rights were violated. Our focus can be only to develop policies that promote an integrated society, understanding that it will be impossible to fully untangle the web of inequality that we've woven.

The challenge is more difficult because low-income African Americans today confront not only segregation but also the income stagnation and blocked mobility faced by all Americans in families with low or moderate incomes. Historically, African Americans have made progress mostly when opportunity is expanding for all and whites are less fearful of competition from others. Thus, to provide an adequate environment for integration efforts, the United States also needs a full employment policy, minimum wages that return to their historic level and keep up with inflation, and a transportation infrastructure that makes it possible for low-income workers to get to jobs that are available. This book is not the place to argue for these and similar policies, but I would be remiss if I pretended that desegregation was compatible with economic stress and insecurity.

I hesitate to offer suggestions about desegregation policies and remedies because, imprecise and incomplete though they may be, remedies are inconceivable as long as citizens, whatever their political views, continue to accept the myth of *de facto* segregation. If segregation was created by accident or by undefined private prejudices, it is too easy to believe that it can only be reversed by accident or, in some mysterious way, by changes in people's hearts. But if we—the public and policy makers—acknowledge that the federal, state, and local governments segregated our metropolitan areas, we may open our minds to considering how those same federal, state, and local governments might adopt equally aggressive policies to desegregate.

# III

ONLY IF we can develop a broadly shared understanding of our common history will it be practical to consider steps we could take to fulfill our obligations. Short of that, we can make a start. Several promising programs are being pursued in some jurisdictions. Civil rights and fair housing organizations in most cities advocate and, in many cases, help to implement reforms that begin to ameliorate the worst effects of *de jure* segregation. While we attempt to build public and political support for the more far-reaching remedies, we should advance the presently possible reforms as well. We might begin with high school and middle school curricula. If young people are not taught an accurate account of how we came to be segregated, their generation will have little chance of doing a better job of desegregating than the previous ones.

One of the most commonly used American history textbooks is *The Americans: Reconstruction to the 21st Century*. A thousand-page volume, published by Holt McDougal, a division of the publishing giant Houghton Mifflin Harcourt, it lists several well-respected professors as authors and editors. The 2012 edition has this to say about residential segregation in the North: "African Americans found themselves forced into segregated neighborhoods." That's it. One passive voice sentence. No suggestion of who might have done the forcing or how it was implemented.

*The Americans* also contains this paragraph: "A number of New Deal programs concerned housing and home mortgage problems. The Home Owners Loan Corporation (HOLC) provided government loans to homeowners who faced foreclosure because they couldn't meet their loan payments. In addition, the 1934 National Housing Act created the Federal Housing Administration (FHA). This agency continues to furnish loans for home mortgages and repairs today."

The authors do not mention that an enduring legacy of the HOLC was to color-code every urban neighborhood by race so that African Americans would have great difficulty getting mortgages. That the FHA suburbanized the entire nation on a whites-only basis is overlooked. The textbook does acknowledge that "a number of" New Deal agencies—the truth is that it was virtually all—paid lower wages to African Americans than to whites but fails to refer to the residential segregation imposed by the government's public housing projects.

*United States History: Reconstruction to the Present*, a 2016 textbook issued by the educational publishing giant Pearson, offers a similar account. It celebrates the FHA's and VA's support of single-family developments and gives Levittown as an example of suburbanization without disclosing that African Americans were excluded. It boasts of the PWA's bridge, dam, power plant, and government building projects but omits describing its insistence on segregated housing. Like *The Americans*, it employs the passive voice to avoid explaining segregation: "In the North, too, African Americans faced segregation and discrimination. Even where there were no explicit laws, **de facto segregation**, or segregation by unwritten custom or tradition, was a fact of life. African Americans in the North were denied housing in many neighborhoods."

This is mendacious. There was nothing unwritten about government policy to promote segregation in the North. It was spelled out in the FHA's *Underwriting Manual*, in the PWA's (and subsequent agencies') racial designation of housing projects, in congressional votes on the 1949 public housing integration amendment, and in written directives of federal and state officials.

With very rare exceptions, textbook after textbook adopts the same mythology. If middle and high school students are being taught a false history, is it any wonder that they come to believe that African Americans are segregated only because they don't want to marry or because they prefer to live only among themselves? Is it any wonder that they grow up inclined to think that programs to ameliorate ghetto conditions are simply undeserved handouts?

# IV

IN 2015, the Obama administration unveiled a rule to implement an underappreciated provision of the 1968 Fair Housing Act that requires jurisdictions that receive federal funds to "affirmatively further" the purposes of the law.

The rule instructed cities, towns, and suburbs to assess their concentrations (or absence) of disadvantaged populations and identify goals to remedy segregated conditions. The rule seemed to assume that segregated white communities want to do the right thing but don't have adequate information to do so. Giving suburbs around the country the benefit of the doubt may have been a smart way to encourage them to fulfill their "affirmatively furthering" obligations; left unsaid was what HUD might do if suburbs don't take steps necessary to advance integration. Did the Obama administration plan to deny federal funds to suburbs that remain segregated?

Police killings of young black men in 2014 and 2015 called renewed attention to our racial divide. The presidential election of 2016 revealed that the nation was almost evenly split between those who believe that we've done too much to remedy racial inequality and those who believe we've done not nearly enough. In early 2017, congressional Republicans proposed legislation to prohibit enforcement of the "affirmatively furthering" rule. But even if the rule were to survive, or if a future administration reintroduces it, effective remedies for racial inequality will be unlikely unless the public is disabused of the *de facto* myth and comes to understand how government at all levels insulted our constitutional principles regarding race.

## V

IN 1970, stung by riots in more than a hundred cities by angry and embittered African Americans, HUD secretary George Romney tried to pursue integration more vigorously than any other administration, either before or since. Observing that the federal government had imposed a suburban "white noose" around urban African American neighborhoods, Romney devised a program he called Open Communities that would deny federal funds (for water and sewer upgrades, green space, sidewalk improvements, and other projects for which HUD financial support is needed) to suburbs that hadn't revised their exclusionary zoning laws to permit construction of subsidized apartments for lower-income African American families. The anger about Open Communities among voters in the Republican Party's suburban base was so fierce that President Nixon reined in Romney, required him to repudiate his plan, and eventually forced him from office.

George Romney undertook his desegregation initiative only a few years after a series of civil rights measures had been enacted into law and after the assassinations of Martin Luther King, Jr., and other civil rights leaders and activists. It followed upon the release of a widely discussed report on the causes of African American rioting, published by an investigatory commission appointed by President Johnson and chaired by Illinois governor Otto Kerner. Because of all this attention to the suppression of African Americans and to the federal government's partial responsibility for it, many Americans were receptive to Romney's argument, although they were not sufficiently numerous or influential for him to prevail. Today many fewer Americans are familiar with the extent of *de jure* segregation. The intellectual and political groundwork has not been laid for a revival of the George Romney program or for the Obama administration's more modest 2015 rule. Americans are unaware of the *de jure* segregation history that makes the rule necessary.

# VI

IT IS not difficult to conceive of ways to rectify the legacy of *de jure* segregation. In what follows, I'll suggest a few, first some that could not be enacted in today's political environment, and then some modest reforms that are still not politically possible but are within closer reach.

We might contemplate a remedy like this: Considering that African Americans comprise about 15 percent of the population of the New York metropolitan area, the federal government should purchase the next 15 percent of houses that come up for sale in Levittown at today's market rates (approximately $350,000). It should then resell the properties to qualified African Americans for $75,000, the price (in today's dollars) that their grandparents would have paid if permitted to do so. The government should enact this program in every suburban development whose construction complied with the FHA's discriminatory requirements. If Congress established such a program and justified it based on the history of *de jure* segregation, courts should uphold it as appropriate.

Of course, no presently constituted Congress would adopt such a policy and no presently constituted court would uphold it. Tax-payers would rebel at the cost, as well as at the perceived undeserved gift to African Americans. I present this not as a practical proposal but only to illustrate the kind of remedy that we would consider and debate if we disabused ourselves of the *de facto* segregation myth.

# VII

THE SEGREGATION we should remedy is not only that of low-income families but that of middle-class African Americans who currently reside in towns like Lakeview, where Vince Mereday settled and which is still today 85 percent African American; or Roosevelt, Long Island (currently 79 percent African American), another predominantly black middle-class town near where other Mereday relatives found homes; or Prince George's County (65 percent African American) outside Washington, D.C.; or Calumet Heights (93 percent African American) outside Chicago.

Middle-class suburbs like these are attractive to many African Americans, and no policy should force them to integrate against their will. But we should provide incentives for integration because these suburbs have disadvantages for their residents and for the rest of us. The most important disadvantage is that they are frequently adjacent to low-income communities. About one-third of middle- and upper-income black families now live in neighborhoods bordering severely disadvantaged areas, while only 6 percent of income-similar white families do so. Black middle-class adolescents living in such close proximity to ghettos must resist the lure of gangs and of alienated behavior if they aspire to duplicate their parents' middle-class status. Even if they avoid such a trap, youth growing up in predominantly African American communities, even middle-class ones, will gain no experience mastering a predominantly white professional culture in which they, as adults, will want to succeed.

Federal subsidies for middle-class African Americans to purchase homes in suburbs that have been racially exclusive are the most obvious incentive that could spur integration. Again, such assistance is both politically and judicially inconceivable today. Although government financial aid of this kind is still out of reach, advocates of integration can express their support in very local and even informal ways. If one, not the only one, of the reasons that middle-class African Americans hesitate to integrate is their expectation of hostility (from subtly hostile neighbors, from police who follow their sons home), then community welcoming committees that, among other actions, insist upon appropriate police training could be useful. Making a point, perhaps even a requirement, of advertising houses for sale in such neighborhoods with real estate agents who do business in segregated African American communities could also help.

# VIII

ANOTHER REMEDY would be a ban on zoning ordinances that prohibit multifamily housing or that require all single-family homes in a neighborhood to be built on large lots with high minimum requirements for square footage. These rules prevent both lower-income and middle-class families from settling in affluent suburbs. Exclusionary zoning ordinances were partly motivated by unconstitutional racial animosity. Banning them is not only good public policy but constitutionally permissible, if not at the federal level, then by states.

Alternatively, less extreme than an outright ban on exclusionary zoning, Congress could amend the tax code to deny the mortgage interest deduction to property owners in suburbs that do not have or are not taking aggressive steps to attract their fair share of low- and moderate-income housing, both multiunit and single family, whether for rental or sale. A fair share is one that is close to that of low- and moderate-income families in the suburb's metropolitan area, or as a constitutional remedy, the share of African Americans in the metropolitan area. How "close" is "close to" in a region with a substantial African American population? Perhaps plus or minus 10 percent. The New York metropolitan area has an African American population of about 15 percent today. If we used a plus-or-minus-10-percent rule, then any suburb whose African American population was less than 5 percent should be considered segregated and required to take steps to integrate. For any community whose African American population was greater than 25 percent, special incentives should be offered to help families move to integrated towns or to attract nonblack families to live there.

Complementing a ban on exclusionary zoning is a requirement for inclusionary zoning: a positive effort to integrate low- and moderate-income families into middle-class and affluent neighborhoods. Two states, New Jersey and Massachusetts, currently have "fair share" requirements, based on income, not on race. They address the isolation of low-income families in urban areas and their absence from middle-class suburbs. They make a contribution to integration but do not take the additional step of helping to integrate middle-income African American families into white middle-class suburbs. Legislation in New Jersey requires suburbs that do not have a "fair share" of their metropolitan area's low-income housing to permit developers to build multiunit projects that are frequently subsidized either with Section 8 or Low-Income Housing Tax Credit funds. Similar legislation in Massachusetts requires developers in towns without a fair share of subsidized housing to set aside units in middle-income projects for low-income families. Developments that do so are permitted more units per acre than would otherwise be allowed. Douglas Massey and his colleagues, in *Climbing Mount Laurel*, describe one such successful project in a New Jersey suburb of Philadelphia. Disproving fears of the area's middle-class residents, the project did not bring crime into the town of Mount Laurel, diminish the quality of its public school, or otherwise harm the community's character. If other states were to adopt legislation like that in New Jersey and Massachusetts, it would be a significant step toward the integration of all low-income families, not only African Americans.

Some municipalities have "inclusionary zoning" ordinances that accomplish at a local level what the New Jersey and Massachusetts programs do statewide. The regulations usually require developers to set aside a share of units in new projects for low- or moderate-income families. As in Massachusetts, the developers are offered an incentive (higher density than is normally permitted, for example) to comply. The ordinances are sometimes effective, but unless they are implemented on a metropolitan-wide basis, their value as an integration tool is limited. If an inclusionary zoning ordinance applies only to a single town, developers can avoid its requirements and serve the same housing market by building instead in a neighboring town without such rules.

Montgomery County, Maryland, has a strong countywide inclusionary zoning ordinance. Like most such regulations, it requires developers in even the most affluent communities to set aside a percentage of units (in the case of Montgomery County, 12 to 15 percent) for moderate-income families. It then goes further: the public housing authority purchases a third of these set-aside units for rental to the lowest-income families. The program's success is evidenced by the measurably higher achievement of low-income African American children who live and attend school in the county's wealthiest suburbs. Montgomery County's program should be widely duplicated.

# IX

In 1993, a quarter century after the Fair Housing Act was enacted, John Boger, a University of North Carolina law professor, lamented the subsequent lack of progress toward residential integration. He suggested a national "Fair Share Act" that would require every state to establish mechanisms to ensure that each of its suburban or municipal jurisdictions houses a representative share of the African American as well as low- and moderate-income population in its metropolitan region. Professor Boger proposed that homeowners in jurisdictions that did not make progress toward such racial and economic integration would lose 10 percent of their mortgage interest and property tax deductions. The penalty would increase in each year of a jurisdiction's noncompliance with fair share goals until the entire deduction would be lost.

If enacted, the plan would give citizens a powerful economic incentive to press their local officials to take reasonable steps toward integration. But the idea was not intended to be punitive. Professor Boger argued that the Internal Revenue Service should keep funds equivalent to the lost deductions in an account at the Treasury, reserving these funds for helping segregated communities whose residents had lost those deductions to develop public housing or low- and moderate-income subsidized housing. Because Professor Boger's purpose was not to challenge the *de facto* segregation myth, he did not add that such reserved funds could also be used to subsidize the middle-class or even affluent African Americans to reside in suburbs they could not otherwise easily afford. But in view of the *de jure* origins of suburban segregation, this too would be an appropriate use of the withheld taxpayer deductions. Professor Boger's proposal for a Fair Share Act is no less timely today than when he first advanced it.

# X

SUCCESSFUL CIVIL rights lawsuits have led to a few innovative programs that integrate low-income families into middle-class neighborhoods. In 1995 the American Civil Liberties Union of Maryland sued HUD and the Baltimore Housing Authority because as these agencies demolished public housing projects, they resettled tenants (frequently with Section 8 vouchers) almost exclusively in segregated low-income areas. The lawsuit resulted in commitments by the federal and local governments to support the former residents in moving to high-opportunity suburbs. The authority now funds an increased subsidy, higher than the regular Section 8 voucher amount, to families that rent in nonsegregated communities throughout Baltimore County and other nearby counties. Participants can use their vouchers in neighborhoods where the poverty rate is less than 10 percent, the population is no more than

30 percent African American or other minority, and fewer than 5 percent of households are subsidized. The mobility program not only places voucher holders in apartments; it also purchases houses on the open market and then rents them to program participants. It provides intensive counseling to the former public housing residents to help them adjust to their new, predominantly white and middle-class environs. Counseling covers topics such as household budgeting, cleaning and maintenance of appliances, communicating with landlords, and making friends with neighbors.

Those who have participated in this Baltimore program left communities with average poverty rates of 33 percent and found new dwellings where average rates were 8 percent. In their former neighborhoods, the African American population was 80 percent; in their new ones it is 21 percent. However, only a small proportion of former public housing tenants can participate in the program. Most use their Section 8 vouchers as do recipients nationwide: to subsidize living in already segregated low-income areas.

A similar program arose from a lawsuit filed in 1985 by a civil rights group against the Dallas Housing Authority and HUD over their use of the public housing or Section 8 programs to perpetuate segregation. Here too the case settlement provides families with a higher-value voucher when they relocate to a non-segregated suburb where the poverty rate is low and where public school students are high performing. A Dallas civil rights group (the Inclusive Communities Project) uses settlement funds for security deposits and counseling services to help families make the adjustment from racially separate public housing and Section 8 neighborhoods to integrated suburban environments. As in Baltimore, the Dallas program desegregates only a small percentage of families who are eligible for housing assistance.

A few other cities also now have modest programs (some also resulting from settlements in lawsuits that challenged how the Section 8 program reinforces segregation) that assist voucher holders in moving to lower-poverty areas.

Several municipalities and states outlaw flat refusals by landlords to lease to Section 8 voucher families, and those jurisdictions seem to be making a bit more progress toward integration. To allow owners to claim they are not discriminating by race when renters are turned away solely because they are subsidized makes a mockery of the Fair Housing Act. Such discrimination should be prohibited everywhere.

The Section 8 voucher program is not an entitlement. Many more eligible families don't receive vouchers than do, because Section 8 budgetary appropriations are too small. In 2015 approximately one million families had vouchers—but another 6 million who qualified went without them. There are long waiting lists for vouchers in every city that has a large African American low-income population. Indeed, in many cities, the waiting lists have been closed. So, in addition to prohibiting discrimination against voucher holders, Congress should appropriate funds to provide vouchers for all whose low-income status qualifies.

The housing subsidy that the federal government gives to middle-class (mostly white) homeowners is an entitlement: any homeowner with enough income to file a detailed tax return can claim a deduction both for property taxes and mortgage insurance. The government does not tell homeowners that only the first few who file can claim the deductions and the rest are out of luck because the money has been used up. But that is how we handle the Section 8 subsidy for lower-income (mostly African American) renters.

So long as a shortage of vouchers persists, Congress should require that local housing authorities establish a preference for tenants who volunteer to use their Section 8 benefits to find apartments in integrated, low-poverty neighborhoods. To make this possible, other reforms are necessary.

Voucher amounts are normally set to permit leasing of apartments whose rents are close to the median for a metropolitan area. But rental amounts that are typical for a metropolitan area overall are too low for leasing in most low-poverty neighborhoods. So voucher amounts will have to be increased if programs like Baltimore's are to expand nationwide, and more dollars—for security deposits, for example—made available as well. Large numbers of counselors and social workers will have to be hired and trained. Funds will also have to be authorized to enable authorities to purchase single-family homes for some former public housing residents.

In Baltimore the court order compelled HUD to come up with such funds. Expanding this program will require congressional action.

In its waning days, the Obama administration announced that HUD would begin calculating Section 8 voucher amounts for smaller areas than a full metropolis. Section 8 recipients would receive larger subsidies to rent apartments in higher-cost, middle-class neighborhoods and smaller subsidies to use in low-income neighborhoods where rents are lower. As this is written, it is too soon to know whether the new administration will maintain or reverse this new policy.

Other, more technical reforms of the Section 8 program could also help. For example, the vouchers are usually administered by a city housing authority that has no right to permit the vouchers to be used outside city limits. Vouchers can't contribute much to integration unless such jurisdictional rules are eliminated and the program is organized on a metropolitan basis.

State policy could also improve the potential of Section 8 to promote integration. Illinois presently extends a property tax reduction to landlords in low-poverty neighborhoods who rent to voucher holders. Other states should do likewise.

The federal Department of the Treasury should require states to distribute the Low-Income Housing Tax Credits to developers building in integrated high-opportunity neighborhoods. In segregated areas, a project that purports to help revitalize the community should be approved only as part of a coordinated urban development program that includes transportation infrastructure, job creation, inclusionary zoning, supermarkets, community policing, and other characteristics of healthy neighborhoods. But when developers have claimed to use tax credits to upgrade urban neighborhoods, what they have most frequently meant is bringing modern housing to an impoverished community. New construction is fine, but it can also reinforce segregation.

Fifty years of experience has shown that mobilizing the funds and support for revitalizing low-income communities is as politically difficult as integrating suburbs, so we continue to have more tax credit projects, and more Section 8 housing in segregated neighborhoods, without the surrounding community improvements that were promised. Revitalization does generally occur when a neighborhood becomes attractive to the middle class, but all too often the gentrification that follows does not include strict enforcement of inclusionary zoning principles, and it gradually drives the African American poor out of their now-upgraded neighborhoods and into newly segregated inner-ring suburbs.

## XI

FRANK AND Rosa Lee Stevenson raised three daughters in their segregated Richmond neighborhood, where average student performance was among the lowest in the state of California. When the girls were in the primary grades in the late 1950s and early 1960s, African American children composed only 22 percent of Richmond's elementary school population, but six of the district's elementary schools were over 95 percent African American.

Schools in Richmond were segregated primarily because federal and local housing policies had segregated the city itself. But Richmond school officials took additional measures to ensure that African American children did not attend the same school as white children. For example, the Peres school, with a 93 percent black enrollment in 1967, was situated west of the railroad tracks in a neighborhood that included three blocks that had remained white. The school board carved the three-block strip out of the Peres attendance zone and assigned students who lived there to attend the all-white Belding school, across the railroad tracks.

The school that the Stevenson daughters attended, Verde Elementary in unincorporated North Richmond, was west of the railroad tracks and not far from the oil refinery. The school had originally been constructed in 1951 to prevent black students from attending nearby schools in white neighborhoods. Verde was still 99 percent African American in 1968 when it became so overcrowded that the school district had to respond. Meanwhile nearby schools in white neighborhoods had many empty seats as a growing number of white families left Richmond for the suburbs. But instead of allowing African American children to occupy those seats, the district decided to build an addition to Verde. This was such an obvious attempt to perpetuate segregation that civil rights groups sued. The trial judge ordered integration and later told an interviewer that he had been offended by the racially biased testimony of a school board member who defended the district's policy.

Instead of appealing the judge's decision, the district agreed to a desegregation plan that modified attendance zones. But before the policy could be implemented, voters elected an anti-integration majority to the school board, which then reneged on its commitment. Instead, it adopted a voluntary program in which African American children could choose to attend a predominantly white school. By 1980 only one in six black children had done so. These were generally children with the most educationally sophisticated and motivated parents. Their transfers left schools in Richmond's black neighborhoods with the most disadvantaged students, those with the lowest academic performance and greatest behavioral challenges. Even today, as low-income Hispanic families replace African Americans in North Richmond, all students at the Verde School receive subsidized lunches, and 58 percent of its parents have not completed high school.

Richmond's school board could easily segregate its elementary schools because Richmond's neighborhoods were segregated, but for junior and senior high schools, the district created artificial boundaries that prevented many African American students from enrolling in their local schools. Instead, the district transported them to predominantly African American schools that were already more congested than the white ones. Whites also had to travel longer distances to avoid attending heavily African American schools nearer their homes. The assistant superintendent explained at a 1958 public meeting called to protest the segregation that the boundaries "assign to [mostly black] Richmond Union High School the bulk of students who can benefit from the shop program there and . . . the existing boundaries of [mostly white] Harry Ells High School are valid because the students who are grouped there are those who can profit from the academic program."

Civil rights protests forced the school district to redraw the high school attendance boundaries in 1959, but because of neighborhood segregation, African Americans remained concentrated in two of the eleven junior high schools and in Richmond High School. That's where Terry, the youngest of the Stevenson girls, graduated in 1970. Off and on, she took community college courses but never completed a college degree. She worked all her life, in day care centers and as a nursing assistant, and had six children of her own.

Terry Stevenson's two sons are warehouse workers. Of her four daughters, two are certified nurse assistants, one answers phone inquiries at a bank, and one is a security guard. Terry Stevenson's sisters also have children. They include a paralegal working at a law firm, a pharmacist assistant, a clerical worker at a government social service agency, and a department store sales clerk.

What might have become of these Stevenson grandchildren if their parents had grown up and attended school in an integrated Milpitas, not in a *de jure* segregated Richmond? Should they now have partners with similar occupations, their household incomes are unlikely to rise above the fourth income quintile of Americans. How much farther on the socioeconomic ladder would they have been able to climb if they had grown up in a well-educated household as a result of Terry and her sisters being permitted to attend a high school that was designed for students "who can profit from the academic program," rather than one that instead offered manual training? How different might the lives of the Stevenson grandchildren have been were it not for the federal government's unconstitutional determination to segregate their grandparents, and their parents as well? What do we, the American community, owe this family, in this and future generations, for their loss of opportunity? How might we fulfill this obligation?

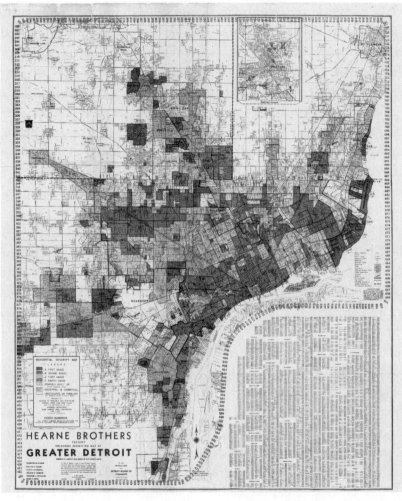

*A New Deal housing agency drew maps of metropolitan areas nationwide. Neighborhoods where African Americans resided were colored red to caution appraisers not to approve loans. This map is of Detroit.*

# EPILOGUE

----------------------------------

WHEN CHIEF JUSTICE John Roberts wrote that if residential segregation "is a product not of state action but of private choices, it does not have constitutional implications," he set forth a principle. But the principle supported his conclusion—that government remedies for segregation were impermissible—only because he assumed an inaccurate factual background: that residential segregation was mostly created by private choices.

We need not argue with the chief justice's principle; his jurisprudence is flawed mainly because he and his colleagues got their facts wrong. Residential segregation *was* created by state action, making it necessary to invoke the inseparable complement of the Roberts principle: where segregation is the product of state action, it has constitutional implications and requires a remedy.

Just like Supreme Court justices, we as a nation have avoided contemplating remedies because we've indulged in the comfortable delusion that our segregation has not resulted primarily from state action and so, we conclude, there is not much we are required to do about it. Because once entrenched, segregation is difficult to reverse, the easiest course is to ignore it.

It's not that private choices haven't also been involved. Many Americans had discriminatory beliefs and engaged in activities that contributed to separating the races. Without the support of these private beliefs and actions, our democratically elected governments might not have discriminated either. But under our constitutional system, government has not merely the option but the responsibility to resist racially discriminatory views, even when—especially when—a majority holds them. In the twentieth century, federal, state, and local officials did not resist majority opinion with regard to race. Instead, they endorsed and reinforced it, actively and aggressively.

If government had declined to build racially separate public housing in cities where segregation hadn't previously taken root, and instead had scattered integrated developments throughout the community, those cities might have developed in a less racially toxic fashion, with fewer desperate ghettos and more diverse suburbs.

If the federal government had not urged suburbs to adopt exclusionary zoning laws, white flight would have been minimized because there would have been fewer racially exclusive suburbs to which frightened homeowners could flee.

If the government had told developers that they could have FHA guarantees only if the homes they built were open to all, integrated working-class suburbs would likely have matured with both African Americans and whites sharing the benefits.

If state courts had not blessed private discrimination by ordering the eviction of African American homeowners in neighborhoods where association rules and restrictive covenants barred their residence, middle-class African Americans would have been able gradually to integrate previously white communities as they developed the financial means to do so.

If churches, universities, and hospitals had faced loss of tax-exempt status for their promotion of restrictive covenants, they most likely would have refrained from such activity.

If police had arrested, rather than encouraged, leaders of mob violence when African Americans moved into previously white neighborhoods, racial transitions would have been smoother.

If state real estate commissions had denied licenses to brokers who claimed an "ethical" obligation to impose segregation, those brokers might have guided the evolution of interracial neighborhoods.

If school boards had not placed schools and drawn attendance boundaries to ensure the separation of black and white pupils, families might not have had to relocate to have access to education for their children.

If federal and state highway planners had not used urban interstates to demolish African American neighborhoods and force their residents deeper into urban ghettos, black impoverishment would have lessened, and some displaced families might have accumulated the resources to improve their housing and its location.

If government had given African Americans the same labor-market rights that other citizens enjoyed, African American working-class families would not have been trapped in lower-income minority communities, from lack of funds to live elsewhere.

If the federal government had not exploited the racial boundaries it had created in metropolitan areas, by spending billions on tax breaks for single-family suburban homeowners, while failing to spend adequate funds on transportation networks that could bring African Americans to job opportunities, the inequality on which segregation feeds would have diminished.

If federal programs were not, even to this day, reinforcing racial isolation by disproportionately directing low-income African Americans who receive housing assistance into the segregated neighborhoods that government had previously established, we might see many more inclusive communities.

Undoing the effects of *de jure* segregation will be incomparably difficult. To make a start, we will first have to contemplate what we have collectively done and, on behalf of our government, accept responsibility.

*In the 1930s and 1940s, University of Chicago trustees (chairman Harold H. Swift, center) instructed chancellor Robert Maynard Hutchins (right) to ensure that neighborhoods near the campus were segregated. His father, William James Hutchins (left), president of the interracial Berea College in Kentucky, unsuccessfully advised his son to reject the demand.*

# APPENDIX

# FREQUENTLY
# ASKED QUESTIONS

A DECADE HAS PASSED since I began considering the account this book sets forth. During that time, I've consulted with friends, colleagues, and housing specialists. These discussions have influenced my thinking and, in some cases, modified my argument. But I've also encountered some objections that did not cause me to change my views. In what follows, I share many of these objections and my response to them.

*You have painted a portrait of unconstitutional policies to segregate metropolitan areas, pursued in the twentieth century by government officials from the president to local police officers. But that was then; this is now. You can't apply today's standards to yesterday's leaders, can you?*

We can judge yesterday's leaders by standards that were readily available to them in their own time. Whether from cowardice, expediency, or moral failure, they ignored prominent contrary voices.

African Americans consistently denounced their unconstitutional treatment. If you dismiss their protests on the ground that whites' "standards of the time" meant ignoring black opinion, consider that many whites also condemned government promotion of segregation.

In 1914, as Woodrow Wilson was segregating federal offices, the National Council of Congregational Churches adopted a resolution condemning his policy. Howard Bridgman, editor of *The Congregationalist and the Christian World* wrote to Wilson that his actions violated Christian principles; the editor told his readers that protesting the administration's segregation of the civil service was the "Christian white man's duty." Wisconsin Senator Robert La Follette's magazine (now known as *The Progressive*) published a series of articles protesting Wilson's racial policy.

During the New Deal, although Interior Secretary Harold Ickes oversaw segregated housing projects, he also desegregated the dining room in his department—reversing Wilson's policy. Franklin Roosevelt's labor secretary, Frances Perkins, did the same in her department. The army refused generally to accept skilled African Americans in the Civilian Conservation Corps, but Ickes and his deputy Clark Foreman hired skilled African Americans in CCC camps that were located in national parks, which were controlled by the Interior Department. Foreman also enraged influential politicians by hiring an African American secretary, the first in the federal bureaucracy. In radio broadcast attacks, Georgia governor Herman Talmadge excoriated Foreman for elevating a woman who, in the governor's view, should properly be a janitor.

First Lady Eleanor Roosevelt, at times an outspoken integration advocate, occasionally challenged her husband's administration policy. In 1939 she resigned her membership in the Daughters of the American Revolution after it barred the African American singer Marian Anderson from performing in its hall. She was the first white resident of Washington, D.C., to join the local NAACP chapter. Mrs. Roosevelt's opposition to segregation was so well known (notorious, in many circles) that the FBI sent agents through the South to attempt to verify rumors that black domestic workers had formed "Eleanor Clubs" to advocate for higher wages and the right to eat at the same tables as the families they served.

During World War II, the Boilermakers excluded African Americans, but the United Auto Workers did not. Martin Carpenter, director of the U.S. Employment Service, reacted to Roosevelt's 1941 fair practices order by consolidating separate white and African American employment offices in Washington, D.C. Congressmen threatened to hold up appropriations unless Carpenter abandoned his plan. He did so, but his attempt illustrates that segregation was not a uniform "standard of the time" but only a standard of many.

Some twentieth-century segregationists acknowledged their own hypocrisy. University of Chicago president Robert Maynard Hutchins worked to keep African Americans away from the university vicinity but claimed privately that he disagreed and was only following wishes of the university trustees. Hutchins later said that he "came nearer to resigning over this than over any other issue," but he did not. He understood that invoking "standards of the time" could not justify acquiescence to the trustees' views; he knew better.

If we excuse past leaders for rejecting nondiscrimination standards that were held by some, we undermine our constitutional system. The Bill of Rights and the Civil War Amendments exist to protect minorities and individuals from majority opinion, not from unanimous opinion. But it really doesn't matter whether we blame Woodrow Wilson, Franklin Roosevelt, or their appointees for supporting segregation. No matter how conventional their racial policies were, they violated African Americans' constitutional rights. The consequences define our racially separate living arrangements to this day, so it is up to our generations to remedy them, whether or not we fault particular historical figures.

*I looked up the deed to my home and found it has a restrictive covenant prohibiting "non-Caucasians" from living there. Although the clause is unenforceable, it still bothers me. How can I remove it?*

The difficulty and expense of eliminating restrictions from deeds varies by state. But even where it is practical, deleting them may not be the best approach. The covenants are an important reminder and educational device, which we still need. If you can modify a deed in your state, rather than removing it, you might consider adding a paragraph like this:

> We, [your name], owners of the property at [your address], acknowledge that this deed includes an unenforceable, unlawful, and morally repugnant clause excluding African Americans from this neighborhood. We repudiate this clause, are ashamed for our country that many once considered it acceptable, and state that we welcome with enthusiasm and without reservation neighbors of all races and ethnicities.

*I wasn't even born when all this stuff happened. When my family came to this country, segregation already existed; we had nothing to do with segregating African Americans. Why should we now have to sacrifice to correct it?*

Sherrilyn Ifill, president of the NAACP Legal Defense Fund, once responded to a similar question, saying, "Your ancestors weren't here in 1776, but you eat hot dogs on the Fourth of July, don't you?" What she was trying to convey is that Americans who preceded us fought for our liberty, sometimes giving their lives for it, yet we benefit without making similar sacrifices. When we become Americans, we accept not only citizenship's privileges that we did not earn but also its responsibilities to correct wrongs that we did not commit. It was *our* government that segregated American neighborhoods, whether we or our ancestors bore witness to it, and it is *our* government that now must craft remedies.

*It is normal for people to want to live among others with whom they share a common history and culture. There are neighborhoods that are mostly Jewish, or Italian, or Chinese. We African Americans want our own neighborhoods, too. Why are you trying to force us to integrate?*

I cannot imagine a policy that would "force" African Americans to integrate, but we can offer incentives to do so. There should be subsidies for low-income African Americans who could not otherwise afford to leave minority neighborhoods. Middle-class African Americans who now live in lower-middle-class segregated areas should also receive incentives to move to integrated communities. Still, it is appropriate to wonder why we should go to great expense to persuade people to follow a policy that nobody, black or white, seems to want.

Surveys show that most African Americans prefer integrated neighborhoods. So do whites. But African Americans define an integrated community as one in which from 20 to 50 percent of residents are African American. Whites define it as one where they dominate—and in which only 10 percent of residents are African American. When a neighborhood exceeds an African American presence of more than 10 percent, whites typically start to leave, and soon it becomes overwhelmingly African American. If this is the likely result of attempts to integrate, it is hardly worth the bother.

Ten percent African American, though, is an insufficient integration goal because our major metropolitan areas have greater African American presence than that. In the Atlanta area, African Americans are 32 percent of the population; in Chicago, 17 percent; in Detroit, 23 percent; in New York–New Jersey–Connecticut, 15 percent. If we say that the share of African Americans in a stable integrated community is the average in their metropolitan area, plus or minus 10 percent, then if whites depart a suburb whenever it exceeds 10 percent, stable integration will be impossible. Integration can't work if we try it only where African Americans remain invisible, or nearly so.

The idea that African Americans themselves don't want to integrate is a white conceit. Many thousands of African Americans risked hostility, even violence, when daring to move into predominantly white neighborhoods. This history has generated considerable reluctance by other African Americans to try to follow them. When African Americans move to predominantly white neighborhoods today, they remain more likely to be stopped by police when driving home or kept under unusual surveillance in retail stores when shopping. Teachers are more likely to expect their children to be less capable and to be unqualified for challenging classes. African American pupils are often disciplined severely in integrated schools for minor misbehavior that, in the case of whites, schools ignore.

It is reasonable to expect that many, perhaps most African Americans will choose segregation unless they are welcomed into white communities whose interracial hospitality becomes widely known. Until then, African Americans' avoidance of integration cannot be considered a free choice. Reform of police practices and school academic and disciplinary policies in predominantly white areas is essential, together with incentives for African Americans to take the chance of believing that those reforms are real.

But incentives alone will not suffice. To achieve an integrated society, African Americans too must take greater risks. A partner in a prestigious law firm once explained to me why she opposed my advocacy of integration: "I am a middle-class African American professional woman, and I want to live where I can be comfortable, where there are salons that know how to cut my hair, where I can easily get to my church, and where there are supermarkets where I can buy collard greens."

No affluent middle-class suburb can be fully integrated overnight. So if my lawyer friend moved to an all-white suburb now, she won't find the hairdresser, church, or supermarket she seeks. But once the neighborhood integrates, salons specializing in African American hair will open, and the supermarket will stock greens. She may initially have to return to her old neighborhood for church; this may be a price paid for the benefits of integration to herself, her children, and our nation.

Many white middle-class neighborhoods today have supermarket aisles with traditional Jewish, Italian, and Asian foods, even when Jews, Italians, or Asians remain a minority in the area. These items were not found, though, when the first members of these groups arrived. Some had to be pioneers. The law partner with whom I spoke may not want to be a pioneer, and she shouldn't have to be if that is her choice. But to solve the economic, social, and political problems that *de jure* segregation perpetuates, some will have to go first. Although nobody should be forced to move out of a segregated neighborhood if he or she chooses to remain, government creates many incentives to persuade people to abandon harmful behavior: we tax cigarettes heavily, we subsidize contributions that employees voluntarily make to their own retirement accounts, and we give commuters a faster lane if they choose to carpool. So we should provide incentives for families to choose to seek integrated settings and then support them there. African Americans can reject the incentives and choose to remain segregated, but government should make it easier for them to make a different choice.

Were we ever to become truly integrated and if all "badges and incidents" of slavery are ever eradicated, certainly some neighborhoods would have higher-than-average proportions of African Americans, as there are neighborhoods with higher-than-average proportions of Jews, Italians, Chinese, and other groups. That will be quite a different kind of metropolitan arrangement, however, than the segregated patterns that characterize our cities and suburbs today.

*Why emphasize our obligation to remedy constitutional violations? You should instead present it as an opportunity because everyone benefits from a diverse society.*

All this is true. But we delude ourselves if we think that desegregation can only be a win-win experience for all. There are costs involved, and some may be substantial.

If we require, as we should, the Section 8 and Low-Income Housing Tax Credit programs to facilitate movement of low-income African American families into middle-class communities, those communities may experience an increase in crime. It is more likely to be petty than violent crime, and it won't approach the violence visited upon African Americans to enforce their segregation. Nonetheless, pretending that integration can be cost-free dooms it to backlash when residents of middle-class communities realize they were duped. Integration cannot wait until every African American youth becomes a model citizen.

Affluent suburbs may experience a decline in property values after integration, because racial and economic snobbery is now part of their appeal to buyers.

Offering incentives to encourage African Americans to settle in white neighborhoods will involve substantial financial costs. If we include low-income children in upper-middle-class schools, we will have to divert resources to special counseling and remedial programs, and taxes will have to rise to pay for them or elective programs may have to be cut. If we mislead white parents into thinking that integration will be cost-free, they will be enraged, understandably so, when these costs become apparent.

Affirmative action programs are reasonable ways to address the legacy of state-sponsored segregation. African Americans whose opportunities have been limited because their families were locked in ghettos should be given some compensation in the form of access to jobs and educations that their forebears were denied. But affirmative action is also not without costs. In his book *For Discrimination*, Harvard law professor Randall Kennedy ridicules Barack Obama's claim in *The Audacity of Hope* that affirmative action "can open up opportunities otherwise closed to qualified minorities without diminishing opportunities for white students." Kennedy retorts, "How can that be?" If college slots are limited and affirmative action admits a handful of African Americans who wouldn't otherwise attend, an equal number of nonfavored applicants must be rejected. That number may be small relative to the thousands of qualified applicants denied admission because of space limitations, but it is not zero.

By not acknowledging this cost, we invite opponents of affirmative action to exaggerate it, wildly in some cases, as they did in recent Supreme Court challenges to University of Texas admission procedures that give a tiny advantage to otherwise qualified African Americans. The plaintiff, Abigail Fisher, was a white applicant who was less qualified than African Americans who were admitted. By failing to acknowledge that a few whites might have to give up their places in an affirmative action program, we encourage any white student rejected by an elite university to feel victimized and to blame affirmative action for his or her failure.

Neither the costs nor the benefits of desegregation can be apportioned fairly. African Americans benefiting from an affirmative action boost may not be those who most need it because of segregation. White students who are rejected by an elite university due to affirmative action, but who otherwise would have been admitted, may not be precisely those who owe their qualifications to the legacy of privilege that segregation bequeathed.

Our legal system expects every compensatory transfer to be precisely calibrated to the responsibility of the giver and the victimization of the receiver. *De jure* segregation is too massive a historical wrong to satisfy this principle. Remedying *de jure* segregation will be neither win-win nor neat. We've made a constitutional mess that will not be easily undone. Certainly, integration will benefit all of us, white and African American. But costs will also be involved, and we should accept that those costs are part of our constitutional obligation. Otherwise, integration will be unlikely to succeed.

*Why did leaders whom we consider liberal promote segregationist policies? What was the motivation for administrations from Wilson's to Franklin Roosevelt's to impose segregation? Was it political expediency, or were they personally bigoted?*

It was some of both.

The Franklin Roosevelt and Harry Truman administrations could not enact progressive economic programs without the support of southern Democrats who were committed to white supremacy. President Roosevelt chose John Nance Garner, a segregationist Texan, as his vice-presidential running mate for his first two terms. The selection preserved, at least initially, Democratic unity in support of policies that disproportionately helped whites.

But there was more to it than expediency. President Roosevelt's inner circle included press secretary Steve Early, a committed segregationist who ensured that no racial liberalism crept into presidential statements. The South Carolina segregationist Senator James F. Byrnes was one of Roosevelt's (and later President Truman's) closest confidants, and Roosevelt appointed him to the Supreme Court. After only a year Byrnes resigned to take other administration positions. Had Byrnes remained on the Court when it considered school desegregation in 1954, Chief Justice Earl Warren would have had more difficulty persuading all eight associate justices to support his *Brown v. Board of Education* opinion. Byrnes by then was governor of South Carolina and became a leader of southern resistance to the ruling.

Not only southerners but many northern New Deal officials gave little consideration to African American welfare. For the first two-thirds of the twentieth century, America's national leadership was almost exclusively white, Anglo-Saxon, Protestant, and male, and most were contemptuous of others. Protestants resisted the 1960 presidential candidacy of a Catholic, John F. Kennedy; his narrow victory was a watershed event for that reason. Kennedy's election, perhaps more than Barack Obama's, shattered the white Protestant elite's near-monopoly hold on political power.

The bigotry of this elite was not based merely on social class but also on race. After all, it was the integration of middle-class, not lower-class, African Americans, that most aroused FHA officials. In 1939, the National Association of Real Estate Boards, whose members furnished appraisers to the FHA, prepared a handbook for use in preparing brokers to take exams for licensure by state governments. The handbook warned brokers to be on guard against "a colored man of means who was giving his children a college education and thought they were entitled to live among whites."

*Don't black people have to take more responsibility for their own success? Crime rates in black neighborhoods are high, and so whites will resist integration because they don't want African Americans bringing crime into white neighborhoods. Young men join gangs and will sell drugs, even when jobs are available. Doesn't black ghetto culture have to change before we can consider integration?*

Certainly everyone—black, white, and others—should take greater responsibility for their own success. African Americans are no exception, and neither are white Americans.

Having agreed on that, let's review some facts.

Most African American youths do take responsibility for their own success, and many work "twice as hard" to succeed. This responsibility and added effort frequently pay off—although the payoff is less than it is for whites. In 2014, of young (ages 25–29) adult African Americans, 21 percent of men and 24 percent of women were college graduates. High school completion rates are over 90 percent. This suggests that a focus on the antisocial behavior of a minority of African Americans is too convenient an excuse for not taking steps to integrate the majority.

The "war on drugs," including the mass incarceration of young men and adolescent boys living in low-income African American neighborhoods, began in the 1970s. Current trends predict that as many as one in three African American men born today can expect to spend some time in prison during their lifetimes, most for nonviolent crimes. Considering this, it is surprising that the African American college graduation rate is as high as it is.

As Michelle Alexander reports in her important book, *The New Jim Crow*, young African American men are less likely to use or sell drugs than young white men, but they are more likely to be arrested for drug use or sale; once arrested, they are more likely to be sentenced; once sentenced, they are more likely to receive long jail terms. African American automobile drivers are no more likely than white drivers to change lanes without signaling, but they are more likely to be stopped by police for doing so, and once stopped, they are more likely to be caught up in the penal system, including jail time for inability to pay fines. The Justice Department's investigation of Ferguson, Missouri, police practices found that African Americans were stopped by police more frequently than whites, but of those who were stopped and searched, more whites were found to be carrying illegal drugs than African Americans. If police wanted to increase their chances of finding drugs, they would be better off conducting "stop and frisk" operations in white than in black neighborhoods.

Imprisoning nonviolent offenders in low-income minority neighborhoods has a multigenerational effect. A parent's absence harms a child's early development and academic performance. Once young men leave prison, even after short sentences (and many are not short), they may have permanent second-class status, be unable to vote, get evicted from public housing, and be ineligible for food stamps. Their family relationships are likely frayed if not irreparably broken. Most companies won't hire them. Barred from legitimate jobs, they are exposed to further incarceration when they attempt to earn a living in the underground economy.

We should not overemphasize the extent to which behavioral change can overcome ghetto conditions for which we, the broader community, are responsible. Lead poisoning is an example. Nationwide, African American children have dangerous and irreversible lead-in-blood levels at twice the rate of white children. The difference is attributable mostly to being trapped in neighborhoods with deteriorated housing stock, where lead paint peels from walls and lead pipes deliver water to homes and schools. When developing brains absorb lead (which then blocks necessary calcium), children's ability to develop self-control diminishes. Lead poisoning predicts teenagers' risky behaviors and young adults' greater violent or criminal activity. Because Flint, Michigan, used a lead-polluted water supply in 2014 and 2015, for example, we can reasonably predict an uptick in violence when the city's children (most of whom are African American) reach adolescence and young adulthood.

Certainly, it would be better if every young African American man resisted adopting an oppositional and alienated stance. But for all of us, reform of the political and economic institutions that encourage that posture is essential. Neither can wait upon the other.

*Isn't the real reason that African Americans can't escape the ghetto that so many are single mothers who can't or don't raise their children properly? Shouldn't we encourage them to wait until marriage to have children, so they will be better able to raise their children properly?*

Government policies that segregated this nation were directed primarily at African American working- and middle-class two-parent families with children. Frank Stevenson and his family who were prohibited from living in Milpitas, Vince and Robert Mereday and their families who were prohibited from living in Levittown, Wilbur and Borece Gary, Bill and Daisy Myers, Andrew and Charlotte Wade, and thousands like them who were met with police-protected violence when they attempted to occupy their homes, were not single mothers with children. Single parenthood as a reason to resist integration is an afterthought, a rationalization for inaction.

Birth rates of African American women have been declining, much more rapidly for teenagers than for adults. Better education about contraception has helped delay first pregnancies. So have school programs that raise girls' expectations about careers. But women of any race will not delay voluntary pregnancy indefinitely; their childbearing goals cannot be suppressed by moralizing or by education. Higher single-parenthood rates in low-income African American communities mostly result from a shortage of marriage partners for young adult women. Excessive incarceration and joblessness of young black men bear responsibility.

We may think of marriage as a romantic commitment, but it is also an economic institution. Two-parent families are likely to have a higher joint income to support and nurture children. A recent survey found that 78 percent of never-married women of all races who hoped to be married were seeking a spouse with a steady job;

this characteristic was more important than having similar religious beliefs, child-rearing philosophies, education, or race. If a community's young men have high unemployment (or only low-wage work), the mothers of their children will have little incentive to marry them. Today, among African Americans between the ages of twenty-five and thirty-four who have never been married, there are fifty-one employed males for every hundred females. For whites, Asians, and Hispanics, the number of employed men is approximately equal to the number of women. Unless the number of working, criminal-record-free men in African American neighborhoods increases, we are unlikely to succeed in reducing the number of women there who have children without the means to support and nurture them well.

White women have rising single-parenthood rates, but they also frequently have resources to hire assistance they need to raise children on their own. Also, a larger proportion of white than black "single" mothers are cohabiting with their children's father; the institution of marriage has been declining among whites faster than the rate of intact two-parent families.

A curious aspect of white racial bigotry—the greater tendency of white women than men to marry black partners—exacerbates the problem. Of African American men who married in 2010, 24 percent married a woman who was not African American. But of African American women who married in that year, only 9 percent married a man who was not African American. This unique imbalance among race and ethnic groups has been consistent since the early twentieth century, when interracial marriages were even rarer than today. When gender-based intermarriage differences are added to higher incarceration and unemployment rates of young African American men, it is apparent that single motherhood among African Americans will remain high.

There are well-designed educational programs that aim to teach better parenting skills to low-income African American mothers, but Congress has not funded them on more than a token experimental scale. It is a bit cynical to say that we can't support the integration of African American women into middle-class neighborhoods until they become better mothers, then fail to provide the support they want and need. And we have no right to wait until every low-income and poorly educated mother develops perfect parenting skills before we move to desegregate metropolitan areas. Middle-class whites aren't perfect caregivers either, but for their children to succeed, the mothers only have to be half as good.

*Why do you only talk about African Americans? Don't other minorities face discrimination as well? Don't Hispanics also live in segregated communities?*

Two distinct problems are easily confused. One, the subject of this book, is the *de jure* segregation of African Americans that has yet to be remedied. The other is growing economic inequality, including housing prices and rents that are unaffordable in many middle-class communities to families of all races and ethnicities.

Although our history includes government-organized discrimination and even segregation of other groups, including Hispanics, Chinese, and Japanese, it was of a lesser degree, and is in the more distant past, than the *de jure* segregation experienced by African Americans.

First- and second-generation Hispanics (mostly Mexican but also from other Latin American countries) frequently live in ethnically homogenous low-income neighborhoods. But for the most part, few have been "segregated" in those neighborhoods—forced to live there by private discrimination or by government policies designed to isolate them.

Low-income immigrants have always lived for the first few generations in ethnic enclaves where their language is spoken, familiar foods are accessible, ethnic churches are nearby, and rent is relatively cheap for overcrowded apartments. This was the history of Irish, Jewish, Italian, Polish, Greek, and other immigrant groups that came to the United States with few skills but were willing to work hard at low wages to achieve economic security and ensure better lives for their children. It could not have been otherwise.

Unskilled and poorly educated immigrants could not easily survive if dispersed throughout a foreign, unfamiliar, native population. In the third generation and beyond, descendants of immigrants typically have left ethnic neighborhoods and assimilated into the broader society. Assimilation does not mean losing a cultural identity, but the primary identity of these later generations has been as Americans.

To a considerable extent, this pattern characterizes twentieth-century Hispanic immigrants as well. Data are sparse that disaggregate results by immigrant generation, but what little we have supports this conclusion. For example, in 2010, 26 percent of all Hispanic newlyweds married non-Hispanics; for those born here (the second and subsequent generations), the rate was 36 percent. For the third generation and beyond, the rate is likely to be 40 percent and perhaps more. But data for black families, who have been Americans for centuries, are quite different: theirs is less than half the intermarriage rate of second-generation Hispanics.

Some studies conclude that Hispanic (and in particular Mexican) educational and economic improvement "stalls" after the second generation and that immigrants are not blending into the "white" middle class. These studies are flawed because they rely on surveys that ask respondents if they are "white," "African American," "Hispanic," or "Asian" (or some other category). If third-generation-and-beyond Hispanics reply that they are "white," data on their education and income are not included in the "Hispanic" category. The most assimilated descendants of Mexican immigrants—those with the most education or highest incomes and those who have married non-Hispanics—are more likely to cease identifying themselves as Hispanics, resulting in underestimates of the third-generation-and-beyond's assimilation.

Mexican immigrants, Mexican Americans, and Puerto Ricans were also sometimes segregated *de jure* by government policy, brutalized by police, prohibited from entering white eating, retail, or entertainment establishments, and mistreated when they served in the armed forces. In some cases, especially in Texas, they were segregated in schools. Today many low-income Hispanic youth living in neighborhoods of concentrated disadvantage have a toxic relationship with police that is similar to that of African American youth, and for many of the same reasons.

Yet horrific though our treatment of Mexican immigrants and Puerto Ricans has sometimes been, it is not comparable to our treatment of African Americans. In many communities, restrictive covenants prohibited sales not only to African Americans but also to Hispanics (and frequently to Jews, the Irish, Asians, and others deemed "non-Caucasians"). Yet judges often deemed Mexican Americans to be "Caucasians" and not subject to exclusion by restrictive covenants. As the twentieth century progressed, property and residency restrictions mostly faded away for all except African Americans. Only African Americans have been systematically and unconstitutionally segregated for such a long period, and with such thorough repression, that their condition requires an aggressive constitutional remedy.

Certainly, Hispanics still suffer discrimination, some of it severe. Bilingual education programs smooth the transition to English for low-income immigrant children, but nativist-driven campaigns have severely restricted the use of this proven pedagogy. Nearly one in four Hispanics seeking to buy or rent homes still meet with discrimination from real estate agents or landlords. In some cases, municipal officials target Hispanic immigrant households for selective building code enforcement. Under the eye of regulators, banks discriminatorily marketed subprime loans to Hispanic as well as to African American families.

Although in many respects the experience of low-income immigrant Hispanics is similar to that of earlier European immigrant groups, those groups experienced periods of broadly shared prosperity. After European immigrants, or their descendants, returned as veterans from World War II, production and nonsupervisory workers experienced a quarter-century of wage growth that averaged 2.3 percent a year, helping them to establish firm footings in the American middle class. Since 1973, there has been no wage growth whatsoever for production and nonsupervisory workers.

This trend, not unremedied *de jure* segregation, is what may prevent late twentieth-century immigrants from fully following in the path of those who came before.

In metropolitan areas, many first- and second-generation Hispanics live in neighborhoods with high proportions of poor and low-income families. Good social policy should facilitate their movement, as soon as they are ready, out of such low-opportunity neighborhoods. The reforms needed to restrain the Section 8 and Low-Income Housing Tax Credit programs from confining African Americans to high-poverty and poorly resourced neighborhoods should do the same for recent Hispanic immigrants.

Creating greater opportunity for low-income Hispanic immigrants is sound social policy; creating greater opportunity for African Americans is sound social policy as well but is also constitutionally required to remedy *de jure* segregation.

A healthy American society requires both desegregation of African Americans and a more egalitarian, growth-oriented economy to benefit all low-income families. *De jure* segregation and blocked economic opportunity are two distinct problems. We should address each one.


*Isn't all your talk about desegregating neighborhoods a form of "social engineering"? When government tries to enact such transformations, aren't there often unintended and harmful consequences?*

Desegregation would attempt to reverse a century of social engineering on the part of federal, state, and local governments that enacted policies to keep African Americans separate and subordinate. Too few whites were terribly concerned with that kind of social engineering, and it's a bit unseemly to make that objection now.

Without minimizing the unfairness that some may suffer as an unintended consequence of desegregation, we should not be more concerned with that unfairness than with the harm that befalls African Americans, and all of us, when we fail to cleanse the nation of a residential organization that is incompatible with the letter and spirit of our Constitution.

*The biggest problem facing African Americans today is the gentrification of their neighborhoods, leaving low-income families nowhere to go. What can we do about that?*

As higher-income whites rediscover the benefits of urban life, demand for housing in many formerly African American and immigrant neighborhoods is rising. Higher rents and property taxes force lower-income families to leave. Before all leave, gentrification seems to create integrated communities. But this phenomenon is mostly temporary, lasting only until the replacement of lower-income with higher-income families is complete.

Most low-income families forced out of gentrifying neighborhoods have nowhere else to go, except to a few segregated suburbs where they soon become concentrated because other locales prohibit or excessively restrict the construction of affordable units. If apartments exist in middle-class suburbs, rents are usually too high for families displaced from urban areas, or else landlords are permitted to discriminate against African Americans and Hispanics in the guise of refusing to accept Section 8 vouchers.

Gentrification would be a positive development if it were combined with inclusionary zoning policies to preserve affordable housing in every neighborhood. But such policies are rare or weak. Inclusionary zoning should also be required of presently exclusionary suburbs. Were that to happen, all neighborhoods could make progress toward integration.

*The writer Ta-Nehisi Coates says we should pay reparations to African Americans. Is that what you are proposing?*

In several articles in *The Atlantic*, Ta-Nehisi Coates has made a "case for reparations" to African Americans who continue to suffer the effects of slavery and segregation. In a January 2016 article, Coates reported surveys showing that 64 percent of white Americans think the legacy of segregation is either a "minor factor" or "no factor at all" in today's white-black wealth gap. Until Americans overcome this collective amnesia, Coates writes, it is pointless to debate specific proposals. If we do overcome this amnesia, then we can have productive conversations about how to address that legacy.

I prefer the term *remedies* to *reparations* to describe policies that could make African Americans, and all Americans, whole for the constitutional violations that segregated the nation. To my ear, and it may only be mine, *reparations* sounds more like a generalized one-time payment to African Americans for their exploitation.

We cannot compensate for *de jure* segregation through litigation—rather, it will require a national political consensus that leads to legislation. But the concept of *remedies* to make victims whole is a familiar one in our legal system. I also prefer the term *remedies* because they also include policies that do not involve payments. While we should subsidize homeownership for African Americans in suburbs from which they were once banned, we should also require repeal of exclusionary zoning ordinances that prevent the construction of affordable homes in such suburbs. "Affirmative action" in education and employment is also constitutionally required to remedy *de jure* segregation.

But I have no quarrel with Coates's preference for the term *reparations*. If you prefer to think of the policies we should follow as being reparations, not remedies, I won't disagree. What's important is that until we arouse in Americans an understanding of how we created a system of unconstitutional, state-sponsored, *de jure* segregation, and a sense of outrage about it, neither remedies nor reparations will be on the public agenda.

*Isn't your argument completely unrealistic? Supreme Court justices will never go for it.*

The observation that the Supreme Court "follows the election returns" may be too simple, but Supreme Court justices certainly do come to new understandings only after a substantial portion of informed opinion has done so. Yet although reparations cannot be won by lawsuits, the courts do have a role. Were Congress, for example, to enact a "Fair Share Plan," opponents would challenge it, insisting that such a policy would be "reverse discrimination" and violate the Fourteenth Amendment. A future, better-educated Court would be called upon to reject this argument, as well as to rule that the plan was an appropriate exercise of congressional power under Section 2 of the Thirteenth Amendment, the clause that authorized Congress to abolish the badges of slavery, of which none other is as important as segregated neighborhoods.

Whether a future Court is better educated is entirely up to us.

# AUTHOR'S NOTE AND ACKNOWLEDGMENTS

-------------------------------------------------------------------

FOR MOST of the last thirty years, I've had the privilege of association with the Economic Policy Institute (EPI), which has supported development of *The Color of Law*. The support was unwavering, even before it became apparent to me, and to Lawrence Mishel, the president of EPI, that residential racial segregation underlay much of the economic inequality that EPI is dedicated to exposing. It is to Larry Mishel that I, and this book, owe the greatest debt of gratitude.

Along with Larry Mishel, EPI's communications department has ensured that my previous books and articles, predicates for *The Color of Law*, got the best editing, design, and distribution. When I didn't know what a blog was and stubbornly refused to learn, EPI's communications director, Elizabeth Rose, gently prodded me toward publishing my work more informally, as well as in traditional ways. Without EPI's support, this book could not, and would not, have been written.

Other institutions also helped. In 2009–10 I had the privilege of participating in a year-long seminar (led by Professors Rob Reich of Stanford University and Danielle Allen, now at Harvard) at the Institute for Advanced Study in Princeton. As I described in Chapter 9, I had been ruminating at the time about the Supreme Court's *Parents Involved* decision, in which the Court rejected school desegregation efforts because, it claimed, schools were racially homogenous only because their neighborhoods were "*de facto*" segregated through no fault, or little fault, of state policy. At the Institute for Advanced Study, seminar participants developed research proposals for new directions in their work, and I decided to look further into my hunch that the "*de facto*" basis of the *Parents Involved* decision was seriously flawed. I concluded the seminar by writing a proposal that summarized what I had learned. Seminar papers were published as chapters in *Education, Justice, and Democracy* (2013), edited by Allen and Reich. *The Color of Law* is little more than a fuller documentation of the claims made in that chapter.

My feeling that *de jure* residential segregation was at the root of the nation's ongoing racial problems in education and other fields had its own roots. Fifty years ago, as a very young man, I worked as an assistant to Harold (Hal) Baron, research director of the Chicago Urban League. Alexander Polikoff, the attorney representing Dorothy Gautreaux in her suit against HUD and the Chicago Housing Authority (I described this litigation in Chapter 2), had obtained a discovery order permitting Hal to search the authority's archives. Correspondence and board minutes going back thirty years were boxed up and stored in the basement of one of the Robert Taylor Homes high-rise towers. I spent part of a hot summer in that basement, collecting evidence that the government had purposely used public housing to ensure that African Americans were concentrated away from white neighborhoods. This experience planted the seeds of my skepticism regarding the contemporary Supreme Court's belief in *de facto* segregation.

Just as this book was going to press, Hal Baron passed away. *The Color of Law* is one of his progeny. I wish he could have seen it. I hope he would have been proud to take credit.

In 2010, I began to spend considerable time in Berkeley, California, because my children (and grandchildren) had all settled in the San Francisco Bay Area. When I described the theme of my research to Christopher Edley, then dean of the University of California (Berkeley) School of Law, he offered to host me as a senior fellow at the law school's Chief Justice Earl Warren Institute on Law and Social Policy. Although the position was unpaid (my support came from the Economic Policy Institute), the Warren Institute provided me with academic library privileges and a series of wonderfully talented research assistants. I'll say more about these terrific students further on, but here I want to stress in the strongest possible terms that without Dean Edley's and the Warren Institute's support, this book would not have been possible. Thanks, Chris.

The Warren Institute ceased to operate in December 2015. At that point, the Haas Institute for a Fair and Inclusive Society at the University of California, led by director john powell and assistant director Stephen Menendian, enthusiastically agreed to a similar appointment, also with library privileges and graduate research assistants. Early in my research, Professor powell was particularly influential when he insisted that I pay more attention to the implications of the discussion in *Jones v. Mayer* regarding the Thirteenth Amendment. I did, and the result should be apparent.

Collaboration with Stephen Menendian has been especially fruitful, and I am gratified to be able to thank him. On one occasion, on behalf of a national group of housing scholars, we collaborated to draft an amicus brief submitted to the U.S. Supreme Court for the case in which it upheld the use of a "disparate impact" standard for evaluating violations of the Fair Housing Act (*Texas Dept. of Housing v. Inclusive Communities Project*). Much of our brief drew on an early draft of this book, and Justice Anthony Kennedy's majority opinion in June 2015 cited the brief in support.

On several occasions I had the opportunity to make joint presentations on the themes I was developing in *The Color of Law* with Sherrilyn Ifill, the thoughtful, charismatic president and director-counsel of the NAACP Legal Defense Fund (LDF). As our collaboration developed, the LDF named me a fellow of its recently established Thurgood Marshall Institute in April 2016, and this fellowship supported me in the final editing of the book. I am grateful for this honor and support to Ms. Ifill and to the other friends and colleagues I have made at the LDF during this fellowship.

*The Color of Law* makes the argument that government actions to create a system of *de jure* segregation were explicit, never hidden, that they were systematic and, not so long ago, well known by anyone who paid attention. As I describe in an introduction to the Bibliography, several prominent and authoritative books have recounted this history. My purpose has not been to plow new ground but to call attention to this body of work and to ask all of us to confront it together. Nonetheless, I have also dug up some relatively obscure documents, not because they were needed to prove the case—the authoritative earlier books I've mentioned did that quite well—but only to illustrate it. In several instances, I could not have dug these documents up without the assistance of the skilled and indefatigable research librarians at the University of California (Berkeley) School of Law. It would be easy to say that they are too numerous to list here, but I received such important assistance from them, on so many occasions, that I want to express my gratitude, first to Dean Rowan, director of Reference and Research Services, and then to his colleagues: Doug Avila, Joseph Cera, Georgia Giatras, Ellen Gilmore, Marlene Harmon, Marci Hoffman, Keri Klein, Michael Levy, Edna Lewis, Mike Lindsey, Ramona Martinez, Gary Peete, Christina Tarr, I-Wei Wang, and Jutta Wiemhoff. To each of you, thanks.

At the Wellfleet, Massachusetts, public library, Naomi Robbins could find a book hidden anywhere in the state, if only I said I'd like to see it. Other helpful librarians and curators included Veronica Rodriguez, curator, and Elizabeth Tucker, lead park ranger, at the Rosie the Riveter/WWII Home Front National Historical Park; and Dana Smith, director of the Daly City History Museum.

The most personally gratifying aspect of researching and writing this book has been the opportunity to work with young people, both undergraduates and graduate students, who served as my research assistants. Of these, Summer Volkmer and Cara Sandberg did the most to influence my thinking. They are now well advanced in successful legal careers, but I had the opportunity to benefit from their insights when they were second-year law students. Each provided crucial memoranda that led to the "*de jure*" argument made in this book. They each showed me where my argument went beyond existing precedent and conventional legal thinking. Neither is responsible for how I eventually framed the argument, but both, while still in law school, had great intellectual courage and self-confidence. Both indulged my desire to develop a theory, not for litigation that could be successful with a current Court, but that (I came to believe) should be successful with a Court that was more faithful to constitutional requirements. They didn't try to assure me that I could get away with it, but neither did they tell me I was crazy.

My association with Lul Tesfai, a public policy graduate student now also embarked on a career as a policy analyst, was especially rewarding. Lul explored archives in, among others, the Bancroft Library at the University of California and in the public libraries of Alameda, Santa Clara, and San Mateo Counties. She attended meetings of the retirement club of the UAW local union in Milpitas and conducted additional literature reviews. She guided me to Westlake in Daly City so I could see this 1950s segregated suburb for myself, and she took me to the local historical society where we pored over old newspaper clippings together. Without her hard work and nuanced understanding of the kinds of documents that would be helpful, this book could not have illustrated with such detail the *de jure* segregation that developed in the San Francisco area.

Sarah Brundage, another public policy graduate student, worked on this book as it was nearing completion. She double-checked endnotes and source citations, a task for which she was overqualified. But she also prepared an exhaustive background report for me on how government policy knowingly isolated African Americans in Baltimore from integrated employment and housing opportunities. I regret that her extensive work had to be reduced to only a paragraph in this book, in which I discuss the inadequacy of Baltimore's transportation system; the paragraph does not adequately display her commitment to justice in housing policy or her remarkable perseverance.

When Sarah graduated and moved on to a career as a housing policy analyst, an incoming graduate student, Kimberly Rubens, picked up the clean-up tasks, doing an equally competent job, including work on the index and searches for photographs.

At the University of California at Berkeley, I had the opportunity to supervise a group of undergraduate research "apprentices," to whom I assigned research into various topics related to the subject of this book. I was capably assisted by a law student (now also a practicing attorney), Sonja Diaz, from whom the undergraduates learned far more about research techniques than they could from me. The reports that they produced were quite helpful to me in organizing the research. I very much appreciate the work that each of them performed. My thanks go to Joyce Chang, Gabriel Clark, Tim Copeland, Daniel Ganz, Javier Garcia, Ana Hurtado-Aldana, Symone McDaniels, Matthew Mojica, Kayla Nalven, Jonathan Orbell, Aveling Pan, Genevieve Santiago, Pauline Tan, and Arielle Turner. These students have now graduated, and I've lost track of them. But if they see this book, I hope they can take some pride in their contributions.

In 2011 Deborah Stipek, then dean of the School of Education at Stanford, invited me to teach a course the following year on the topic of this book to upper-level undergraduates and master's students. I designed the course as a research seminar and invited my students to look into topics like those that my Berkeley apprentices were investigating. My teaching assistant, Ethan Hutt, now a professor at the University of Maryland, guided the Stanford students through their research, and largely due to his dedication and insight, many wrote excellent reports, reinforcing conclusions I had come to and sometimes summarizing secondary sources of which I hadn't been aware. I can't list all the Stanford students who developed reports, but a few stand out and deserve my special thanks: Rivka Burstein-Stern, Lindsay Fox, Laurel Frazier, Jaclyn Le, Terence Li, Sarah Medina, Ximena Portilla, Victoria Rodriguez, and Nicole Strayer. Terence grew up in Hunters Point, and his insights, combined with additional research, were especially valuable. Like my Berkeley apprentices, these students have now gone their various ways, but I hope they become aware of this expression of appreciation.

To understand how public housing was purposely segregated from its inception in the 1930s, I spent some time in the archives of the New York City Housing Authority at LaGuardia Community College. The archivist, Douglas DiCarlo, guided me in my searches; without him, my time there would have been much less efficient and fruitful. When I no longer had time to spend in New York City, a Cornell University undergraduate, Candice Raynor, followed up and obtained additional documents. Thanks to each of them.

Jeffrey Guyton, co-president of Community District Education Council 30 (Queens, New York), helped dig up additional evidence of New York City public housing segregation. And when I visited his office, Jim Sauber, chief of staff of the National Association of Letter Carriers, provided documentation of U.S. Post Office union segregation in New York City.

Christian Ringdal, then a graduate student, undertook on my behalf a search of UAW archives at the Walter Reuther Library of Wayne State University. Mike Smith, archivist of the library, provided additional documents that I was able to identify from his descriptions. Together with minutes and correspondence I located at the San Francisco office of the American Friends Service Committee (see my entries for this source in the Bibliography, and my thanks to Stephen McNeil, assistant regional director of the San Francisco AFSC office in the endnote to page 116, ¶ 2), the documents that Christian Ringdal and Mike Smith found enabled me to piece together the account of the search for integrated housing in Milpitas in the mid-1950s. My thanks to each of them.

I could have told the story of *de jure* segregation without the help of Frank Stevenson, but it would have been a drier, less accessible tale. I am so grateful for his several meetings with me, despite his declining health. Mr. Stevenson passed away on June 28, 2016, at the age of ninety-two. In writing his story, I could not bring myself to refer to him as "Stevenson," consistent with the style rules for a book like this. He was "Mr. Stevenson" to me, and I refer to him in that way in these pages. In a few other cases where I have great respect for scholars or heroes of the struggle for integration, I also employ honorific terms. If this seems jarring to you, don't blame my editors, blame me.

When I began to research the fruitless experiences of African American Ford workers who attempted to find nearby housing when their jobs moved to the suburbs, I intended to focus not only on Frank Stevenson but on a Ford employee with similar experiences when the company's assembly plant in Edgewater, New Jersey, moved to suburban Mahwah. Jessica Pachak, a Cornell University undergraduate, found important documents related to Mahwah in the papers of Paul Davidoff at the Cornell University library archives. Davidoff was the president of the Suburban Action Institute that reported extensively on segregation of the New York City suburbs. I visited the Mahwah Museum and benefited from the enormous generosity of its then-president, Thomas Dunn, who during my visit and subsequently provided me with the fruits of his own substantial research into the shortage of affordable housing in suburban Bergen County. Lizabeth Cohen's *A Consumer's Republic* provides a wealth of information about policies of segregation in suburban New Jersey. Her book's source citations lead a reader to even more. Professor Cohen generously allowed me unfettered freedom to rummage through her files and notes from the preparation of her important book. When it became necessary for me to narrow the scope of *The Color of Law*, I had to forgo inclusion of much of what I learned from the Davidson papers, the archives at the Mahwah Museum, and from Tom Dunn and Lizabeth Cohen. But I am grateful to them for giving me the opportunity to consider this important material.

Jenna Nichols, an undergraduate at Rutgers University, working under the supervision of Professor David Bensman, engaged in an independent study of segregation in Bergen County. When we terminated that investigation, she devoted her efforts to reading and summarizing mid-twentieth-century NAACP archives that had just been made available online. She found important nuggets, including the letter written by Thurgood Marshall to President Truman, protesting the continued practice of segregation by the FHA after *Shelley v. Kraemer* made such practice even more blatantly contemptuous of constitutional rights than it had been previously.

After reading a work of scholarship or journalism related to this book's themes, I never hesitated to follow up with the author, if still living, when I hoped to dig deeper. Often this led to extensive correspondence and telephone discussion. I am grateful to all who assisted me in this way. They include (in addition to those mentioned elsewhere in these acknowledgments): Richard Alba, David Beito, Karen Benjamin, Nicholas Bloom, Calvin Bradford, Mark Brilliant, Aaron Cavin, Bill Cunningham, Stephanie DeLuca, Allison Dorsey, Peter Dreier, David Freund, Margaret Garb, Bunny Gillespie, Colin Gordon, Donna Graves, James Gregory, Trevor Griffey, Dan Immergluck, Ann Moss Joiner, Andrew Kahrl, Arthur Lyons, Tracy K'Meyer, Doug Massey, Diane McWhorter, Molly Metzger, Liz Mueller, J. Thornton Mills III, Kimberly Norwood, Allan Parnell, Wendy Plotkin, Alex Polikoff, Garrett Power, John Relman, Jan Resseger, Herb Ruffin, Jacob Rugh, John Rury, David Rusk, Barbara Saad, Amanda Seligman, Cornelia Sexauer, Thomas Shapiro, Patrick Sharkey, Catherine Silva, Greg Squires, Todd Swanstrom, David Thompson, Lorri Ungaretti, Valerie Wilson, and John Wright. There are doubtlessly others I've overlooked, and I regret this.

If there was a question I didn't know how to answer, Phil Tegeler, executive director of the Poverty and Race Research Action Council, could always be counted upon to point me in the right direction. U.S. Appeals Court Judge David Tatel, in his earlier career, represented plaintiffs in an important school desegregation case in St. Louis. He asked his former law firm to dig out his working files from its archives, and these included valuable evidence. Thank you, Judge Tatel.

For nearly six years I accumulated research on the history of state-sponsored segregation, but without the clear intent of producing a summary book like this one. Instead, when I was not doing further research, my time was spent writing short articles and giving lectures on the topic. Then, in the spring of 2015, Ta-Nehisi Coates contacted Larry Mishel to persuade him to persuade me to put further research aside and produce a book that was accessible to the general public. Once I acceded to this suggestion, Ta-Nehisi put me in touch with his agent, Gloria Loomis, of the Watkins-Loomis Agency. Gloria instantly saw the value of a book like this and passed some chapters on to Bob Weil at the Liveright imprint of W. W. Norton, who accepted the project with enthusiasm. Without Ta-Nehisi, Gloria, and Bob, this book could not have happened, and to each of them I am grateful.

Finding and selecting photographs to illustrate this book, and then obtaining permission to use them, was a task far above my pay grade. I am fortunate to have been referred to photo researcher Hilary Mac Austin, without whom this book would have been unending pages of print. Thanks, Hilary.

While I was developing the research, and then the manuscript that eventually emerged as *The Color of Law*, I took many opportunities to publish articles based on my ongoing investigations. Some appeared as magazine or journal articles, some as chapters of edited books, some as online commentaries or research reports. I have made no effort to artificially change wording in this final book version so as to pretend that it is so "original" that its precise words have never before appeared in print. All these articles, book chapters, commentaries and reports are archived or referenced on the website of the Economic Policy Institute. There are too many of these previously published works to list here, but if readers go to the EPI website and find wording identical to that used in this book, I make no apologies: it has been my intent to express the analysis in the most effective way I know how, as often as I can.

One group of previously published articles (covering policy from the Truman through the Nixon administrations) was co-authored with University of Massachusetts professor Mark Santow, who has consented to my again drawing on his important archival research. Thank you, Mark.

I am indebted to those who read early drafts of the complete manuscript and made careful suggestions to improve it. Almost all of their suggestions have been adopted, and in cases where I failed to adopt some, I endorse without reservation the obligatory disclaimer that I alone am to blame for the book's deficiencies. I am deeply indebted to these readers—David Bernstein, Sherrilyn Ifill, Stephen Menendian, Larry Mishel, Leila Morsy, David Oppenheimer, Judith Petersen, and Florence Roisman.

In previous writing, I have benefited from relationships with several great editors. Each has proven to me, on multiple occasions, that you can indeed make a silk purse from a sow's ear. For this book, three—Bob Kuttner, Sara Mosle, and Kit Rachlis—read and made important editorial criticisms and suggestions regarding this manuscript. Bob suggested the book's title, both a metaphor and an allusion. Kit devoted several weeks to intense work with me on a detailed structural and line edit. Before submitting the book to my publisher, I flew to Los Angeles so Kit could sit side by side with me and improve the writing and argument, word by word and line by line. If you find any silk in *The Color of Law*, it is his more than mine. He is truly a coauthor of this book.

On top of all that, Bob Weil at Liveright devoted his summer vacation to making the presentation of this material even more logical, clear, and persuasive. Without his careful effort, all the work I and my colleagues and my students put into this project might have been wasted. Thanks, Bob.

My debt to Bob Weil includes gratitude for the staff he and his colleagues at Liveright have assembled—art director Steve Attardo, who designed the book jacket; copy editor Janet Biehl; managing editor Nancy Palmquist; project editor Anna Mageras; production manager Anna Oler; and above all, Marie Pantojan, who oversaw the entire editing and production process and made sure everything fit together.

It is usual in pages like these to acknowledge the support of family, but its conventionality does not diminish my gratitude. My wife, Judith Petersen, never once complained about the hours, days, months, and years when I ignored obligations to her because of my obsession with this work. My children, too, were unfailingly understanding. Thankfully, this tolerance was partly due to our shared belief that the message of this book is important. I hope they know that I know how lucky I am.

And there is another debt. Although I have noted that my interest in this topic stemmed from perplexity about the Supreme Court's *Parents Involved* ruling, that's not the full story. My interest originated much earlier. As a young boy growing up in New York in the 1940s and '50s, my world was forever transformed when Jackie Robinson started playing for the Brooklyn Dodgers. Doris Kearns Goodwin, in *Wait Till Next Year*, describes how the experience of being a devoted Dodgers fan at that time shaped her (and unbeknownst to her, my) worldview in a way that guided our adulthoods. So thank you, Mr. Robinson, and Mr. Rickey, too.

# NOTES

------------------------

S OURCE CITATIONS ARE reported by page and full paragraph
 number. Sources citing evidence described in a particular paragraph are assembled in a single note identified by that paragraph.
Citations applying to a description in a continuation paragraph are
identified in a note referring to the page on which that paragraph
began. To avoid needless repetition of citations, in cases where a
description of an incident continues for more than one paragraph,
source citations may be consolidated in a single note referring to the
first paragraph of that description. In some cases where I felt that
readers would benefit from broader contexts or from more easily
accessible secondary sources, more than one source may be cited in
support of a claim in the text.

### FRONTISPIECE

When in his second inaugural address, delivered in January, 1937, President
Franklin D. Roosevelt said, "I see one-third of a nation ill-housed, ill-clad, ill-
nourished," he was referring primarily to white working- and lower-middle-class
families. His administration's public housing programs were intended to address
their needs. The photo shows the president handing keys to the Churchfield family for their apartment in the whites-only Terrace Village project in Pittsburgh,
constructed by the United States Housing Authority and the city's housing
agency.

PREFACE

p. viii, ¶ 3    *Civil Rights Cases* 1883. The 1866 law stated that citizens of any race had equal rights to purchase or rent property and that an individual who denied such a right was guilty of a misdemeanor. The 1866 law was reenacted in 1875; it was the 1875 version that the Supreme Court specifically rejected.

p. xii, ¶ 1    *Milliken v. Bradley* 1974, 757; *Bradley v. Milliken* 1971, 587, 592.

p. xii, ¶ 3    *Parents Involved in Community Schools v. Seattle School District No. 1, et al.* 2007, 736. Internal quotation marks omitted.

p. xiii, ¶ 1    *Freeman v. Pitts* 1992, 495–96.


CHAPTER 1:
## If San Francisco, Then Everywhere?

p. 5, ¶ 2    Record 1947, 18 (table IV), 26, 32–33; Johnson 1993, 53. Of fifty unemployed black Richmond workers surveyed in 1947, only six had worked as farm laborers before migrating to Richmond; another four had worked as independent farmers. The black migrants to Richmond were "above the average in occupational background and education, and ... had abilities and potentials for which there was no outlet in the areas from which they migrated." A 1944 survey of black migrants throughout the Bay Area found educational attainment of nearly nine years.

p. 5, ¶ 3    Moore 2000, 84–85; Graves 2004, unpaginated.

p. 5, ¶ 4    Johnson 1993, 128–29; Moore 2000, 84–85; Alancraig 1953, 89.

p. 6, ¶ 3    Johnson 1993, 107, 222; Record 1947, 9; Barbour 1952, 10; Woodington 1954, 83–84. Of the 13,000 African Americans remaining in Richmond in 1952, 80 percent still resided in temporary war housing, compared to about 50 percent of the white population.

p. 7, ¶ 1    Moore 2000, 89; White 1956, 2.

p. 7, ¶ 2    Wenkert 1967, 24–26; Johnson 1993, 129.

p. 8, ¶ 1    Stevenson 2007, 1-00:36:13; Moore 2007, 77; NPS online. The plant has been converted by the National Park Service into the Rosie the Riveter World War II Homefront National Historical Park, mostly commemorating the women who worked there during the war (and who were fired or pressured to quit when army veterans returned looking for jobs).

p. 9, ¶ 1    PG&E 1954, 2; Grier and Grier 1962, 4; Munzel 2015.

p. 10, ¶ 3    As whites left Richmond, the African American population grew to nearly half the city total by 1980. Since then it has declined and is now less than a quarter. African Americans have been supplanted both by low-income Hispanic immigrants and by affluent whites who have been driving up rents in parts of the city, making those neighborhoods unaffordable for low-income families. Many African Americans have left, to disperse not into integrated communities but into new increasingly African American suburbs, like Antioch.

p. 10, ¶ 4   Stegner 1947; Benson 1996, 153; Friend and Lund 1974, 19–22; Treib and Imbert 1997, 150.

p. 12, ¶ 2   Leppert 1959, 657; Williams 1960a, 11; Alsberg 1960, 637; Johnson 1960, 722, 725; German, 1955; Williams 1960b, 483. Although I have no direct evidence (e.g., a board resolution) that the real estate board had an official "blackballing" policy applied to agents who sold to African Americans in white neighborhoods, several witnesses at the 1960 U.S. Civil Rights Commission hearings in San Francisco reiterated that agents refused to sell to African Americans from a belief that blackballing would follow. Franklin Williams, a California assistant attorney general, stated that "several [brokers or agents] have told us of their fear of being 'blackballed' or otherwise ostracized if they practiced democracy in their business." Williams also described that many agents believed that their real estate board deemed selling to African Americans in white neighborhoods to be an "unethical" practice, subjecting the violator to expulsion from the board. In a survey of area real estate agents, one was asked, "Can't you sell a home to a Negro?" The agent answered, "No; not in a white area, or we would be blackballed by other realtors."

p. 13, ¶ 1   Leler and Leler 1960.

p. 13, ¶ 3   Williams 1960a, 11; Alsberg 1960, 638–39.


CHAPTER 2:
## Public Housing, Black Ghettos

p. 17, ¶ 2   Sard and Fischer 2008, 16 (fig. 6), Technical Appendix tables 2b, 3b2; Atlas and Dreier 1994. As of 2008, nearly one-third of all public housing units nationwide were in low-poverty neighborhoods (where fewer than 20 percent of households were poor). Only one-fourth of all units were in high-poverty neighborhoods (where more than 40 percent of households were poor). By 2008, of metropolitan area public housing units outside New York City, only 9 percent were in projects with more than 500 units, and one-third were in projects with 100 units or fewer. However, of the 9 percent of units in large projects, two-thirds were in high-poverty neighborhoods. Of the one-third in projects with 100 units or fewer, only 10 percent were in high-poverty neighborhoods.

In 1935, Secretary of the Interior Harold Ickes described the nation's first civilian public housing as "intended to be self-liquidating. With the exception of [a few projects], the money used in financing this low-cost housing will be returned to the Treasury through the collection of rents." As time went on, the proportion of subsidized to unsubsidized projects grew, but construction of middle-class projects continued for another two decades.

p. 18, ¶ 1    Bloom 2008, 8, 176–77, 209; NYCHA 1970; Vale 2002, 24–25, 74–80, 102.

p. 18, ¶ 2    Ben-Joseph online; Dunn-Haley 1995, 38ff; Jackson 1985, 192; Donohue 2014–15. The U.S. Housing Corporation (USHC), the federal agency with responsibility for war worker housing in the First World War, built projects for whites only in Bremerton, Washington; Bridgeport, Connecticut; Camden, New Jersey; Chester, Pennsylvania; Kohler, Wisconsin; Mare Island, California; and Wilmington, Delaware, to name a few. It is possible that some of the projects were all white because there were few African Americans working in the munitions plants that the housing served. Portsmouth, New Hampshire, though, is one example of government-sponsored segregation: African Americans were working in war-related jobs but were denied access to the Atlantic Heights housing complex that the USHC developed for white workers. In Niagara Falls, New York, the USHC built separate projects for Italian Americans and Polish Americans.

p. 19, ¶ 2    Fishel 1964–65, 114; Houston and Davis 1934, 290–91.

p. 19, ¶ 3    Fishel 1964–65; Kifer 1961, 5–31.

p. 20, ¶ 1    Kifer 1961, 27, 35–41.

p. 20, ¶ 2    Fishel 1964–65, 116; Guzda 1980, 32.

p. 20, ¶ 3    Radford 1996, 100–1 (table 4.2); Alancraig 1953, 20. Not included in these totals are two projects in Puerto Rico and one in the Virgin Islands, designated for "natives."

p. 21, ¶ 1    Hirsch 2000a, 209; Hirsch 2005, 58–59; Connerly and Wilson 1997, 203; Miller 1964, 65; Mohl 2001, 321. The Miami civic leader was a retired judge, John C. Gramling, who negotiated with the Public Housing Administration on behalf of the Dade County Housing Authority.

p. 21, ¶ 2    Moore 2000, 14, 19–21.

p. 21, ¶ 4    Holliman 2008.

p. 22, ¶ 1    Heathcott 2011, 89–90, 94. The neighborhood was about 65 percent white in 1930; the African American population was growing and was greater than 35 percent when the neighborhood was demolished.

p. 23, ¶ 1    Hughes 1940, 30–31; ECH 2011; PWA 1939, 283 (table 15); Cleveland Historical online; Rotman online; Weaver 1948, 75–76.

p. 23, ¶ 2    Radford 1996, 100–1 (table 4.2); Weaver 1948, 74; *NYT* 1936. Nationwide, there was nothing hidden about the government's explicit segregation policy. *The New York Times* described the Harlem River Houses as having been established to accommodate "574 Negro families."

p. 23, ¶ 3      USHA 1939, 7–8.

p. 24, ¶ 1      McGhee 2015, 15–16, 24, 26; Busch 2013, 981–83; Busch 2015. The housing authority installed outdoor clotheslines on the Rosewood Courts site, assuming that women who resided in the project would work as domestics and laundresses for Austin's white population. A third segregated project, for Mexican Americans, was constructed in a neighborhood adjoining the Eastside black ghetto. The city plan did not call for segregating the Mexican American population into a single zone, although the public housing project contributed to their greater isolation.

p. 24, ¶ 2      Bowly 1978, 24; Hirsch 1983. 1998, 14; Choldin 2005. The racial identification of these projects was reinforced by their naming. Julia C. Lathrop and Jane Addams were white, early-twentieth-century social workers and reformers whose careers were devoted to serving low-income white immigrant populations. Ida B. Wells, an African American, was one of the founders of the NAACP. Such use of naming to identify projects or neighborhoods by race has continued into more recent times, as many cities have renamed boulevards going through African American neighborhoods after Martin Luther King, Jr. Many fewer boulevards going through white communities are named after him.

p. 25, ¶ 3      Vale 2002, 37, 55, 80; USCCR 1967, 65.

p. 26, ¶ 1      Cunningham 16–19; Stainton and Regan 2001, 12.

p. 26, ¶ 2      Weaver 1948, 171–74. In 1945, the federal government finally accepted a small number of African American families in Willow Run housing, after setting aside a segregated section for them. In 1946, African Americans were finally permitted to live throughout the project. By this time, however, it was too late for a substantial integration program to take hold. With the end of the war, jobs at the bomber plant were disappearing, and many white families were returning home. Unfilled vacancies developed in the white sections of the project, so permitting African Americans to occupy these units did not deny any white workers and their families the preferential treatment to which they had been accustomed. Eventually, as more white families departed, many to return to the rural communities and smaller towns from which they had migrated, the Willow Run project became increasingly black. African American workers had come to Willow Run not only for jobs but also to escape racial violence and exploitation in the South. For them, returning home when bomber plant jobs disappeared was not an attractive option.

p. 26, ¶ 3      This is another example of how the government used naming to identify projects by race. Because the project was intended for African Americans, it was named after Sojourner Truth, an African American abolitionist before and during the Civil War.

p. 26, ¶ 4     Franklin Roosevelt's administration was notorious for creating multiple agencies with overlapping jurisdictions. In a 1939 reorganization, the USHA became part of the Federal Works Agency (FWA). The FWA then was given direct responsibility for Lanham Act projects, even where there was no local housing authority participating.

Accounts differ regarding the number killed or wounded in the Sojourner Truth riot. I rely here on Robert Weaver's (1948, 92–94) because his is closer to contemporaneous. If, as other accounts have it (e.g., Funigiello 1978, 99, citing Shogan and Craig's 1964, *The Detroit Race Riot*), large numbers were killed, not wounded, I assume that Weaver would have known about it. Weaver was the most important African American official of the federal government during World War II, responsible for monitoring the interests of African Americans in employment, training and housing. Sugrue (1996, 2005, 74), closely confirming Weaver, reports that "at least 40 people were injured, 220 arrested, and 109 were held for trial—all but three black." Other accounts of the Sojourner Truth incident include Goodwin 1994, 326–27; White 1942; Foreman 1974.

p. 27, ¶ 2     Sugrue 1996, 2005, 80, 85; Sugrue 1995, 569, 571–72.

p. 27, ¶ 3     Weaver 1948, 199–200. A more recent account (Broussard 1993, 175–76) seems to contradict Weaver's and states that the Hunters Point project was thoroughly integrated. I accept Weaver's claim of segregation because it is nearly contemporaneous and because Weaver was in a position to know (and was probably involved in) the controversy over segregation in Hunters Point (see note to page 26, ¶ 4, above). For the role of Robert Weaver, see Hill 2005. Possibly Broussard categorized Hunters Point as integrated because it included both black and white units, although the project was internally segregated. The description of Hunters Point as integrated may stem from the period just after the war when, as in Willow Run in Michigan (see note to page 26, ¶ 2, above), vacancies in the white units developed as the occupants found private housing and African Americans were permitted to occupy the vacant units.

p. 28, ¶ 2     Broussard 1993, 177, 179, 222; Johnson, Long, and Jones 1944, 22; *Banks v. Housing Authority of City and County of San Francisco* 1953; Weaver 1948, 168–69; Alancraig 1953, 74–75.

p. 29, ¶ 2     France 1962, 39–40, 58 (n. 23); Wirt 1974, 251; Link 1971, 53; Alancraig 1953, 93–96; Broussard 1993, 223–225; *Banks v. Hous-*

*ing Authority of City and County of San Francisco* 1953; Quinn 1960, 550. There is no other plausible explanation than hypocrisy for policies that announced nondiscrimination and then fulfilled the promise by admitting only a few other-race families to segregated projects. In 1939, for example, the New York City Housing Authority adopted a nondiscrimination policy, but like policies in Boston and San Francisco, it, too, was nominal, assigning a token few other-race families to otherwise single-race projects to support a claim that they were integrated. In the borough of Queens, the Housing Authority built the Woodside Houses in 1949, a project for white middle-class families in a mostly white neighborhood, but included a handful of African American families. A few miles away, the South Jamaica Houses, built in a mostly African American neighborhood, included a handful of whites. The Housing Authority explained that its policy was to respect "existing community patterns" and that it had concluded that the South Jamaica project should house minorities because it was "located in a neighborhood having a preponderance of colored people" (Bloom 2008, 87). The most prominent example of a tormented public official in this regard was Elizabeth Wood, who led the Chicago Housing Authority from 1937 to 1954, all the while urging board members to cease segregating while dutifully implementing its discriminatory policies. She was eventually fired by the Chicago Housing Authority for disclosing these conflicts to the press (see also discussion and note on page 146).

p. 31, ¶ 1    Davies 1966, 108; Julian and Daniel 1989, 668–69; Hirsch 2000b, 400–1; von Hoffman 2000, 309. At the time of the debate, Douglas and Humphrey were freshmen senators, having been elected to their first terms only six months earlier. They became national leaders of the liberal wing of the Democratic Party. It must have been particularly galling to Senator Humphrey to feel that he had to compromise with segregation to get the housing bill passed. The previous year, as mayor of Minneapolis, he had defied President Truman and his party leadership at the Democratic National Convention by leading liberals in a demand that the party platform denounce racial segregation. Losing the fight in committee, he took it to the floor of the convention. He told delegates, "I do not believe that there can be any compromise on the guarantees of the civil rights . . . in the minority report." In defiance of southern states' insistence on their right to impose racial segregation, he added: "The time has arrived in America for the Democratic Party to get out of the shadow of states' rights and to walk forthrightly into the bright sunshine of human rights." The delegates adopted his minority report, leading to a walkout of southern Democrats and their formation of a separate party (the Dixiecrats) that ran South Carolina governor Strom Thurmond as a 1948 third-party presidential candidate, on a pro-segregation platform. Defying all predictions, President Truman won reelection against Republican Thomas Dewey, Dixiecrat Strom Thurmond, and Henry Wallace, who ran a left-wing campaign as a Progressive Party candidate. Humphrey was elected to two more Senate terms, then went on to win election as Lyndon Johnson's vice-presidential running mate in 1964. But when Humphrey himself ran as the Democratic presidential nominee four years later, he lost liberal support because of what many of his friends and allies believed was his compromise of principle in refusing to speak out against President Johnson's pursuit of victory in the Vietnam War. It contributed to his defeat by Richard Nixon for the presidency.

The 1949 Housing Act was intended as a slum clearance as well as a public housing measure. It required the demolition of one slum unit for every public housing unit built. Although this provision was not always followed, the legislation would do little to add to the supply of housing for African Americans. This is another reason for skepticism about the wisdom of Douglas's and Humphrey's compromise with segregation.

| | |
|---|---|
| p. 32, ¶ 2 | Hirsch 2000b, 401, 406, 417–18. |
| p. 32, ¶ 3 | von Hoffman 2000, 320. |
| p. 32, ¶ 4 | *James v. Valtierra* 1971; Murasky 1971, 115–16; UPI 1971; Herbers 1971. States that required some form of referendum prior to construction of public housing included Alabama, California, Colorado, Iowa, Minnesota, Mississippi, Montana, Oklahoma, Texas, Vermont, Virginia, and Wisconsin. |
| p. 33, ¶ 1 | USCCR 1961, 111. |
| p. 33, ¶ 2 | Hirsch 2000a, 218; Abrams 1955, 30–32. |
| p. 33, ¶ 3 | Bartelt 1993, 135–36; Hogan 1996, 48. |
| p. 34, ¶ 1 | *Kennedy v. Housing Authority of Savannah* 1960. |
| p. 34, ¶ 2 | Flournoy and Rodrigue 1985. |
| p. 34, ¶ 4 | *Hills v. Gautreaux* 1976; Polikoff 2006, 98, 148, 153; Orfield 1985. |
| p. 35, ¶ 2 | In 1987, more than a decade after the Supreme Court case, President Ronald Reagan nominated Bork to fill a Supreme Court vacancy. A fierce controversy ensued in the Senate, and Bork failed to win confirmation. |
| p. 36, ¶ 1 | PRRAC 2005; Daniel & Beshara online; *Banks v. Housing Authority of City and County of San Francisco* 1953; Berger 1998; Mohl 2001, 345. A Home Box Office miniseries, *Show Me a Hero*—based on the 1993 book by Lisa Belkin, *Show Me a Hero: A Tale of Murder, Suicide, Race and Redemption*—describes the |

resistance of Yonkers to the federal appeals court decision and the city's eventual half-hearted compliance.

p. 36, ¶ 2    Abrams 1951, 327; Hirsch 2005, 59–60; Nixon 1973. But Nixon's was an exaggerated stereotype. Segregated public housing perpetuates racial isolation, with all the attendant problems that characterize low-income minority neighborhoods where disadvantage accumulates. But from the perspective of families in desperate need of housing, segregated housing is preferable to none. The long waiting lists for public housing in most cities are testament to the continued desirability and popularity of public housing for families whose incomes are too low to purchase or rent housing in the private market. The choice should not be, as it was for Congress in 1949, between segregated high-rise public housing and no housing. The choice should be between segregated public housing and integrated (by race and income) public housing in integrated neighborhoods.

p. 37, ¶ 2    Johnson 1993, 105.

## CHAPTER 3:
## Racial Zoning

p. 39, ¶ 1    Logan et al. 2015, 26 (fig. 4); Logan and Stults 2011. Residential racial segregation is difficult to define and thus to measure precisely. The most common demographic description is the "index of dissimilarity" that calculates the share of African Americans living in a neighborhood with other groups, compared to their share of their metropolitan area. This index, however, shows an increase in "integration" when poor Hispanic immigrants move into a predominantly black neighborhood. For understanding the *de jure* segregation of African Americans, the dissimilarity index is not a useful tool. What we should be most concerned with is the extent to which African Americans and the white majority live among one another. By this standard, integration decreased in both rural and urban areas in every region of the country from 1880 to 1950, when measured by the chances of having an opposite-race neighbor or by the share of opposite-race residents who lived in a resident's neighborhood, i.e., the exposure of whites and blacks to one another. An analysis of population in ten of the largest American cities from 1880 to 1940 finds that in 1880, the neighborhood (block) on which the typical African American lived was only 15 percent black; by 1910 it was 30 percent, and by 1930, even after the Great Migration, it was still only about 60 percent black. By

1940 the local neighborhood where the typical African American lived was 75 percent black. Another analysis, using a different definition of neighborhood, found that in 1950 the average African American nationwide lived in a neighborhood that was 35 percent white, a figure that remains approximately the same today.

p. 41, ¶ 2    Hennessey 1985, 103–10; Smith 1994, 144–50; Simkins 1944, 63, 270; Kantrowitz 2000, 69, 121, 143; Dew 2000; Kingkade 2015. These historical accounts differ on the details of how many were killed, the order of the attacks by the Red Shirts, resistance by African Americans (who were organized into a militia), actions of the governor, and the precise location of the events. Older versions are more sympathetic to Tillman. It can be assumed only that the text here is approximately correct.

p. 41, ¶ 4    Loewen 2005, 9; Lang 1979, 50, 57.

p. 42, ¶ 1    Lang, 1979; Ogden 2007.

p. 42, ¶ 2    Loewen 2005; Palm Beach online. Explicit town ordinances were not unknown. The Historical Society of Palm Beach County reports: "A 1939 Guide to Florida said of Belle Glade, 'A municipal ordinance requires that all Negroes, except those employed within the town, be off the streets by 10:30 p.m. On Saturdays they are permitted to remain in the business district until midnight.' Other towns had similar restrictions."

p. 42, ¶ 3    This book can't delve into the history of this period in detail, but it is no secret and has been told by several popular writers. Sixty years ago, C. Vann Woodward described the growth of segregation in *The Strange Career of Jim Crow*. More recently, in *Redemption*, Nicholas Lemann recounted the violent suppression of African Americans as Reconstruction ended. James Loewen's *Sundown Towns* tells how, throughout the nation, African Americans were violently expelled and then barred from communities where they had previously lived. Loewen has assembled substantial information on racial violence in towns throughout the nation and has posted it online. The Montana page on this site as of January 2017 is at sundown .tougaloo.edu/sundowntownsshow.php?state=MT. For information on other states, click on the map at sundown.tougaloo.edu/ content.php?file=sundowntowns-whitemap.html.

p. 43, ¶ 2    Wolgemuth 1959, 159–67; King 1995, 9–17; Weiss 1969, 63–65; *NYT* 1914; Kifer 1961, viii; *Chicago Defender* 1932.

p. 44, ¶ 2    *NYT* 1910.

p. 44, ¶ 3    Pietila 2010, 24; Power 1983, 303–4.

p. 45, ¶ 1    *Crisis* 1917; Silver 1997, 27, 32; Power 1983, 310; Rabin 1989, 106; Wehle 1915.

p. 45, ¶ 2    *Buchanan v. Warley* 1917. The Court's opinion, by Justice William R. Day, also acknowledged that racial zoning denied African Americans equal protection, but this was not the basis of the Court's decision.

p. 46, ¶ 1    Whitten 1922; Randle 1989, 43; Rabin 1989, 107–8; Freund 2007, 66; Atlanta 1922, 10.

p. 46, ¶ 2    *Bowen v. City of Atlanta* 1924.

p. 46, ¶ 3    Thornbrough 1961, 598–99; *Harmon v. Tyler* 1927.

p. 47, ¶ 1    *Richmond v. Deans* 1930; Williams 2015.

p. 47, ¶ 2    *Birmingham v. Monk* 1950; Williams 1950; Greenberg 1959, 278.

p. 47, ¶ 3    Greenberg 1959, 278; Palm Beach online; *Dowdell v. Apopka* 1983; Rabin 1987.

p. 48, ¶ 4    Flint 1977, 50, 103, 114, 119, 207, 322, 345–57, 394; Gordon 2008, 122–28.

p. 51, ¶ 1    Freund 2007, 76–78; Chused 2001, 598–99; Advisory Committee on Zoning 1926.

p. 51, ¶ 2    American City Planning Institute 1918, 44–45; Freund 2007, 73–74. Olmsted Jr. was the son of Frederick Law Olmsted, the renowned nineteenth-century park designer. In using the term "racial divisions," Olmsted Jr., like many national planning leaders in those years, was referring to distinctions between whites and European immigrants as well as between whites and African Americans. The Protestant, mostly Anglo-Saxon elite considered southern and central Europeans (including Catholics like Italians and Slavs, and Jews) to be "swarthy" and "dark-skinned" and of a different race than northern Europeans. Over time, however, the elite and its planners came to accept European immigrants as "white" (although subject to some continued prejudice), but firm opposition to "mingling" with African Americans persisted.

p. 51, ¶ 3    Hancock 1988, 200–1. The quotation comes from a memorandum that Bettman, the lead author, issued in 1933 for the American City Planning Institute, of which he was then a member.

p. 52, ¶ 1    McEntire 1960, 245.

p. 52, ¶ 2    Freund 1929, 93.

p. 52, ¶ 3    *Euclid v. Ambler* 1926, 394–95; Freund 2007, 83.

p. 53, ¶ 2    *Dailey v. Lawton* 1970.

p. 53, ¶ 3    *Arlington Heights v. Metropolitan Housing Corp.* 1977; Mandelker 1977, 1221 (n. 15).

p. 54, ¶ 2    Collin and Collin 1997, 226–27.

p. 55, ¶ 3    Sides 2003, 113; *Los Angeles Sentinel* 1947c; *Los Angeles Sentinel* 1947a; *Los Angeles Sentinel* 1947b.

p. 56, ¶ 1    Collin and Collin 1997, 227–28.

p. 56, ¶ 2    Collin and Collin 1997, 230; Clinton 1994.

CHAPTER 4:
## *"Own Your Own Home"*

p. 60, ¶ 1      Vale 2007, 20; Cannato 2010; Hayward 2013, 121–22.

p. 60, ¶ 2      Hutchison 1997, 194; Better Homes in America, 1926; *NYT* 1922; Pelo 1922. The American Construction Council was founded in 1922 at the behest of Secretary of Commerce Herbert Hoover, with Roosevelt as its first president. This was the first public activity that Roosevelt, formerly the Democratic candidate for vice president in 1920, undertook after contracting polio. Roosevelt's purpose was the "building up of public confidence in the construction industry," something that was supposedly lacking because of poor employment conditions owing to the seasonal nature of construction work, where wages and employment were good in the summer months and poor in the winter. It is difficult to understand how Roosevelt planned to overcome this obstacle. He suggested that somehow he would manage to move labor from states like New York to states like Georgia in the winter and the reverse in the summer. Such shifting of labor around would, he said, result in lowered construction costs. Roosevelt proposed to accomplish this by getting representatives of all the industries and labor unions that were involved in construction around a table, with Secretary Hoover at the head, to work out a solution. I won't speculate about the feasibility of Roosevelt's idea. Suffice it to say that the American Construction Council didn't last long. But what I find most interesting about this incident is the presence of Roosevelt, as the construction industry representative, on Hoover's Better Homes advisory council. It suggests that, as early as 1922, a working relationship existed between future president Hoover and future president Roosevelt around their joint commitment to getting working- and middle-class white Americans into single-family units.

p. 60, ¶ 3      Freund 2007, 75; Hutchison 1997, 193; Wright 1981, 197–98; Lands 2009, 126. I say that Better Homes representatives "probably" told this to audiences because I have not been able to identify the source of Wright's reference to avoidance of "racial strife" as a benefit of homeownership. I infer that the source was a pamphlet published by the Better Homes organization or by the Commerce Department giving guidance to local Better Homes committees. Understandably, Professor Wright no longer has copies of documents she used in her research thirty-five years ago.

p. 61, ¶ 1      Hoover 1932, xi; Hoover 1931.

p. 61, ¶ 2      Ford 1931, 615, 617; Gries and Taylor 1931, 92–95. These public and private leaders probably also considered European immigrants as persons to be avoided. See note to p. 51, ¶ 2, above.

p. 61, ¶ 3     Ecker 1932, 46; Kushner 2009, 31.

p. 62, ¶ 2     Johnson 1932, 114–15. The frontispiece of the report was an admiring photo of the "Paul Laurence Dunbar Apartments for Negroes at Harlem, New York City," an illustration of good housing for African Americans. The Dunbar Apartments had been built by John D. Rockefeller a few years before the Hoover conference.

p. 63, ¶ 2     Jackson 1985, 196–97.

p. 63, ¶ 4     Freund 2007, 115.

p. 64, ¶ 2     Jackson 1985, 200.

p. 65, ¶ 1     FHA 1936, Part II, Section 233; FHA 1935, Sections 309–12.

p. 65, ¶ 2     Jackson 1985, 207; Abrams 1955, 30; FHA 1935, Section 229; FHA 1938, Part II, Section 909 (e), Section 935. Highway planners shared this objective. In Chicago, for example, they modified the original design of the Dan Ryan Expressway, shifting it by several blocks for the purpose of creating a "firewall" between the slowly expanding African American area and white neighborhoods.

p. 65, ¶ 3     FHA 1938, Part II, Section 951.

p. 66, ¶ 1     FHA 1947, Part II, Section 12, 1215 (4) (d), Part III Section 13, 1315, 1320 (1), 1320 (2); Hirsch 2000b, 413; FHA 1952, Section 131. In its 1947 *Underwriting Manual*, the FHA made deferral to the racial prejudices of a neighborhood's residents a federal government principle. Having removed from this edition an absolute declaration that racial mixing made lending in a neighborhood too risky, the manual stated that additional risk was "not necessarily involved" in neighborhood racial change. When would such additional risk be involved? Only if the FHA "determined [that] the mixture will render the neighborhood less desirable to present and prospective residents."

p. 66, ¶ 2     Freund 2007, 130–31.

p. 66, ¶ 3     Williams 1959; Hirsch 2005, 50.

p. 69, ¶ 1     Goodwin 1994, 169, 329–30.

p. 69, ¶ 2     There were a few areas in Nassau County open to African Americans, but severe overcrowding led to unsanitary and dilapidated conditions. One such neighborhood was Bennington Park, in the Village of Freeport, where Vince Mereday's uncle Charles settled. In 1946 the New York State Housing Commission declared Bennington Park the worst slum in the state and offered Freeport a loan to build new public housing. The loan would have cost the village nothing, because African Americans in Bennington Park were employed, and were living there not because they couldn't afford decent housing but because they were excluded from it. Their rents in public housing would have been sufficient to enable

Freeport to repay the loan without dipping into the public treasury. The village submitted the proposed loan to a referendum and
permitted only Freeport property owners to vote. The property
owners rejected the proposal by nearly a 2–1 margin. An interview with Charles Mereday who, like his brother Robert, worked
at Grumman during the war, then formed his own trucking company at war's end, is reported in Baxandall and Ewen 2000, 171–
73.

p. 70, ¶ 1    Jackson, 231–45 (Chapter 13); Yardley 2009; Bobker and Becker
1957; Lambert 1997; Cotter 1951; *NYT* 1950b; *NYT* 1951; Williamson 2005, 48; Baxandall and Ewen 2000, 175–76. William Levitt, however, did not feel differently. He was a more-than-willing
participant in an FHA policy to prohibit racial integration in
suburbs for which it provided financial support. In 1950, Levitt
canceled the rental leases of two white families because their children had African American playmates who visited. (The NAACP
sought to enjoin the evictions, but New York State courts declined
to intervene.) Indeed, Levitt told an interviewer that a desire to
avoid middle-class African American neighbors was what had
first motivated him to move and then to build in the suburbs: "a
couple of centuries [after black people were first brought as slaves
to this continent], as they moved into the north, they moved onto
the same street we lived on in Brooklyn. Next to us a black assistant DA moved in. Fearing a diminution of values if too many
came in, we picked up and moved out. We then got into the suburbs, into building." Nonetheless, Levitt claimed that he was not
prejudiced: "As a Jew, I have no room in my mind or heart for
racial prejudice. But . . . I have come to know that if we sell one
house to a Negro family, then ninety to ninety-five percent of our
white customers will not buy into the community."

A film made about another Levitt development, *Crisis in Levittown, PA*, shows both opposition to and support for integration
by residents, with the opposition in the majority. Nonetheless,
the interviews suggest that Levitt's estimate of 90 to 95 percent
being so against integration that they would refuse to purchase
his homes is exaggerated, especially in view of the serious housing
shortage faced by lower-middle-class white and black families. In
fact, there was active and vocal resistance in the Levittowns to the
builder's and FHA's segregation policy. In the first Long Island
development, for example, a residents' Committee to End Discrimination in Levittown distributed leaflets against "Jim Crow-
ism." When Levitt continued to include racial deed restrictions
after the Supreme Court declared them unenforceable, the committee, along with outside civil rights groups, campaigned against

his policy and, two years after the ruling, finally forced him to cease requiring the clauses.

If the FHA had made nondiscrimination a condition of all developments it financed for these families, whites who refused to purchase in an integrated Levittown for racial reasons would have had few, if any, other options.

p. 70, ¶ 2    Hirsch 2000a, 208.

p. 70, ¶ 4    Larrabee 1948, 86.

p. 72, ¶ 1    Clark 1938, 111; Weiss 1987, 147–51; Jackson 1985, 208–9, 238; *Levitt v. Division Against Discrimination* 1960, 523.

p. 72, ¶ 3    VerPlanck 2008; Hope 2011, 32, 58; Jackson 1985, 238; *Architectural Forum* 1947; Baxandall and Ewen 2000, 122; Houlihan 2010, 10–13. Another was Park Forest in suburban Chicago, built by Philip Klutznick. The FHA subsidized its construction in 1946, and although Klutznick described his project as integrated, it was 1959 before the first African American family bought a home there.

p. 73, ¶ 1    Sexauer 2003, 180, 199, 210–11, 215, 226–28, 232.

p. 74, ¶ 1    Jackson 1985, 209; Sugrue 1993, 113; USCCR 1961, 67–68.

p. 74, ¶ 2    Hirsch 2005, 55–56.

p. 75, ¶ 2    USCCR 1973, 3, 5.

## CHAPTER 5:
### *Private Agreements, Government Enforcement*

p. 76    In the photograph, developer Henry Doelger smiles at FHA district director McGinness as his wife positions the spike. Although the ceremony took place almost a year after the Supreme Court's decision prohibiting enforcement of restrictive covenants, the FHA continued to finance the subdivision despite its ban on sales to African Americans.

p. 78, ¶ 1    Jackson 1985, 76.

p. 79, ¶ 3    Jackson 1985, 177–78; Nichols 1923, 174; Colby 2012, 91–93: Hayward 2013, 114–17.

p. 79, ¶ 4    Dean 1947, 430 (table II).

p. 80, ¶ 1    Weaver 1948, 250, 247; Sugrue 1995, 557.

p. 80, ¶ 2    *Lyons v. Wallen* 1942.

p. 80, ¶ 3    Silva 2009.

p. 80, ¶ 4    Pates 1948; *Claremont Improvement Club v. Buckingham* 1948.

p. 81, ¶ 1    Miller 1965b, 2–3.

p. 81, ¶ 2    Thompson 2014.

p. 81, ¶ 3    Kushner 1979, 562–66; McGovney 1945, 6–11.

p. 82, ¶ 1    Power 2004, 791–92, 801–2; Power 1983, 315; *California Eagle* 1943a.

p. 82, ¶ 2     *Corrigan v. Buckley* 1926.

p. 82, ¶ 3     Bartholomew 1932, 50, 57–58; Weiss 1989; Monchow 1928, 50, 72–73. The 1928 review written by Helen Monchow was published by the Institute for Research in Land Economics and Public Utilities. At the time, the institute was the most influential national urban planning organization. The review quoted extensively from the recent (1926) Supreme Court opinion (*Corrigan v. Buckley*) upholding the validity of deeds that prevented resales to African Americans: "This contention (that the covenant is void in that it is contrary to and forbidden by the 5th, 13th, and 14th Amendments) is entirely lacking in substance or color of merit. The fifth Amendment is a limitation only upon the powers of the general government and is not directed against the action of individuals. The thirteenth Amendment involving slavery and involuntary servitude, that is, a condition of enforced compulsory service of one to another, does not in other matters protect the individual rights of persons of the negro race. And the prohibitions of the fourteenth Amendment have reference to state action exclusively and not to any action of private individuals. It is state action of a particular character that is prohibited. Individual invasion of individual rights is not the subject matter of the amendment."

p. 83, ¶ 2     FHA 1935, Part II, Sections 309–12.

p. 83, ¶ 3     FHA 1936, Part II, Sections 284 (2)–(3).

p. 84, ¶ 2     Johnson 1993, 92. For Peninsula Housing Association sources, see notes to p. 10, ¶ 4; for St. Ann sources, see notes to p. 73, ¶ 1; for Levittown sources, see notes to pp. 70, ¶ 1, and 72, ¶ 1. Dean 1947, 430–31. Hirsch 2000a, 207–9, concludes that the FHA made restrictive covenants a "virtual precondition for federally insured mortgages." For particular loan guarantees, the FHA required restrictive covenants, but as a general policy the FHA strongly recommended such covenants. A builder could commit not to sell to African Americans even if no racial covenant was attached to the deed. The FHA did insure some loans without covenants. A very small number of loans in African American neighborhoods were FHA insured, as were a small number in integrated neighborhoods.

p. 85, ¶ 1     Dean 1947, 430.

p. 85, ¶ 2     The distinction between the legality of a private contract and the unconstitutionality of its enforcement was not considered in the 1926 decision. The 1926 case arose in the District of Columbia, so in *Corrigan* the Court only ruled on whether covenants were lawful under the Fifth, not the Fourteenth Amendment.

p. 85, ¶ 3     In the Washington, D.C., case *Hurd v. Hodge*, the Supreme Court based its decision not on the Constitution but on the Civil Rights

Act of 1866. Its position was still that the Civil Rights Act of 1866 prohibited racial discrimination only by government, not by private individuals, but once federal courts got involved, enforcement of racial covenants was government action. Twenty years later, in *Jones v. Mayer*, the Court recognized that the Civil Rights Act of 1866 also applied to private discrimination, because Congress passed the act to implement the Thirteenth Amendment that, the Court recognized, prohibited not only slavery but the badges and incidents of slavery. Thus, while not technically accurate, it is reasonable to say that federal court enforcement of restrictive covenants, or federal agency promotion of such covenants, violated not only the Civil Rights Act of 1866 but the Thirteenth Amendment to the Constitution as well.

| | |
|---|---|
| p. 86, ¶ 2 | Hirsch 2000a, 211–14; Marshall 1949, 8. |
| p. 86, ¶ 3 | Streator 1949. |
| p. 86, ¶ 4 | Will 1949, 1; Marshall 1949, 7–8; 12. |
| p. 87, ¶ 1 | Will 1949, 2–3. |
| p. 87, ¶ 2 | Hirsch 2000a, 212–13. |
| p. 88, ¶ 1 | Hinton 1949. |
| p. 88, ¶ 2 | Davies 1966, 125; Polikoff 2006, 113; Hirsch 2000a, 213. |
| p. 88, ¶ 3 | Wood, 1949; Miller 1965b, 6. |
| p. 89, ¶ 1 | *Weiss v. Leaon* 1949; *Correll v. Earley* 1951. |
| p. 90, ¶ 1 | Making an adjustment with the Consumer Price Index for all urban consumers helps us to understand the homes' affordability for working- and lower-middle-class families. With such an adjustment, Westlake house prices in current (2016) dollars were about $99,000 (in 1949) and $114,000 (in 1955). Damages of $2,000 paid to each of eight neighbors would total about $140,000 in current dollars. Median family income is now about $60,000, about twice what it was (in current dollars) in 1950. Property selling for about two to three times median income is affordable for working- and lower-middle-class families, especially if FHA or VA mortgages are available. Homes for sale in the Westlake subdivision of Daly City with two bedrooms and one bath are now (early 2016) being sold for $450,000 to $800,000. The difference between the current dollar price paid in the early 1950s and the sale prices of the same houses today, less any investments in home improvements, represents the equity appreciation gained by white families who bought into Westlake sixty years ago. |
| p. 90, ¶ 2 | *Barrows v. Jackson* 1953; Gotham 2000, 624; Silva 2009. If you live in a single-family house built before 1953 in a major metropolitan area, go to the office of your county clerk or recorder of deeds, and ask for a copy of any deed restrictions that apply to your home. In many cases, sandwiched between landscaping and |

paint color specifications (or prohibitions of tanning skin, hides, or leather), you will find a racial restriction. If you want to see samples, the Seattle Civil Rights Project maintains a website that includes an inventory of whites-only suburban developments that ring that city, including examples of restrictive covenants.

p. 90, ¶ 3    *Mayers v. Ridley* 1972; Greenberg 1959, 283–86.

p. 91, ¶ 1    Supreme Court justices do not explain why they excuse themselves from participating in particular cases, but scholars are in agreement that in this instance the reason was that each of the three lived in homes that were racially restricted. Some or all of the six justices that participated in deciding the case may also have lived in restricted neighborhoods; declining to participate in a case is solely up to a justice.

Unlike *Shelley v. Kraemer*, the 1953 *Barrows v. Jackson* decision (extending *Shelley* to prohibit covenants providing monetary damages instead of eviction) was not unanimous. Among the dissenters was Chief Justice Fred Vinson, who insisted that suits to recover damages from violated covenants should be permitted to continue. A few months later, he was replaced as chief justice by Earl Warren who, after rehearing the school desegregation cases, marshaled a unanimous Court to ban separate black and white schools in *Brown v. Board of Education*.

## CHAPTER 6:
### White Flight

p. 93, ¶ 1    Kimble 2007, 404.

p. 93, ¶ 2    Hoyt 1939, iii, 62; Kimble 2007.

p. 94, ¶ 1    Laurenti 1960, 12–15, 37, 51–53; Laurenti 1952, 327. Charles Abrams (1951, 330) identified a 1948 *Washington Business Review* article by Rufus S. Lusk as the source of the statement that "the infiltration of Negro[es]" tends to appreciate property. However, Abrams's citation is incorrect, and I have not been able to identify the source. Because Abrams was a respected and generally credible midcentury housing expert, I have accepted that his quotation from the Lusk article is accurate, although his source citation is not. Another 1948 *Washington Business Review* article (*WBR* 1948, 17), describing the increase in Washington, D.C.'s, population, did observe that "[w]hen [the Negro] first goes into a neighborhood, prices may be higher, but eventually values are apt to be depressed. This is not always true because the high class colored who now live on T Street west of 14th maintain their homes well." Throughout the period that the FHA attempted to exclude

African Americans from white neighborhoods, other voices refuted the agency's belief in the inevitability of property value declines associated with African American ownership or residence. In 1945, an article in another professional journal with which FHA staff would have been familiar, the *Review of the Society of Residential Appraisers*, stated that because of the shortage of housing available to African Americans, neighborhood home prices increased from 60 to 100 percent within three years of integration. An article in the same journal the following year stated, "It is a fact, the axiom that colored infiltration collapses the market is no longer true." In 1952, the FHA's own former deputy chief appraiser in Los Angeles wrote in the same journal that "it was [previously] commonly believed by nearly all that the presence of Negroes or other minorities in a neighborhood was a serious value-destroying influence. . . . There are many locations where such generalizations are no longer true." The author of the *Appraisal Journal* article cited in the text, Luigi Laurenti, was a professor of economics at the University of California at Berkeley who analyzed 10,000 property transfers in San Francisco, Oakland, and Philadelphia. About half were in a test group of neighborhoods that were integrating, and the other half in a control group of neighborhoods that were all white. In a 1960 report, he stated that in 41 percent of the cases, prices in the test group and control group remained similar. In 44 percent, prices in the test group moved higher than those in the control group. In 15 percent, prices in the test group declined relative to those in the control group. Laurenti also reviewed studies of Chicago, Detroit, Kansas City, and Portland (Oregon) and found similar trends. He observed that frequently the social status of African Americans moving into white neighborhoods was higher than that of their new white neighbors.

p. 95, ¶ 1   "Vitchek" 1962; McPherson 1972; Colby 2012, 75; Baxandall and Ewen 2000, 183–86; Sugrue 1995, 560.

p. 97, ¶ 1   Satter 2009; Satter 2009b, 2, 8.

p. 97, ¶ 2   McPherson 1972; "Vitchek" 1962; Seligman 2005. I am aware of no nationwide study documenting where the contract-buying system was prevalent. The cities listed here have been identified in city-specific studies. "Norris Vitchek" stated that blockbusting was prevalent in Baltimore, Boston, Cleveland, Detroit, New York City, Philadelphia, St. Louis, Washington, D.C., "and other cities and in some of their suburbs" as well as in Chicago. He does not specifically say, however, that the blockbusting system included contract sales in all those cities, although the inflated prices to which homes were sold to African Americans, and the refusal of banks to issue conventional or FHA-insured mortgages to African American buyers, makes it likely that it did. Seligman 2005 refers to blockbusting in Buffalo. For additional discussion of contract buying, see also Coates 2014.

p. 98, ¶ 1    Satter 2004, 42; Greenberg 1959, 301; Sugrue 1993, 112; Drake and Cayton, 1945 (rev. and enlarged, 1962), 179; Taylor 1994, 180; Gordon 2008, 84–86; Moore 1963. Nationwide, local real estate boards generally threatened to expel agents and brokers if they sold to African Americans in white neighborhoods. A number of actual expulsions, without any reaction from state regulatory commissions, made the threats real. In 1921, the Chicago Real Estate Board promised that "[i]immediate expulsion . . . will be the penalty paid by any member who sells a Negro property in a block where there are only white owners." In 1948 the Seattle Real Estate Board expelled a member for selling a home in a white neighborhood to an interracial couple. In 1955, the St. Louis Real Estate Exchange notified brokers and agents that "no Member of our Board may, directly or indirectly, sell to Negroes . . . unless there are three separate and distinct buildings in such block already occupied by Negroes. . . . This rule is of long standing [and is our interpretation of] the Code of Ethics of the National Association of Real Estate Boards." The Missouri State Real Estate Commission considered that brokers were guilty of professional misconduct and subject to loss of license if they sold to African Americans in white neighborhoods. Note to p. 12, ¶ 2 describes the general fear among real estate agents south of San Francisco during the 1950s that they would be "blackballed" if they sold to African Americans in white neighborhoods. In 1963, the Sarasota, Florida, Real Estate Board expelled a member for selling a home to an African American physician in a white neighborhood.

CHAPTER 7:
## IRS Support and Compliant Regulators

p. 100    When a few African Americans moved into the white middle-class neighborhood of Park Hill in Denver, real estate agents undertook a campaign to panic homeowners to sell at a discount. The agents then resold the homes to African Americans at a premium. Joni Noel, a white Denver schoolteacher who grew up in Park Hill, told me that in the late 1950s and early 1960s, real estate agents "were insistent and obnoxious. They called, they left cards. They knocked on the door. They mailed flyers. They had neighborhood meetings at schools, churches, and lodges. They made it very clear as they were pounding the For Sale signs in the ground next door and down the street that if we didn't move we would be left in a ghetto and our home would be worthless and our lives would be in danger." This activity could not have been unknown to the Colorado real estate licensing agency, but it took no action.

p. 102, ¶ 2    Spratt 1970.

p. 102, ¶ 3    Coleman 1982, 31–32.

p. 103, ¶ 1    *Bob Jones University v. United States* 1983, 586 (n. 24); Coleman 1982, 86, 127. The income tax system established by the Revenue Act of 1913, whose relevant provisions continue to this day, exempted from taxation churches, universities, and other "corporations, companies, or associations organized and conducted solely for charitable, religious, or educational purposes, including fraternal beneficiary associations." The Revenue Act of 1917 permitted individual donors to deduct from their own income taxes contributions to tax-exempt organizations. Regulations of the Department of the Treasury that guide IRS decisions define charitable organizations that are eligible for tax exemption as those that, inter alia, work "to eliminate prejudice and discrimination."

The Supreme Court has ruled that "allowance of a deduction cannot be permitted where this result 'would frustrate sharply defined national or state policies proscribing particular types of conduct, evidenced by some governmental declaration thereof.'" Even before the Fair Housing Act of 1968, housing discrimination was unlawful under Section 1982 of the Civil Rights Acts of 1866. So although public attention was not focused on housing discrimination from the 1920s until the 1960s, granting a tax exemption to institutions that operated in violation of Section 1982 was contrary to "national or state policy" as well as a violation of the Fifth Amendment.

The *Bob Jones* case specifically concerned whether a racially discriminatory *educational* institution could receive tax-exempt status. The Court's ruling was rooted in a recognition of national policy to eliminate school segregation, but the reasoning equally applies to government support, through tax policy, for any racially discriminatory institution.

p. 103, ¶ 2    Cote Brilliante Presbyterian Church online; Wright 2002, 77; Long and Johnson 1947, 82.

p. 104, ¶ 1    Miller 1946, 139; Brilliant 2010, 97. Neighborhood homeowners' associations themselves are rarely tax-exempt; nor are contributions to them tax deductible. However, businesses seeking to protect their neighborhoods from integration sometimes inappropriately deducted contributions to segregation groups as business expenses. The Seattle Civil Rights Project has posted a copy of a 1948 leaflet distributed by the Capitol Hill Community Club of Seattle in which it solicited contributions for legal expenses incurred in the course of updating racially restrictive covenants in its neighborhood. The leaflet promises that contributions for this purpose are tax deductible as business expenses. I don't know how widespread this practice was, or if it was sufficiently common that the IRS should have taken notice.

p. 104, ¶ 3　Long and Johnson 1947, 53, 83.

p. 105, ¶ 1　Plotkin 1999, 75, 118–19; Long and Johnson 1947, 74, 83. Wendy Plotkin to author, May 12, 2016.

p. 105, ¶ 3　Brilliant 2010, 94.

p. 105, ¶ 4　Hirsch 1983, 1998, 144–45; Plotkin 1999, 122–30. Arnold Hirsch concludes: "More than a passive supporter of these groups, the university was the spark and driving force behind them."

p. 106, ¶ 2　*NYT* 1938; Greenhouse 1969. In 1968, twenty-four years after Parkchester opened for whites-only, the New York City Commission on Human Rights issued a formal complaint charging Metropolitan Life with a "deliberate, intentional, systematic, open and notorious" policy of refusing to rent to African Americans or Puerto Ricans. For the first twenty-two of those years, not a single nonwhite family was permitted to rent in Parkchester.

p. 106, ¶ 3　Caro 1975, 968; *NYT* 1947c; Weaver 1948, 227; Henderson 2000, 122; *Dorsey v. Stuyvesant Town Corporation* 1949; USCCR 1961, 121; Bagli 2010; *NYT* 1947a; *NYT* 1947b.

p. 107, ¶ 1　*NYT* 1947c; McEntire 1960, 264; *Fordham Law Review* 1957, 681; *NYT* 1950a; Buckley 2010; CUR 2011. Data for Stuyvesant Town include its adjoining twin project, Peter Cooper Village.

p. 107, ¶ 2　Caro 1975, 968. Robert Moses estimated that 37 percent of evictees from Stuyvesant Town and several similar demolitions were African American or Puerto Rican, about three times their share of the city's population. Robert Caro, the Moses biographer, considers the Moses estimate low.

p. 108, ¶ 1　USCCR 1961, 36–37.

p. 108, ¶ 2　USCCR 1961, 42, 49–51, 45.

p. 109, ¶ 1　*Davis v. Elmira Savings Bank* 1896, 283. And see also *Franklin National Bank v. New York* 1954, 375: "The United States has set up a system of national banks as federal instrumentalities."

p. 109, ¶ 2　Immergluck and Smith 2006.

p. 109, ¶ 3　Warren 2007; Nguyen 2011.

p. 110, ¶ 3　Bradford 2002, vii, 37, 69. Lower-income borrowers are those whose income is less than 80 percent of the median income in their metropolitan area. Higher-income borrowers are those whose income is more than 120 percent of the median. A predominantly African American (or white) census tract is one where at least 75 percent of residents are African American (or white).

p. 111, ¶ 1    Brooks and Simon 2007; Avery, Canner, and Cook 2005. Other studies (e.g., Squires, Hyra, and Renner 2009; Bocian and Zhai 2005) find similar racial disparities. These data are only suggestive. We would expect minority borrowers, on average, to have lower rates of qualification for conventional loans than white borrowers because, on average, minorities have less advantageous economic characteristics (income, assets, employment, etc.) that are relevant to creditworthiness. The data disparities, however, are so large that it is probable, though not certain, that creditworthiness alone cannot explain them.

           Hispanic borrowers were also disproportionately exploited by aggressively marketed subprime loans.

p. 111, ¶ 2    Powell 2010; Donovan 2011; National Coalition for the Homeless et al. 2009.

p. 112, ¶ 2    Memphis and Shelby County 2011, 34, 33.

p. 112, ¶ 3    Baltimore 2011, 21–22.

p. 113, ¶ 1    *Cleveland v. Ameriquest* 2009, 26.

p. 113, ¶ 3    Stevenson and Goldstein 2016; *NYT* 2016. Census Bureau data show that African American homeownership rates fell from 50 percent in 2004 to 42 percent in 2016, while white rates fell only from 76 percent to 72 percent.

p. 113, ¶ 4    Some critics charged that the housing bubble and subsequent collapse was caused not merely by federal regulators' failure to restrain irresponsible and racially targeted subprime lending but also by active federal encouragement of the practice. According to this theory, the federal government pressured banks to increase lending to low-income and minority borrowers, with the threat of government sanctions under the Community Reinvestment Act of 1974 if banks did not do so. The critics claimed that banks were unable to satisfy government regulators' demands for more loans in minority communities without lending to unqualified home-owners. This is an unpersuasive claim. It cannot explain why, for example, so many subprime loans were issued to minority borrowers who qualified for conventional loans. The Community Reinvestment Act (CRA) applied only to banks and thrift institutions that accepted consumer deposits. Such banks represented only a small share of institutions that made subprime loans that were foreclosed after the housing bubble collapsed in 2008. Barr (2009, 172) finds that only about 25 percent of all subprime loans were made by institutions covered by the CRA. Most were made by independent mortgage bankers and brokers who were not covered by the law. Many of those loans were then purchased by non-depository institutions, such as Lehman Brothers or Bear Stearns, who could have been under no pressure to do so by CRA regulators. Nonetheless, although the CRA could not have been responsible for the housing bubble, regulators did not interfere with racially motivated subprime targeting when banks and thrifts did engage in it.

CHAPTER 8:
*Local Tactics*

p. 115, ¶ 1    Johnson 1993, 91–93; Hayward Area Historical Society online; Stiles 2015; Self 2003, 113. David Bohannon's leading role as a mass-production builder was confirmed by his election, in 1941, as the first president of the National Association of Home Builders. Later, his contribution to racial segregation went unmentioned when, in 1958, he was elected national president of the influential research group for planners, the Urban Land Institute (praising him as "one of the West Coast's most successful land developers and community builders"); or when he was selected, in 1986, as the annual honoree of the California Homebuilding Foundation and a member of its Hall of Fame for having "enriched the home-building industry through innovation, public service, and philanthropy."

p. 115, ¶ 2    *Architectural Forum* 1945; San Lorenzo Village, mid-1950s.

p. 116, ¶ 1    Devincenzi, Gilsenan, and Levine 2004, 24–26.

p. 116, ¶ 2    Moore 2000, 110. The AFSC's Social-Industrial Committee was chaired during much of the period discussed here by Clark Kerr, chancellor of the University of California at Berkeley. He was a prominent advocate of racial integration and was also admired for refusing to fire faculty who had refused to sign an anti-Communist loyalty oath. But in 1964 he became the symbol of opposition to students' right to "free speech" on campus, during protests against segregation and the Vietnam War. He was later denied appointment as secretary of health, education, and welfare by President Lyndon Johnson because the FBI deemed him subversive.

In 2013, Stephen McNeil, the assistant regional director of the AFSC's western regional office in San Francisco, permitted me to comb through, read, and copy its relevant files from the 1940s and 1950s. The documents cover the AFSC's efforts to assist Ford's African American workers when the plant was located in Richmond and later when they sought housing in the Milpitas area.

Much of the account in Section I of Chapter 8 relies on information in the minutes and correspondence of the AFSC's San Francisco executive committee and Social-Industrial Committee, including reports of Phil Buskirk who directed these efforts, supervised by Kerr's committee.

After my research at the San Francisco AFSC office was completed, the organization shipped all its files from this period to AFSC headquarters in Philadelphia for archiving. I cannot identify the present archive location of specific minutes, reports, and correspondence on which my account relies. However, my description of the search for racially integrated housing in the Milpitas area is based in important respects on these AFSC records, although letters and minutes are not individually described in the notes that follow here. Where publicly available sources are available, I cite them, but in many cases these are less informative than the AFSC documents.

p. 116, ¶ 3    Sources for the account of efforts to find integrated housing near Milpitas, beginning with this paragraph and continuing through the description of the opening of Sunnyhills, include, in addition to San Francisco office AFSC documents: Bernstein 1955; Bloom 1955a; Bloom 1955b; Briggs 1982, 5–9, 12; Callan 1960, 800–1; *Daily Palo Alto Times* 1955; Grant 1992; Grier and Grier 1960, 80–85; Grier and Grier 1962, 7–11; Hanson 1955; Harris 1955a; Harris 1955b; Oliver 1955; Oliver 1957, 3–5; Oliver and Callan 1955; *San Francisco News* 1955; *San Jose Evening News* 1955; *San Jose Mercury* 1955; *San Jose News* 1957; Self 2003, 114; Stevenson 2013, 2015; UAW 1979; USCCR 1961, 136–37.

p. 117, ¶ 2    Several sources repeat the story of a town near the Ford plant that increased its minimum lot size from 6,000 to 8,000 square feet to prevent an integrated project from being built. But I've not been able to identify the town by name.

p. 119, ¶ 3    Mort Levine, who had been editor of the *Milpitas Post* at the time, told me in a March 6, 2013, interview that he did not believe that the sewer connection fees were increased for racial reasons, but rather that the original calculation had been flawed. I have no way to evaluate the accuracy of this statement, but the irregular procedure by which the meeting to raise the fee was convened, as well as the open racial motivations of other participants, suggest that the decision was at least in part racially motivated, if not entirely so.

p. 120, ¶ 1    Although California had no open housing law at the time, Brown may have relied on the equal protection clauses of the state or federal constitutions, or perhaps on an argument based on two earlier California Supreme Court rulings (e.g., *James v. Marinship* 1944,

739) that racial discrimination is "contrary to the public policy of the United States and this state [and that the] United States Constitution has long prohibited governmental action discriminating against persons because of race or color." Brown's complaint, however, never got to the stage of an actual filing.

p. 120, ¶ 3    In 1950, a provision permitting FHA insurance of loans to cooperatives was added to the National Housing Act, and in 1959 projects that were originally constructed as separate units were permitted to convert to co-ops and gain the benefits of the lower rates that followed from FHA endorsement. It was to take advantage of this provision that the UAW converted its Sunnyhills project to a cooperative. It is unclear why the FHA was willing to support integrated developments if they were organized as co-ops but not if they were individually owned. Section 213 was designed to encourage construction of lower-cost units for working-class families. Perhaps the FHA was willing to tolerate integration in lower-priced working-class developments from a belief that such a policy would not undermine its promotion of segregation in more middle-class suburbs. More likely, I think, is that administrators of Section 213 projects, favorable toward cooperatives, were more liberal on racial issues than administrators of the regular FHA program, who mostly came to the government from the real estate industry. In earlier years, when the FHA refused to endorse integrated co-ops (as in the case of the cooperative that Wallace Stegner helped to lead, or the co-op that Lombard, Illinois, families tried to establish), the cooperatives had to appeal to regular FHA administrators. Now, in the 1950s and 1960s, they had a special group within the FHA to which their banks could apply.

p. 121, ¶ 1    *Milpitas Post* 1955 or 1956.

p. 121, ¶ 3    Theobold 2004; Smith 1967, 600; Reagan 1967, 592. The Trailmobile plant moved from Berkeley to Fremont, a town adjacent to Milpitas. The plant manager's explanation for not hiring African American workers may not have been well founded. The general counsel of the U.S. Commission on Civil Rights asked the personnel manager of a Fremont furniture manufacturer (that also had workers who commuted from their homes in Oakland) whether absenteeism from long-distance commuting was a serious problem. The manager responded, "I think that we probably have a greater degree of tardiness and absenteeism among our employees who probably live closer in. We find that in most cases. The people across the street are the ones that are always late."

p. 123, ¶ 1    Grier and Grier 1960, 86–87; *Chester Times* 1955; *Chester Times* 1956; *Evening Bulletin* 1955.

p. 123, ¶ 3    USCCR 1961, 132–34; *Progress v. Mitchell* 1960, 712; Lathers 1960;

*Time* 1959; *Time* 1960. The federal court also found that the developer did not have "clean hands" because it proposed to maintain a quota system of 80 percent white and 20 percent black purchasers, and to require contracts to compel purchasers to resell the property only to subsequent buyers of the same race, to maintain the project's racial balance. Such contracts would be unenforceable in court. This squeamishness about racial quotas as a means of transitioning to an integrated society has since characterized federal court approaches to race. The federal courts previously did not hesitate to approve quotas of 100 percent white and zero percent black, and they now felt no obligation to come up with practical ways to undo that history. This decision was a harbinger of today's jurisprudence, in which Chief Justice John Roberts asserts that the way to end discrimination by race is simply to end discrimination by race.

p. 124, ¶ 3    USCCR 1961, 135–36; *Creve Coeur v. Weinstein* 1959, 404.

p. 125, ¶ 1    Herbers 1970; Ayres, 1971; Rosenthal 1971a; Rosenthal 1971b; Gordon 2008, 147–50; *Park View Heights v. Black Jack* 1972; *U.S. v. Black Jack* 1974, 1185 (n. 3), 1186 (internal quotation marks have been eliminated and emphasis added).

p. 127, ¶ 2    Mohl 2000, 230–34.

p. 128, ¶ 2    Schwartz 1976, 485 (n. 481).

p. 128, ¶ 3    *Garrett v. Hamtramck* 1974, 1239, 1246 (italics added); USCCR 1961, 100; *Garrett v. Hamtramck* 1975, 1156–57.

p. 129, ¶ 2    Mohl 2001, 340–44; Mohl 1987, 14.

p. 129, ¶ 3    Mohl 2000, 239.

p. 130, ¶ 1    McWilliams 1949; *California Eagle* 1943b; Sides 2003, 124; *California Eagle* 1954. A similar rezoning had been attempted several years before at the behest of economically pressed property owners who sought white renters, but it had been vetoed by Los Angeles's mayor.

p. 131, ¶ 1    USCCR 1961, 99–100; Mohl 2000, 231; Schwartz 1976, 483; Mohl 2002, 16–18.

p. 132, ¶ 2    Busch 2013, 981–83; McGhee 2015, 6, 7, 15, 21–22; Koch & Fowler 1928, 57; Busch 2015.

p. 133, ¶ 3    Benjamin 2012b. Karen Benjamin provided additional detail and documents regarding the use of school placements to segregate Raleigh and Atlanta in e-mail correspondence and telephone calls with me in November 2015. I am especially grateful to her for providing me with a copy of the Atlanta School Board minutes of July 9, 1919.

p. 135, ¶ 1    Benjamin 2012a.

p. 136, ¶ 1    Benjamin 2013. Karen Benjamin plans to develop these accounts in greater detail in a forthcoming book, *Segregation Built to Last: Schools and the Construction of Segregated Housing Patterns in the New South.*

CHAPTER 9:
*State-Sanctioned Violence*

p. 139, ¶ 1   Beckles online; Moore 2000, 116–18; Barbour 1952, 26; Rolling-wood Improvement Association Board 1952; Wenkert 1967, 44; *Toledo Blade* 1952; *Milwaukee Journal* 1952.

p. 140, ¶ 3   Kushner 2009, 83, 88, 91, 100–1, 116, 136–37, 140, 147, 154, 157, 163, 167–70, 175, 181–82; Yardley 2009; Bobker and Becker 1957; Weart 1957.

p. 142, ¶ 2   In 1969 York, Pennsylvania, the city to which the Myers family retreated, was the site of a violent confrontation between whites and African Americans. It resulted in the deaths of a policeman and of an African American woman who took a wrong turn and drove through a white neighborhood. The woman's death was not investigated until 2000, when alleged perpetrators were arrested, including the city's then mayor. A police officer in 1969, he was accused of distributing ammunition to the civilians who killed the woman, and he admitted having shouted "white power" to incite the civilians to riot. But more than thirty years after the fact, witnesses' testimony about the distribution of ammunition was not persuasive to an all-white jury, and the mayor was acquitted; two civilians who fired shots that killed the woman were convicted.

p. 143, ¶ 4   Rubinowitz and Perry 2002, 350; Spear 1967, 22.

p. 144, ¶ 1   Tuttle 1970, 266–82; Bell 2008, 540; Rubinowitz and Perry 2002, 381.

p. 144, ¶ 3   Hirsch 1983, 1998, 52–53. Weaver (1948, 96) reports that all forty-six were arson-bombings.

p. 145, ¶ 1   *Time* 1951; Hirsch 1983, 200; Wilkerson 2010, 373–75; Loewen 2005, 10–11; Coates 2014.

p. 145, ¶ 2   The charges against Harvey Clark and his associates were later dropped.

p. 145, ¶ 3   Hirsch 1995, 537 and throughout; Hirsch 1983, 1998, 97–99. Donald and Betty Howard were the first African American family to move in to the Trumbull Park Homes. They could do so only because Betty Howard was fair-skinned, and the project manager accepted her application without realizing that she "might be Negro." Once the Howards' residence was a *fait accompli* and neighbors belatedly decided that the family was African American, the violence began. After the Howards moved in to Trumbull Park, the authority accepted a few other African Americans into the project. The housing authority had an official policy of non-discrimination but followed an actual policy of segregation.

p. 146, ¶ 1   Royko 1971, 123–37.

p. 146, ¶ 2   Sugrue 1993, 111–12; Zineski and Kenyon 1968, 6.

p. 147, ¶ 1    Bauman 1987, 161–62.

p. 147, ¶ 2    Rubinowitz and Perry 2002, 381; Sides 2003, 102–6; Miller 1965b, 5; Miller 1965a, 11; Robertson 1952; Wilkerson 2010, 232, 330, 331.

p. 147, ¶ 3    Bell 2008, 543, 546–47; Smothers 1990.

p. 148, ¶ 2    Braden 1958; Fosl 1989.

p. 150, ¶ 2    *Marshall v. Bramer* 1987. Two perpetrators, one of whom was the brother-in-law of the Klan member at whose home a Klan rally was held, were convicted of committing the initial firebombing. The Marshalls were attempting to identify the perpetrators of the arson attack that destroyed their home. The Marshalls were unsuccessful, but if a police department where twenty officers were Klan members wanted to identify the perpetrators, it could surely have done so.

## CHAPTER 10:
### Suppressed Incomes

p. 154, ¶ 4    Wilkerson 2010, 50–54, 150–53, 160–72; Lemann 1991, 17–23, 48.

p. 154, ¶ 5    Blackmon 2008, 7, 9, 91, 94, 289, 381; McPherson 1996.

p. 155, ¶ 1    Wilkerson 2010, 161, 556.

p. 155, ¶ 3    Katznelson 2005; Wolters 1969, 143; Dowden-White 2011, 175.

p. 156, ¶ 1    Houston and Davis 1934, 291; Fishel 1964–65, 113.

p. 156, ¶ 2    Fishel 1964–65, 113–14; Katznelson 2013, 241–42; Davis 1933, 271.

p. 157, ¶ 1    Fishel 1964–65, 115; Kifer 1961, 3–61; Foreman 1974; Hills 2010, 27–28.

p. 158, ¶ 1    Wolters 1969, 143, 148–52.

p. 159, ¶ 1    Archibald 1947, 130–31.

p. 159, ¶ 2    Wenkert 1967, 16–17; Brown 1973, 1; Johnson 1993, 46–48.

p. 159, ¶ 3    Stevenson 2007, 2–00:08–13. Johnson, Long, and Jones 1944, 67; Goodwin 1994, 228. In a memo to Eleanor Roosevelt during a 1941 strike for union recognition at a Ford plant in Dearborn, Michigan, Mary McCleod Bethune (director of Negro affairs in the National Youth Administration and founder of the National Council of Negro Women) wrote that Ford had earned the loyalty of African American workers (who at first opposed and refused to participate in the strike) because Ford had employed "more Negroes in skilled and semi-skilled capacities than any other auto manufacturer."

p. 159, ¶ 4    Wollenberg 1990, 74; Johnson 1993, 65, 69; Moore 2000, 54; Quivik undated 162ff; Goodwin 1994, 247.

p. 160, ¶ 1    Moore 2000, 59–60; Johnson 1993, 71–73; Quivik undated, 162–69; Johnson, Long, and Jones 1944, 71–72; Marshall 1944, 77; Archibald 1947, 83–84; Record 1947, 11; Broussard 1993, 157; Rubin 1972, 35.

p. 160, ¶ 2    Quivik undated, 164; Marshall 1944, 77–78; Northrup 1943, 206–8.

p. 160, ¶ 3    *Postal Record* 2011, 8ff. Racial discrimination by recognized federal unions was banned by Presidential Executive Order 10988, January 17, 1962.

p. 161, ¶ 2    *Independent Metal Workers* 1964.

p. 161, ¶ 3    Burns 1970, 123–24; Goodwin 1994, 246–53; Broussard 1993, 148–51.

p. 163, ¶ 1    Burns 1970, 264; *Afro American* 1942. Because he took positions such as urging the mob to refrain from violence against Andrew Wade, Ethridge had a national reputation as a racial liberal. He died in 1981, and a *New York Times* obituary eulogized him as "one of the most respected figures in American journalism," adding that "[l]ong before it was fashionable, or even safe, Mr. Ethridge denounced racism and repression and condemned the poverty he saw in a nation of plenty. Small, round-faced and pink-cheeked, he spoke out in a lyrical Southern accent against prejudice and provincialism."

p. 163, ¶ 2    Moore 2000, 54–55; France 1962, 68.

p. 163, ¶ 3    Broussard 1993, 151–52, 154–57; Broussard 2001, 198; Ungaretti 2012, 126–27; Angelou 1969, 2015, 258ff. It seems from the context of Maya Angelou's autobiography that she was about sixteen when she got the streetcar job, in 1943 or 1944. She stated that she was "hired as the first Negro on the San Francisco streetcars," but Audley Cole, a motorman, and perhaps other African Americans preceded her in 1942. Angelou may have meant that she was the first African American conductress.

p. 165, ¶ 1    Wollenberg 1981, 269–71; Moore 2000, 61; Wollenberg 1990, 78–82; France 1962, 69–72; Quivik undated, 164–66; Johnson 1993, 73; *James v. Marinship* 1944, 739.

p. 166, ¶ 1    Johnson 1993, 81; Foner 1974, 247; Goodwin 1994, 246–47; Whelan et al. 1997 (not paginated re: St. Louis plant); O'Neil 2010.

p. 167, ¶ 2    Katznelson 2005, 136–37; Herbold 1994–95; Onkst 1998; Turner and Bound 2002; Tygiel 1983, 59ff; Vernon 2008. The historical novel *OK, Joe* by Louis Guilloux (translated by Alice Kaplan) reports that African American GIs in liberated France who were accused of rape were frequently executed, while white GIs accused of identical crimes were lightly punished or sent home. If the disparity in treatment was equally extreme for discharge status, then African Americans, who were disproportionally discharged with less-than-honorable status, were disproportionately disqualified for GI Bill job training, employment, and educational benefits.

p. 168, ¶ 1    Myrdal 1944, 417–18; de Graaf and Taylor 2001, 28.

p. 168, ¶ 2    Sugrue 1993, 107–8. Even if Michigan's law had been vigorously enforced, and it was not, 1955 was too late to enable African Americans to participate fully in the postwar employment and housing construction booms.

p. 168, ¶ 3   USCCR 1967, 119 (n. 78), 55–57; Hayes 1972, 78 (table 4-2).

p. 169, ¶ 1   Swarns 2015.

p. 170, ¶ 1   Bremer et al. 1979, 24–26. The report actually says that the chances were less than one in a thousand. Because the researchers' data calculations are no longer available, and the possibility of a typographical error cannot be excluded, I use the more conservative estimate of one in a hundred.

p. 170, ¶ 3   Lyons 1982, 74.

p. 170, ¶ 4   Oldman and Aaron 1965, 42 (table III), 48. West Roxbury is near but not adjacent to Roxbury.

p. 171, ¶ 1   Karhl 2015, 13 (fig. 1).

p. 171, ¶ 2   Little 1973, 2 (table A), 12 (table 1.2)

p. 171, ¶ 4   Karhl 2015; Capps 2015.

p. 172, ¶ 3   Hughes 1940, 27; Clark and Perlman 1947, 30; Kimble 2007, 422; Woofter 1928, 126–27. The FHA defined overcrowding as more than one person per room and doubling-up as more than one family sharing a single housing unit.

p. 173, ¶ 2   Velie 1946, 112, 17; Weaver 1948, 119.

p. 173, ¶ 3   Weaver 1948, 36–37, 60–61.

p. 174, ¶ 1   Weaver 1948, 104, 119. Brown et al. (2003, 22–25) refer to this process as African Americans' "disaccumulation of wealth," in contrast to whites' accumulation of wealth in housing.

p. 174, ¶ 3   Dunn 2013; Rosenhaus 1971; Herbert 1971; SAI 1972; Nix, undated.

## CHAPTER 11:
### *Looking Forward, Looking Back*

p. 177, ¶ 2   Mondale 2015; Schill and Friedman 1999; Hannah-Jones 2013; Tegeler 2013. Throughout this book, FHA refers to the Federal Housing Administration, not to the Fair Housing Act.

The floor leader for the Fair Housing Act in the Senate was Walter Mondale, a senator from Minnesota who later served as vice president under Jimmy Carter and was the Democratic nominee for president in 1984. In 1968, as they had done successfully in 1966, southern Democrats engaged in a filibuster against the bill. Senator Mondale was one vote short of the sixty-seven needed to end debate (to invoke "cloture"). The vice president at the time was Hubert Humphrey, serving under Lyndon Johnson. Recently, Mondale recalled how he got the Fair Housing Act passed in the

Senate. "So I went to Humphrey, and I said, 'What do I do?' He said 'call Lyndon Johnson,' so I called the president (which you don't do every day), and I told him our predicament. He said, 'Well, do you know of any vote that could be cast for this where the person wouldn't be hurt, where they would not have any trouble politically?' And I said, 'Well, the senator from Alaska could do it, but he's against cloture. But he also wants a housing project in downtown Anchorage,' and the president said 'Thank you' and hung up. So the next morning we're on the floor: 'Will we get cloture?'—most people didn't think we would do it—and just as the vote tally was ending I saw the senator from Alaska come through the back door and vote 'aye' and we passed fair housing, we got the cloture on the fourth vote, no votes to spare but we got it! Then the bill went to the House."

Enforcement of the Fair Housing Act has been weak, but neither has it been absent. Middle-class African Americans are now minimally present in many predominantly white suburbs. (Levittown is now 1 percent African American.) Under the 1968 act, individuals who had suffered from housing discrimination could file complaints with the Department of Housing and Urban Development (HUD), but the department could attempt only to "conciliate" the parties; it had no enforcement powers. Complainants could file private lawsuits with punitive damages capped at $1,000. The Department of Justice could file civil suits against systematic perpetrators of discrimination but not on behalf of single individuals. The Fair Housing Act was amended in 1988 to establish a system of HUD administrative law judges to resolve presumptively valid complaints that came from state and local fair housing agencies, but HUD's enforcement activities have been focused more on discrimination based on family status and disability than on race. Audit studies (where matched pairs of African American and white testers pose as potential buyers or renters and attempt to secure housing) continue to show ongoing racial discrimination in housing.

p. 179, ¶ 1 Santow and Rothstein 2012; Rothstein 2013, 14 (table 7); Orfield et al. 2016, 4–5 (table 1). The increased segregation results both from the failure to desegregate neighborhoods and from the declining share of white students in public schools. In New York State, 66 percent of African American students attend schools where fewer than 10 percent of students are white; in Illinois, 60 percent of African American students do so; in Mississippi, it is 45 percent; and in Alabama, 42 percent.

p. 180, ¶ 4 Data are from the Census, with additional analysis by Valerie Wilson, an economist at the Economic Policy Institute.

p. 182, ¶ 1      Baxandall and Ewen 2000, 131, 164. Wealth from the sale of a home consists of the sale price, less the purchase price and any investments made in remodeling during the intervening years. While remodeling was frequently extensive for homes bought in the post–World War II period by returning veterans and other lower-middle-class families, the cost of this remodeling was sometimes modest. Many of the urban men who participated in suburbanization during this period were skilled workers who had craft knowledge and maintenance skills, and who remodeled their homes themselves or with help from neighbors, with less subcontracting costs than might have been expected.

p. 183, ¶ 3      The same is true for children whose parents have incomes anywhere in the distribution. In a perfectly mobile society, not only would the poorest children have the same chance as anyone else to be rich, but the richest children would have the same chance as anyone else to be poor. This is all a bit oversimplified, however. Even in a fully equal opportunity society, if a large number of lower-earning immigrants came to the country, native children born to lower-earning parents would have a better-than-random chance of having adult incomes higher in the income distribution. And conversely, if a large number of higher-earning immigrants came to the country, native children born to lower-earning parents would have a worse chance of having adult incomes higher in the income distribution. A second qualification is that if low-earning parents typically have more children than higher-earning parents, then children born to lower-earning parents would have a better chance of having adult incomes higher in the income distribution. Because we have recently had more lower-wage immigrants than higher-wage immigrants, and because lower-income parents do have more children than higher-income parents, these two qualifications offset each other, if not perfectly.

p. 184, ¶ 1      Lopoo and DeLeire 2012, 6 (fig. 3). These estimates compare the average income of parents over a five-year period with the average income of their children when these children were approximately the same age as the parents were when the initial income data were collected.

p. 184, ¶ 2      Lopoo and DeLeire 2012, 20 (fig. 15). Part of the explanation for the lower mobility of African Americans than whites is probably that, comparing African Americans and whites who are poor during a five-year period of their adulthood, African Americans are more likely than whites to be poor both before and after that five-year period. African American poverty is more likely a permanent or long-term circumstance than white poverty.

p. 184, ¶ 3     Federal Reserve Board online. Microdata analysis by Valerie Wilson of the Economic Policy Institute.

p. 185, ¶ 2     Lopoo and DeLeire 2012, 15 (fig. 11).

p. 185, ¶ 3     Lopoo and DeLeire 2012, 21 (fig. 15).

p. 185, ¶ 5     Wilhelm 2001, 141 (table 4.2).

p. 186, ¶ 2     Sharkey 2013, 27 (fig. 2.1), 38 (fig. 2.6).

p. 187, ¶ 1     Sharkey 2013, 39.

p. 187, ¶ 2     Morsy and Rothstein 2015; Rothstein 2004.

p. 189, ¶ 1     *Baltimore Sun* 1975; Gutierrez et al., 30.

p. 189, ¶ 2     Dresser and Broadwater 2015.

p. 190, ¶ 2     Leviner 2004; Khadduri, Buron, and Climaco 2006, 7.

p. 190, ¶ 3     McClure, Schwartz, and Taghavi 2014; Sard and Rice 2014, 35 (fig. 7); Sard and Rice 2016, 26 (table A-1). The tax credit and Section 8 programs also support housing for senior citizens; projects for the elderly are more likely to be found in middle-class neighborhoods. The text refers only to family units.

p. 191, ¶ 1     ICP 2008.

p. 191, ¶ 2     *Texas Dept. of Housing v. Inclusive Communities Project* 2015.

## CHAPTER 12:
### Considering Fixes

p. 194     Bernestine Williams moved to Plano with a higher-value Section 8 voucher, the result of the 1985 civil rights lawsuit *Walker v. HUD* against the Dallas Housing Authority and HUD. She raised her two children in Plano. College is typical for students who attend schools in integrated communities like Plano, and both of her children are now in college. This is the type of outcome for which the housing mobility programs aim.

p. 195, ¶ 2     Levine et al. 2014; Levine and Stark 2015; American Psychological Association 2015, 27; Wells, Fox, and Cobo 2016. One set of experiments gave groups of financial experts information about the underlying characteristics of simulated stocks. Racially and ethnically diverse groups estimated values for the stocks that were closer to their true values than racially and ethnically homogenous groups. In a brief filed with the Supreme Court in a recent affirmative action case, the American Psychological Association presented summaries of research demonstrating that in discussion groups, "the presence of minority individuals stimulates an increase in the complexity with which students—especially members of the majority—approach a given issue."

p. 196, ¶ 4     CDC 2016; Edozien 2004. The nationwide asthma rate for African American children is 13.7 percent, for white children 7.6

percent. The New York City health commissioner reported in 2004 that while asthma rates overall were declining, "[t]he asthma hospitalization rate among children under 5 years of age living in low-income neighborhoods is four times that of children living in high-income neighborhoods." In that year, asthma was the leading cause of absenteeism in New York City schools.

p. 199, ¶ 1   Danzer et al. 2012, 288, 492, 506.

p. 199, ¶ 4   Lapsansky-Werner et al. 2016, 304, 431–32, 449. The boldface emphasis of "de facto segregation" is how the textbook presents the term, expecting that this will help students remember the importance that the textbook authors assign to the concept.

p. 200, ¶ 2   Sewall (online) attempts to keep track of the most commonly used textbooks. I've looked at many, but not all, of the textbooks he lists.

p. 201, ¶ 1   For a summary account of Romney's Open Communities plan, and its fate, see Santow and Rothstein 2012. It draws on Romney 1969; Herbers 1969; Lilley 1970; Bonastia 2006; Danielson 1976; McDonald 1970; Lamb 2005, and Lemann 1991, 209.

p. 203, ¶ 2   Sharkey 2014, 925 (table 2). The data are from 2000. Sharkey defines a middle-class family as one with annual income of at least $30,000, and a "severely disadvantaged" census tract as one where the concentration of welfare receipt, poverty, unemployment, female-headed households, and young children is more than two standard deviations above the national average.

p. 204, ¶ 2   This is not intended as a fully developed proposal. Metropolitan areas with smaller African American populations would require a different fair share definition. Perhaps, for example, metropolitan areas with a black population of 10 percent should define their suburbs as segregated if their African American population is less than 5 percent.

p. 205, ¶ 1   Racioppi and Akin 2015; O'Dea 2015; Krefetz 2000–1; Herr 2002; Smart Growth America 2016; Massey et al. 2013. In New Jersey until 2008, towns (in practice, towns with wealthier residents) were permitted to evade this requirement by paying other towns to assume their fair share obligations. Legislation prohibiting this arrangement was adopted in 2008. In 2015, the New Jersey Supreme Court, confronted with foot-dragging by wealthy towns and by the governor, removed responsibility for planning fair share developments from towns and made this a judicial function.

The Massachusetts 40B program, adopted in 1969, overrides local exclusionary zoning laws in jurisdictions where less than 10 percent of existing housing is "affordable"—i.e., where rents or purchase payments can reasonably be made by families whose income is 80 percent or less than the area's median income. For developers to take advantage of this flexibility, at least 25 percent of the units in their projects must be permanently affordable, after federal subsidies for low- and moderate-income housing have been used. Since the law's passage, the number of jurisdictions where less than 10 percent of their housing stock is affordable has declined.

p. 206, ¶ 1    Schwartz 2010.

p. 206, ¶ 2    Boger 1993.

p. 207, ¶ 2    Berdahl-Baldwin 2015; Donovan 2015; Darrah and DeLuca 2014. The criteria for participation in the Baltimore program are somewhat more complex than described here but not substantially different.

p. 208, ¶ 3    Berdahl-Baldwin 2015. Other cities with modest programs that assist voucher holders in moving to lower poverty areas include Buffalo, Chicago and Cook County (Illinois), Cincinnati, Connecticut cities that are highly segregated, Minneapolis, Philadelphia, Richmond (VA), San Diego, Seattle (King County), Yonkers, and perhaps others.

p. 208, ¶ 4    Sard and Rice 2014, 38, 51, 53–57; Metzger 2014, 556; McClure, Schwartz, and Taghavi 2014, 3.

p. 209, ¶ 1    Analysis of Housing Choice Voucher eligibility and use from Census and HUD administrative data was provided to author by Alicia Mazzara and Barbara Sard of the Center on Budget and Policy Priorities, May 23, 2016.

p. 209, ¶ 3    Section 8 priorities are presently established for emergencies— for families that must move because of domestic violence, or for homeless families, for example. I do not suggest that a priority for families willing to move to high-opportunity communities should replace emergency preferences, but it should follow them.

p. 209, ¶ 4    Sard and Rice 2014, 38, 51, 54. Perversely, targeting the voucher amount to a metropolitan-wide median rent also results in voucher amounts that are too high for low-income minority neighborhoods. Landlords in those neighborhoods frequently raise their rents above what market conditions support in order to capture this excessive payment.

p. 210, ¶ 1    HUD 2016.

p. 210, ¶ 2    Sard and Rice 2014, 38, 50–53. Section 8 is also needlessly bureaucratic. HUD requires a special health and safety inspection of apartments before voucher recipients can rent them. This is a well-meaning rule, but there can be more efficient coordination between municipalities' regular building and health inspections and the standards established by HUD.

p. 210, ¶ 3    Sard and Rice 2014, 56–57.

p. 210, ¶ 4     For a summary of other advisable reforms in government housing programs, see Tegeler, Haberle, and Gayles 2013.

p. 211, ¶ 1     Kirp 1982, 123.

p. 211, ¶ 2     Rubin 1972, 79.

p. 211, ¶ 3     Rubin 1972, 78, 127–33; Kirp 1982, 121, 123, 128–29, 138.

p. 212, ¶ 1     Kirp 1982, 130–43.

p. 212, ¶ 2     Hamachi 1954, 96.

p. 212, ¶ 3     Kirp 1982, 142–44.


APPENDIX:
## Frequently Asked Questions

p. 220, ¶ 1     Wolgemuth 1959, 166; Unger 2015.

p. 220, ¶ 2     Foreman 1974; Guzda 1980, 32.

p. 220, ¶ 3     Roosevelt online; Goodwin 1994, 370–71.

p. 220, ¶ 4     White 1942, 214.

p. 221, ¶ 1     Ashmore 1989, 307; Mayer 1993, 275–76, 380. In an interview over two decades later, Hutchins recalled that *Shelley v. Kraemer* was decided "a few months" after he decided not to resign. Hutchins's memory, or the notes of his biographer, Milton Mayer, were faulty. *Shelley v. Kraemer* was decided nine years after he made this decision, and during those nine years, the segregation of Chicago' South Side became more rigid.

Segregation wasn't the only issue where Hutchins chose to go along rather than follow his conscience. He was also a pacifist and opponent of American participation in World War II, yet he acceded to requests of the military that he oversee the project to develop the atomic bomb. Mayer was a tough interviewer, and his exchange with Hutchins about the atomic bomb, following their discussion of segregating the university area, is worth reflecting upon before being tempted to succumb to a "standards of the time" explanation for racial segregation:

**Mayer:** I think *you* care . . . that you've been against an awful lot of things that cause war, but when war comes and the bugle blows, it's Hutchins in the front line.

**Hutchins:** That's right.

**Mayer:** With that prospect before you, would you do the same thing again?

**Hutchins:** No.

**Mayer:** Why not?

**Hutchins:** Because I'm brighter now. . . . You get bright too late. There are all kinds of things that I would have done and would not have done if I had been as bright as I am now. Perhaps contributing to the segregation of Chicago was one of those things.

p. 226, ¶ 4    Kennedy 2013, 18; Boddie 2015. In June 2016 the Supreme Court rejected Abigail Fisher's challenge to affirmative action, but ongoing criticisms of affirmative action will undoubtedly continue.

p. 227, ¶ 5    Katznelson 2013, 159–60; Goodwin 1994, 163. Roosevelt told NAACP leader Walter White, "If I come out for the anti-lynching bill, they [the southerners in Congress] will block every bill I ask Congress to pass to keep America from collapsing. I just can't take that risk."

p. 228, ¶ 2    Larson 2011, 30–31, 38, 39, 130, 235; Goodwin 1994, 100, 173, 397; Olson 2013, 381–82. New Deal leaders were not only bigoted against African Americans; many were also anti-Semitic. In the 1930s, a number of Franklin Roosevelt's State and War Department officials were personally sympathetic to Hitler's persecution of Jews in Germany, even if they thought Hitler a bit extreme in his methods. Those officials had little inclination to admit Jewish refugees to the United States or to make impeding the operation of Hitler's death camps a military concern. William J. Carr, assistant secretary of state in charge of the consular service in the Roosevelt administration, referred to Jews as "kikes" and, after a visit to Detroit, complained that the city was full of "dust, smoke, dirt, Jews." To make it difficult, if not impossible, for Jews fleeing Germany to enter the United States, the State Department rigidly enforced a law that required immigrants to provide a police affidavit from their home countries attesting to their good character, a requirement with which Jewish refugees from Nazi Germany could not comply. The diary of Breckinridge Long, head of the State Department's visa department, was "filled with invective against Jews, Catholics, New Yorkers, liberals, and in fact everybody who was not of his own particular background." William F. Dodd, the American ambassador to Germany, said that while he did not "approve of the ruthlessness that is being applied to the Jews here [in Germany] . . . I have said very frankly that they [the Germans] had a very serious problem. . . . The Jews had held a great many more of the key positions in Germany than their numbers or their talents entitled them to." In a meeting with German foreign minister Konstantin von Neurath, Dodd assured him: "[W]e have had difficulty now and then in the United States with Jews who had gotten too much of a hold on certain departments of intellectual and business life." Dodd went on to assure Neurath that some of his State Department colleagues "appreciated the difficulties of the Germans in this respect but they did not for a moment agree with the method of solving the problem which so often ran into utter ruthlessness."

p. 228, ¶ 3    Weaver 1948, 217; Kushner 1979, 599 (n. 118).

p. 229, ¶ 4    For whites, the comparable numbers are 38, 44, and 93 percent. Data on educational attainment are from the U.S. Department of Education, National Center on Education Statistics. The high school completion rate includes students who dropped out and studied for and then took a high school diploma equivalency exam. This may include some who studied for and took the exam while in prison. There is some evidence that labor market outcomes for holders of a diploma equivalent are worse, on average, than outcomes for holders of regular diplomas. However, if dropouts disproportionately come from the bottom of the cohort achievement distribution, then outcomes for holders of equivalency exams are probably better than those of comparable students who remained in school and got regular diplomas. Both for those who took the exam in prison and those who took it without being incarcerated, studying for the equivalency exam is evidence of strong motivation and responsibility.

p. 229, ¶ 5    Lyons and Pettit 2011, 258; Alexander 2010, 6–7, 97; Braman 2004, 33, using data from the Washington, D.C. Department of Corrections, estimates that three in four African American men in that city can expect to spend some time in prison during their lifetimes.

p. 230, ¶ 1    Morsy and Rothstein (2016).

p. 230, ¶ 2    Morsy and Rothstein (2015, 19–22) summarize what is known about racial differences in lead absorption and its effects.

p. 231, ¶ 3    Hamilton et al. 2015, 43 (table 16).

p. 231, ¶ 4    Wang and Parker 2014, 6, 33, 34.

p. 232, ¶ 2    Wang 2012, 9; Merton 1941, 232. Data on marriages of African Americans in 2010 include heterosexual marriages to non-African American partners, including whites, Asians, Pacific Islanders, and Hispanics. A few of these partners were Asian, Native American, or others, but most were white. In 1941, Robert K. Merton reported, "In our samples, such pairings [Negro male—white female] are from three to ten times as frequent as the Negro female—white male combination."

p. 234, ¶ 1    Wang 2012, 8, 9.

p. 234, ¶ 2    Waters and Pineau 2015, 6–7. A panel of the National Academy of Sciences reviewed the problem, concluding, "The hypothesis of ethnic attrition [that more assimilated Hispanics are less likely to identify themselves as Hispanic] suggests that there is in fact educational progress in the third generation, but it is difficult to measure it well."

| | |
|---|---|
| p. 235, ¶ 1 | Miller 1946, 138. Native Americans have a yet different historical and constitutional experience. |
| p. 235, ¶ 2 | Rothstein 1998; Bowdler 2008. |
| p. 238, ¶ 1 | Coates 2014; Coates 2016a; Coates. 2016b; Conyers 2015. Coates recommends legislation introduced by Representative John Conyers (D-MI) in the 2015 congressional session to establish a commission to consider reparations for African Americans. The proposed legislation uses both "remedies" and "compensation" to describe its purpose, calling for a commission to "acknowledge the fundamental injustice" experienced by African Americans, and "to make recommendations to the Congress on appropriate remedies." |

# BIBLIOGRAPHY

THE AVAILABILITY OF sources online continually evolves, and the location of specific documents can often change. For this reason, while many cited sources are available online, I have not attempted to provide specific Web addresses. Rather, I have trusted that the citations provide sufficient information for readers to search for documents with little difficulty. No source citations are provided for easily accessible Census, Bureau of Labor Statistics, and school district data. In a few cases where a document is available only online and I judged that finding it might be difficult, I have provided a Web address, but I can only warrant that it was accurate shortly before this book went to press.

A theme of *The Color of Law* has been that the many aspects of *de jure* segregation were once well known, but we have suppressed memories of this history because addressing it seems too daunting. It has been the purpose of this book to reacquaint readers with this evidence. As the source citations indicate, some of the research that went into the book was original, but mostly I've simply summarized existing, though no longer popular, literature.

Two older works provided an overview of *de jure* segregation that helped me frame my subsequent research and argument that brings together the many facets of *de jure* segregation. They are underrepresented in the source citations, but readers should be aware that I relied heavily on them to develop a framework for the argument. In many cases, it was these books that led me to more detailed sources.

Two overviews influenced me the most: Robert Weaver's *The Negro Ghetto* (1948) and James A. Kushner's book-length law review article, "Apartheid in America" (1980). I read these early in my research and cannot overly stress the extent to which each framed my subsequent research and argument. Kenneth Jackson's *Crabgrass Frontier* (1985) called attention to the role of the FHA in creating whites-only suburbs, not only through its individual mortgage insurance program but with its financing of large-scale developments of segregated housing. Most scholarship in this field can be traced back to this seminal work and to Douglas Massey and Nancy Denton's *American Apartheid* (1993). Two more recent books on the history of segregation in individual cities also helped me develop the overview for this book: Arnold R. Hirsch's *Making the Second Ghetto: Race and Housing in Chicago, 1940–1960*, originally published in 1983 and then updated in 1998; and Thomas J. Sugrue's *The Origins of the Urban Crisis: Race and Inequality in Postwar Detroit* (1996).

My citations of these six sources cannot adequately convey my debt to them. Readers interested in delving more deeply into the themes of *The Color of Law* would be well advised to familiarize themselves with these works before attempting to track down the more narrowly focused items listed in the Bibliography.

I also recommend Michelle Alexander's *The New Jim Crow: Mass Incarceration in the Age of Colorblindness*. Residential segregation underpins our racial problems today, and the mass incarceration of young black men, often without sufficient cause, is the most serious. Integrating the nation residentially is a long-term project, but the criminal justice system's targeting of young men living in black neighborhoods is an urgent crisis that we can, if we have the will, address quickly. Absorbing the analysis of *The New Jim Crow* can be a first step.

## INTERVIEWS

My ACCOUNTS of the personal histories of members of the Stevenson and Mereday families are based on interviews—in person, by phone, and by e-mail—with Pam Harris (niece of Robert Mereday, Jr.), Shirley Haulsey (daughter of Leroy Mereday and sister of Vince Mereday), Robert Mereday, Jr. (son of Robert Mereday), Frank Stevenson and his wife, Barbara, and Terry Stevenson (daughter of Frank Stevenson).

## COURT AND AGENCY CASES

*Arlington Heights v. Metropolitan Housing Corp.* 1977. U.S. Supreme Court, 429 U.S. 252.

*Banks v. Housing Authority of City and County of San Francisco.* 1953. District Court of Appeal, First District, Division 1, California. 120 Cal. App. 2d 1.

*Barrows v. Jackson.* 1953. U.S. Supreme Court, 346 U.S. 249.

*Birmingham v. Monk.* 1950. U.S. Court of Appeals, Fifth Circuit, 185 F.2d 859.

*Bob Jones University v. United States.* 1983. U.S. Supreme Court, 461 U.S. 574.

*Bowen v. City of Atlanta.* 1924. Supreme Court of Georgia, 159 Ga. 145.

*Bradley v. Milliken.* 1971. U.S. District Court, Eastern District of Michigan, Southern Division, 338 F. Supp. 582.

*Brown v. Board of Education.* 1954. U.S. Supreme Court, 347 U.S. 483.

*Buchanan v. Warley.* 1917. U.S. Supreme Court, 245 U.S. 60.

*Civil Rights Cases.* 1883. U.S. Supreme Court, 109 U.S. 3.

*Claremont Improvement Club v. Buckingham.* 1948. District Court of Appeal, First District, Division 2, California. 89 Cal. App. 2d 32.

*Cleveland v. Ameriquest.* 2009. U.S. District Court, Northern District Of Ohio, Eastern Division, 1:08 cv 139.

*Correll v. Earley.* 1951. Supreme Court of Oklahoma, 205 Okla. 366.

*Corrigan v. Buckley.* 1926. U.S. Supreme Court, 271 U.S. 323.

*Creve Coeur v. Weinstein.* 1959. St. Louis Court of Appeals, Missouri, 329 S.W.2d 399.

*Dailey v. Lawton.* 1970. U.S. Court of Appeals, Tenth Circuit, 425 F.2d 1037.

*Davis v. Elmira Savings Bank.* 1896. U.S. Supreme Court, 161 U.S. 275.

*Dorsey v. Stuyvesant Town Corporation.* 1949. Court of Appeals of New York, 299 N.Y. 512, July 19.

*Dowdell v. Apopka.* 1983. U.S. Court of Appeals, Eleventh Circuit, 698 F.2d 1181, February 28.

*Euclid v. Ambler.* 1926. U.S. Supreme Court, 272 U.S. 365.

*Franklin National Bank v. New York.* 1954. U.S. Supreme Court, 347 U.S. 373.

*Freeman v. Pitts.* 1992. U.S. Supreme Court, 503 U.S. 467.

*Garrett v. Hamtramck.* 1974. U.S. Court of Appeals, Sixth Circuit, 503 F.2d 1236.

*Garrett v. Hamtramck.* 1975. U.S. District Court, Eastern District of Michigan, 394 F. Supp. 1151.

*Harmon v. Tyler.* 1927. U.S. Supreme Court, 273 U.S. 68.

*Hills v. Gautreaux.* 1976. U.S. Supreme Court, 425 U.S. 284.

*Hurd v. Hodge.* 1948. U.S. Supreme Court, 334 U.S. 24.

*Independent Metal Workers,* Locals 1 & 2 (Hughes Tool Co.). 1964. National Labor Relations Board, 147 N.L.R.B. 1573.

*James v. Marinship.* 1944. Supreme Court of California, 25 Cal.2d 721.

*James v. Valtierra.* 1971. U.S. Supreme Court, 402 U.S. 137.

*Jones v. Mayer.* 1968. U.S. Supreme Court, 392 U.S. 409.

*Kennedy v. Housing Authority of Savannah.* 1960. Superior Court of Chatham County, Georgia, Case No. 2004 [*Race Relations Law Reporter* 5 (1960): 804–7].

*Levitt v. Division Against Discrimination.* 1960. Supreme Court of New Jersey, 31 N.J. 514.

*Lyons v. Wallen.* 1942. Oklahoma Supreme Court, 191 Okla. 567.

*Marshall v. Bramer.* 1987. U.S. Court of Appeals, Sixth Circuit, 828 F.2d 355.

*Mayers v. Ridley.* 1972. U.S. Court of Appeals, District of Columbia Circuit. 465 F. 2d 630.

*Milliken v. Bradley.* 1974. U.S. Supreme Court, 418 U.S. 717.

*Parents Involved in Community Schools v. Seattle School District No. 1, et al.* 2007. U.S. Supreme Court, 551 U.S. 701.

*Park View Heights v. Black Jack.* 1972. U.S. Court of Appeals, Eighth Circuit, 407 F. 2d 1208.

*Progress Development Corp. v. Mitchell,* 1960. U.S. District Court, Northern District of Illinois, 182 F.Supp. 681.

*Richmond v. Deans.* 1930. U.S. Supreme Court, 281 U.S. 704.

*Shelley v. Kraemer.* 1948. U.S. Supreme Court, 334 U.S. 1.

*Texas Dept. of Housing v. Inclusive Communities Project.* 2015. U.S. Supreme Court, 576 U.S. _.

*U.S. v. Black Jack.* 1974. U.S. Court of Appeals, Eighth Circuit, 508 F. 2d 1179.

*Weiss v. Leaon.* 1949. Supreme Court of Missouri, Division No. 1, 359 Mo. 1054.

## ARTICLES, BOOKS, DISSERTATIONS, STATEMENTS, ARCHIVED MATERIAL

Abrams, Charles. 1951. "The New 'Gresham's Law of Neighborhoods'—Fact or Fiction." *Appraisal Journal* 19 (3), July: 324–37.

Abrams, Charles. 1955. "Housing, Segregation, and the Horne Case." *Reporter* 13, October 6: 30–33.

Advisory Committee on Zoning. 1926. *A Zoning Primer*, rev. ed. Advisory Committee on Zoning, U.S. Department of Commerce. Washington, D.C.: U.S. Government Printing Office.

*Afro American.* 1942. "Ethridge Should Resign from President's FEPC." Baltimore: Vol. 50 (July 11): 4.

Alancraig, Helen Smith, 1953. *Codornices Village: A Study of Non-Segregated Public Housing in the San Francisco Bay Area.* M.A. thesis, University of California.

Alexander, Michelle. 2010. *The New Jim Crow: Mass Incarceration in the Age of Color Blindness.* New York: New Press.

Alsberg, Elsa. 1960. "Statements of Miss Elsa Alsberg, Executive Director, Palo Alto Fair Play Council, and Lee B. Spivak, Real Estate Salesman." In USCCR 1960, 636–57.

American City Planning Institute. 1918. *Proceedings of the Tenth National Conference on City Planning.* St. Louis, May 27–29.

American Psychological Assocation. 2015. "Brief of *Amicus Curiae* the American Psychological Association in Support of Respondents, *Fisher v. University of Texas*," November 2.

Angelou, Maya. 1969, 2015. *I Know Why the Caged Bird Sings.* New York: Random House.

Archibald, Katherine. 1947. *Wartime Shipyard.* Berkeley: University of California Press.

*Architectural Forum.* 1945. "Bohannon Building Team." Vol. 82, June: 172.

*Architectural Forum.* 1947. "The Industrialized House: The Greatest House-Building Show on Earth." Vol. 86 (3), March: 105–13.

Ashmore, Harry S. 1989. *Unseasonable Truths: The Life of Robert Maynard Hutchins.* Boston: Little, Brown.

Atlanta. 1922. *The Atlanta Zone Plan.* City of Atlanta, City Planning Commission.

Atlas, John, and Peter Dreier. 1994. "Public Housing: What Went Wrong?" *Shelterforce* 74, October–November.

Avery, Robert B., Glenn B. Canner, and Robert E. Cook. 2005. "New Information Reported under HUDA and Its Application in Fair Lending Enforcement." *Federal Reserve Bulletin*, Summer: 344–94.

Ayres, R. Drummond, Jr. 1971. "Bulldozers Turn Up Soil and Ill Will in a Suburb of St. Louis." *New York Times*, January 18.

Bagli, Charles V. 2010. "A New Light on a Fight to Integrate Stuyvesant Town." *New York Times*, November 21.

Baltimore (Mayor and City Council of). 2011. "Second Amended Complaint for Declaratory and Injunctive Relief and Damages." In *Baltimore v. Wells Fargo*, Civil Case No. JFM-08-62, filed in U.S. District Court for the District of Maryland, April 7.

*Baltimore Sun.* 1975. "Transit Fears in Anne Arundel" (Editorial). April 22.

Barbour, W. Miller. 1952. *An Exploratory Study of Socio-Economic Problems Affect-*

*ing the Negro-White Relationship in Richmond, California*. National Urban League and United Community Defense Services, November–December.

Barr, Michael S. 2009. "Community Reinvestment Emerging from the Housing Crisis." In "Revisiting the CRA: Perspectives on the Future of the Community Reinvestment Act," *Community Development Investment Review* 4 (1), February.

Bartelt, David. 1993. "Housing the Underclass." In Michael B. Katz, ed., *The Underclass Debate: Views from History*. Princeton: Princeton University Press.

Bartholomew, Harold. 1932. "Planning for Residential Districts. Chapter II. Report of Committee on Subdivision Layout." In John M. Gries and James Ford, eds., *Planning for Residential Districts: The President's Conference on Home Building and Home Ownership*. Washington, D.C.: National Capital Press.

Bauman, John F. 1987. *Public Housing, Race, and Renewal*. Philadelphia: Temple University Press.

Baxandall, Rosalyn, and Elizabeth Ewen. 2000. *Picture Windows: How the Suburbs Happened*. New York: Basic Books.

Beckles, Jovanka. Online. "The Gary Family of Richmond: Fighting for Equality and Standing for Their Rights." Richmond Black History.org.

Bell, Jeannine. 2008. "The Fair Housing Act and Extralegal Terror." *Indiana Law Review* 41 (3): 537–53.

Ben Joseph, Eran. Online. "Workers' Paradise: The Forgotten Communities of World War I. A Research Project by Prof. Eran Ben-Joseph."

Benjamin, Karen. 2012a. "City Planning, School Site Selection, and the Rise of Residential Segregation in the Urban South, 1890–1930." Paper presented at the annual meeting of the American Historical Association, Chicago, January.

——. 2012b. "Suburbanizing Jim Crow: The Impact of School Policy on Residential Segregation in Raleigh." *Journal of Urban History* 38 (2): 225–46.

——. 2013. "Segregation Built to Last: School Construction and the Formation of Segregated Housing Patterns in Interwar Houston." Paper presented at the conference "The Past and Present of Race and Place in Houston, Texas," Rice University, February.

Benson, Jackson J. 1996. *Wallace Stegner: His Life and Work*. New York: Viking.

Berdahl-Baldwin, Audrey. 2015. *Housing Mobility Programs in the U.S. 2015*. Prepared for the Sixth National Conference on Housing Mobility, Chicago, June. Poverty and Race Research Action Council.

Berger, Joseph. 1998. "Judge Orders State to Help Yonkers Pay for Integration." *New York Times*, February 6.

Bernstein, Robert. 1955. "Supervisor Levin Relates Behind-Scenes Maneuvers." *Daily Palo Alto Times*, May 17.

Better Homes in America. 1926. *Guidebook for Better Homes Campaigns in Cities and Towns*. Publication no. 12.

Blackmon, Douglas A. 2008. *Slavery by Another Name*. New York: Doubleday.

Bloom, Irving N. 1955a. "Milpitas Housing Project. Memorandum of Meeting of April 15, 1955" and "Milpitas Housing Project. Memoranda of Meetings on April 18, 1955." Wayne State University, Walter Reuther Archives, UAW Fair Practices and Anti-Discrimination Department Collection, Folder 65-18 "Sunnyhills; memorandum, meeting reports, 1955," April 19.

——. 1955b. "Milpitas Housing Project. Memoranda of Meetings of April 19, 1955" and "Milpitas Housing Project. Memorandum of Special Meeting of the Board of Sanitation District No. 8." Wayne State University, Walter Reuther Archives, UAW Fair Practices and Anti-Discrimination Department Collection, Folder 65-18 "Sunnyhills; memorandum, meeting reports, 1955," April 21.

Bloom, Nicholas Dagen. 2008. *Public Housing that Worked: New York in the Twentieth Century*. Philadelphia: University of Pennsylvania Press.

Bobker, Lee, and Lester Becker. 1957. *Crisis in Levittown, PA*. Dynamic Films.

Bocian, Debbie Gruenstein, and Richard Zhai. 2005. *Borrowers in Higher Minority Areas More Likely to Receive Prepayment Penalties on Subprime Loans*. Center for Responsible Lending, January.

Boddie, Elise C. 2015. "Why Supreme Court Justices Should Celebrate College Diversity, Not Reject It." *New York Times*, December 8.

Boger, John Charles. 1993. "Toward Ending Residential Segregation: A Fair Share Proposal for the Next Reconstruction." *North Carolina Law Review* 71 (5), June: 1573–618.

Bonastia, Christopher. 2006. *Knocking on the Door: The Federal Government's Attempt to Desegregate the Suburbs*. Princeton: Princeton University Press.

Bowdler, Janis. 2008. "Creating a Fair Housing System Available to Hispanic Families." National Council of La Raza, September 22.

Bowly, Devereux, Jr. 1978. *The Poorhouse: Subsidized Housing in Chicago*, 2nd ed. Carbondale and Edwardsville: Southern Illinois University Press.

Braden, Anne. 1958. *The Wall Between*. New York: Monthly Review Press.

Bradford, Calvin. 2002. *Risk or Race? Racial Disparities and the Subprime Refinance Market*. Center for Community Change, May.

Braman, Donald. 2004. *Doing Time on the Outside: Incarceration and Family Life in Urban America*. Ann Arbor: University of Michigan Press.

Bremer, Fred, et al. 1979. *Relative Tax Burdens in Black and White Neighborhoods of Cook County*. School of Urban Sciences, University of Illinois at Chicago Circle, April 24.

Briggs, Wayne E. 1982. *Sunnyhills Methodist Church: A History. 1957–1982*. Sunnyhills Methodist Church, Milpitas.

Brilliant, Mark. 2010. *The Color of America Has Changed*. New York: Oxford University Press.

Brooks, Rick, and Ruth Simon. 2007. "Subprime Debacle Traps Even Very Credit-Worthy; As Housing Boomed, Industry Pushed Loans to a Broader Market." *Wall Street Journal*, December 3.

Broussard, Albert S. 1993. *Black San Francisco: The Struggle for Racial Equality in the West, 1900–1954.* Lawrence: University Press of Kansas.

Broussard, Albert S. 2001. "In Search of the Promised Land: African American Migration to San Francisco, 1900–1945." In Lawrence B. de Graaf, Kevin Mulroy, and Quintard Taylor, eds., *Seeking El Dorado: African Americans in California,* 181–209. Seattle: University of Washington Press.

Brown, Hubert Owen. 1973. *The Impact of War Worker Migration on the Public School System of Richmond, California, From 1940 to 1945.* Ph.D. dissertation, Stanford University.

Brown, Michael K., et al. 2003. *Whitewashing Race: The Myth of a Color-Blind Society.* Berkeley: University of California Press.

Buckley, Cara. 2010. "Tenants and Landlords Criticize Paterson's Rent Regulation Proposal." *New York Times,* May 26.

Burns, James MacGregor. 1970. *Roosevelt: The Soldier of Freedom, 1940–1945.* New York: Harcourt Brace Jovanovich.

Busch, Andrew. 2013. "Building 'A City of Upper-Middle-Class Citizens': Labor Markets, Segregation, and Growth in Austin, Texas, 1950–1973." *Journal of Urban History* 39 (5), September: 975–96.

———. 2015. "Crossing Over: Sustainability, New Urbanism, and Gentrification in Austin, Texas." *Southern Spaces,* August 19.

*California Eagle.* 1943a. "Communiques from the Housing Front: Venice Race-Hate Meet Reported On." Vol. 64 (32), November 18: 1, 2.

———. 1943b. "Sugar Hill Residents Battle to Keep Homes." Vol. 63 (50), March 24: 1.

———. 1954. "Sugar Hill's Fate to Be Decided at Freeway Hearing." Vol. 73 (48), February 18: 1, 10.

Callan, Arnold. 1960. "Statement of Arnold Callan, Subregional Director, Region 6, United Auto Workers." In USCCR 1960: 799–802.

Cannato, Vincent J. 2010. "A Home of One's Own." *National Affairs* 3, Spring.

Capps, Kriston. 2015. "How the 'Black Tax' Destroyed African-American Home-ownership in Chicago." *CityLab,* June 11.

Caro, Robert. 1975. *The Power Broker: Robert Moses and the Fall of New York.* New York: Vintage Books.

CDC. 2016. "National Current Asthma Prevalence (2014)." Centers for Disease Control and Prevention.

*Chester Times.* 1955. "Home Plan Submitted." March 16, p. 28. Online at *Newspaper Archives of Delaware County Library.*

*Chester Times.* 1956. "Court Rule Asked on Harvard Av. in Swarthmore Development Tiff." March 25, p. 1. Online at *Newspaper Archives of Delaware County Library.*

Choldin, Harvey M. 2005. "The Chicago Housing Authority." *Electronic Encyclopedia of Chicago.* Chicago Historical Society.

*Chicago Defender.* 1932. "Roosevelt Exposed as Rapid Jim Crower by Navy Order." October 15, p. 1.

Chused, Richard H. 2001. "Euclid's Historical Imagery." *Case Western Reserve Law Review* 51 (4), Summer: 597–616.

Clark, Charles D. 1938. "Federal Housing Administration Standards for Land Subdivision." *Journal of the American Institute of Planners* 4 (5): 109–12.

Clark, Tom C., and Philip B. Perlman. 1947. "Brief for the United States as Amicus Curiae." *Shelley v. Kraemer*, 334 U.S. 1, December.

Cleveland Historical. Online. *Outhwaite Homes*. Center for Public History and Digital Humanities, Cleveland State University.

Clinton, William J., President. 1994. Executive Order. *Federal Actions to Address Environmental Justice in Minority Populations and Low-Income Populations*. February 11.

Coates, Ta-Nehisi. 2014. "The Case for Reparations." *Atlantic*, May 21.

———. 2016a. "The Case for Considering Reparations." *Atlantic*, January 27.

———. 2016b. "Ta-Nehisi Coates is Voting for Bernie Sanders Despite the Senator's Opposition to Reparations." *Democracy Now*, February 10.

Colby, Tanner. 2012. *Some of My Best Friends Are Black*. Viking.

Coleman, William T., Jr. 1982. Brief of amicus curiae in *Bob Jones University v. United States*, U.S. Supreme Court, 461 U.S. 574, August 25.

Collin, Robert W., and Robin Morris Collin. 1997. "Urban Environmentalism and Race." In June Manning Thomas and Marsha Ritzdorf, eds., *Urban Planning and the African American Community: In the Shadows*, 220–36. Thousand Oaks, Calif.: Sage.

Connerly, Charles E., and Bobby Wilson. 1997. "The Roots and Origins of African American Planning in Birmingham, Alabama." In June Manning Thomas and Marsha Ritzdorf, eds., *Urban Planning and the African American Community: In the Shadows*, 201–19. Thousand Oaks, Calif.: Sage.

Conyers, John. 2015. "H.R.40—Commission to Study Reparation Proposals for African-Americans Act." 114th Congress, 1st session (2015–16).

Cote Brilliante Presbyterian Church. Online. *Our History*.

Cotter, William G. 1951. "Dear Friend." Committee to End Discrimination in Levittown. Levittown Public Library archives.

*Crisis*. 1917. "Segregation." Vol. 15 (2), December: 69–73.

CUR 2011. *NYC Population Change: New York City Demographic Shifts, 2000 to 2010*. Center for Urban Research.

*Daily Palo Alto Times*. 1955. "Work Under Way at Milpitas on Pioneer Inter-Racial Subdivision." April 7.

Daniel & Beshara. Online. *Walker v. HUD*. http://www.danielbesharalawfirm.com/Pages/WalkervHUD.aspx.

Danielson, Michael N. 1976. *The Politics of Exclusion*. New York: Columbia University Press.

Danzer, Gerald A., et al. 2012. *The Americans: Reconstruction to the 21st Century*. Holt McDougal, Houghton Mifflin Harcourt.

Darrah, Jennifer, and Stefanie DeLuca. 2014. "'Living Here has Changed My

Whole Perspective': How Escaping Inner-City Poverty Shapes Neighborhood and Housing Choice." *Journal of Policy Analysis and Management* 33 (2), Spring: 350–84.

Davies, Richard O. 1966. *Housing Reform During the Truman Administration*. Columbia: University of Missouri Press.

Davis, John P. 1933. "What Price National Recovery?" *Crisis* 40 (12), December: 271–72.

de Graaf, Lawrence B., and Quintard Taylor. 2001. "Introduction: African Americans in California History, California in African American History." In Lawrence B. de Graaf, Kevin Mulroy, and Quintard Taylor, eds., *Seeking El Dorado: African Americans in California*, 3–69. Seattle: University of Washington Press.

Dean, John P. 1947. "Only Caucasian: A Study of Race Covenants." *Journal of Land and Public Utility Economics* 23 (4), November: 428–32.

Devincenzi, Robert J., Thomas Gilsenan, and Morton Levine. 2004. *Milpitas: Five Dynamic Decades*. Milpitas, Calif.: City of Milpitas.

Dew, Charles B. 2000. "Tightening the Noose." *New York Times*, May 21.

Donohue, Mary M. 2014–15. "Housing Factory Workers During Wartime." *Connecticut Explored*, Winter.

Donovan, Doug. 2015. "Housing Policies Still Pin Poor in Baltimore, But Some Escape to Suburbs." *Baltimore Sun*, December 13.

Donovan, Shaun. 2011. "Prepared Remarks of Secretary Shaun Donovan during the Countrywide Settlement Press Conference." December 21.

Dowden-White, Priscilla A. 2011. *Groping Toward Democracy: African American Social Welfare Reform in St. Louis, 1910–1949*. Columbia: University of Missouri Press.

Drake, St. Clair, and Horace R. Cayton. 1945 (revised and enlarged, 1962). *Black Metropolis: A Study of Negro Life in a Northern City*. New York: Harper and Row.

Dresser, Michael, and Luke Broadwater. 2015. "Hogan Says No to Red Line, Yes to Purple." *Baltimore Sun*, June 25.

Dunn, Tom. 2013. "Mahwah and Mt. Laurel." Powerpoint presentation, Mahwah Museum, January 12.

Dunn-Haley, Karen. 1995. *The House that Uncle Sam Built: The Political Culture of Federal Housing Policy, 1919–1932*. Ph.D. dissertation, Stanford University.

ECH. 2011. "Central (Neighborhood)." *Encyclopedia of Cleveland History*.

Ecker, Frederick H. 1932. "Report of Committees on Home Finance and Taxation. Chapter I. Financing Home Ownership." In John M. Gries and James Ford, eds,. *Planning for Residential Districts: The President's Conference on Home Building and Home Ownership*. Washington, D.C.: National Capital Press.

Edozien, Frankie. 2004. "Kids Breathing Easier As Asthma Plummets." *New York Post*, January 14.

*Evening Bulletin*. 1955. "Swarthmore Gets Plans for Interracial Development." Philadelphia, April 12: 16.

Federal Reserve Board. Online. "Survey of Consumer Finances 2013."

FHA. 1935 (June 1); 1936 (April 1); 1938 (with revisions to February); 1947 (January 1); 1952 (January). *Underwriting Manual: Underwriting Analysis Under Title II, Section 203 of the National Housing Act*. Federal Housing Administration. Washington, D.C.: U.S. Government Printing Office.

Fishel, Leslie H., Jr. 1964–65. "The Negro in the New Deal Era." *Wisconsin Magazine of History* 48 (2), Winter: 111–26.

Flint, Barbara J. 1977. *Zoning and Residential Segregation: A Social and Physical History, 1910–1940*. Ph.D. dissertation, University of Chicago.

Foner, Philip S. 1974. *Organized Labor and the Black Worker, 1619–1973*. New York: Praeger.

Ford, James. 1931. "Factors of Bad Housing that Contribute to Ill Health." In Blanche Halbert, ed., *The Better Homes Manual*, 614–19. Chicago: University of Chicago Press.

*Fordham Law Review*. 1957. "Constitutional Aspects of Legislation Prohibiting Discrimination in Housing." Vol. 26 (4): 675–83.

Foreman, Clark. 1974. "Interview with Clark Foreman," November 16. *Oral Histories of the American South*, Interview B-0003. Southern Oral History Program Collection (#4007). University Library, University of North Carolina at Chapel Hill.

Fosl, Catherine. 1989. "Interview with Andrew Wade, November 8, 1989." *Anne Braden Oral History Project*, Louie B. Nunn Center for Oral History, University of Kentucky Libraries.

France, Edward Everett. 1962. *Some Aspects of the Migration of the Negro to the San Francisco Bay Area since 1940*. Ph.D. dissertation, University of California.

Freund, David M. P. 2007. *Colored Property: State Policy and White Racial Politics in Suburban America*. Chicago: University of Chicago Press.

Freund, Ernst. 1929. "Some Inadequately Discussed Problems of the Law of City Planning and Zoning." In *Planning Problems of Town, City and Region: Papers and Discussions at the Twenty-First National Conference on City Planning, held at Buffalo and Niagara Falls, New York, May 20 to 23, 1929*, 79–101. Philadelphia: William F. Fell.

Friend, Hallis, and Nancy Lund. 1974. *Ladera Lore*. Ladera, Calif.

Funigiello, Philip J. 1978. *The Challenge to Urban Liberalism: Federal-City Relations During World War II*. Knoxville: University of Tennessee Press.

German, Art. 1955. "Belle Haven Practices Eyed by State Official." *Palo Alto Times*, August 5. Reproduced in USCCR 1960, 645.

Goodwin, Doris Kearns. 1994. *No Ordinary Time: Franklin and Eleanor Roosevelt: The Home Front in World War II*. New York: Simon and Schuster.

Gordon, Colin. 2008. *Mapping Decline. St. Louis and the Fate of the American City*. Philadelphia: University of Pennsylvania Press.

Gotham, Kevin Fox. 2000. "Urban Space, Restrictive Covenants and the Origins of Racial Residential Segregation in a US City, 1900–1950." *International Journal of Urban and Regional Research* 24 (3), September: 616–33.

Grant, Joanne. 1992. "How Milpitas Became Integration 'Showplace.'" *San Jose Mercury News*, May 25: 1B, 5B.

Graves, Donna. 2004. *Mapping Richmond's World War II Home Front.* A Historical Report Prepared For National Park Service Rosie the Riveter/World War II Home Front National Historical Park, July.

Greenberg, Jack. 1959. *Race Relations and American Law.* New York: Columbia University Press.

Greenhouse, Linda. 1969. "Parkchester: Trouble in Paradise." *New York Magazine* 2 (7), February 17: 36–43.

Grier, Eunice, and George Grier. 1960. *Privately Developed Interracial Housing: An Analysis of Experience.* Berkeley: University of California Press.

———. 1962. *Case Studies in Racially Mixed Housing. Sunnyhills, Milpitas, California.* Prepared for Princeton Conference on Equal Opportunity in Housing. Washington, D.C.: Washington Center for Metropolitan Studies.

Gries, John M., and James S. Taylor. 1931. "Property Considerations in Selecting the Home Site." In Blanche Halbert, ed., *The Better Homes Manual*, 87–95. Chicago: University of Chicago Press.

Gutierrez, Roberto, et al. 1990. *Baltimore Metro: An Initiative and Outcome in Rapid Public Transportation.* December 3. Johns Hopkins University.

Guzda, Henry P. 1980. "Frances Perkins' Interest in a New Deal for Blacks." *Monthly Labor Review* 103: 31–35.

Hamachi, Roy. 1954. *Postwar Housing in Richmond, California: A Case Study of Local Housing Developments in the Postwar Period.* Master's thesis, University of California, Berkeley.

Hamilton, Brady E., et al. 2015. "Births: Final Data for 2014." *National Vital Statistics Reports* 64 (12), December 23. National Center for Health Statistics.

Hancock, John. 1988. "The New Deal and American Planning: the 1930s." In Daniel Schaffer, ed., *Two Centuries of American Planning*, 197–230. Baltimore: Johns Hopkins University Press.

Hannah-Jones, Nikole. 2013. "Housing Crisis: Widespread Discrimination; Little Taste for Enforcement." *ProPublica*, June 11.

Hanson, Sam. 1955. "Off the Beat. Inter-Racial Issue Rears Its Ugly Head in Milpitas Housing." *Los Gatos Daily Times*, May 19.

Harris, Michael. 1955a. "Negro-White Project: A Bold Housing Plan for Milpitas." *San Francisco Chronicle*, January 26.

———. 1955b. "Sewer Fees Boosted At Inter-Racial Tract." *San Francisco Chronicle*, May 14.

Hayes, Edward C. 1972. *Power Structure and Urban Policy. Who Rules in Oakland?* New York: McGraw-Hill.

Hayward, Clarissa Rile. 2013. *How Americans Make Race.* New York: Cambridge University Press.

Hayward Area Historical Society. Online. "History of San Lorenzo."

Heathcott, Joseph. 2011. "'In the Nature of a Clinic': The Design of Early Public Housing in St. Louis." *Journal of the Society of Architectural Historians* 70 (1), March: 82–103.

Hennessey, Melinda Meek. 1985. "Racist Violence During Reconstruction: The 1876 Riots in Charleston and Cainhoy." *South Carolina Historical Magazine* 86 (2), April: 100–12.

Herbers, John. 1969. "Romney Making His Greatest Impact Outside Government by Challenging U.S. Institutions." *New York Times*, May 15.

——. 1970. "Housing: Challenge to 'White Power' in the Suburbs." *New York Times*, November 15.

Herbert, Robert M. 1971. "Mahwah Accused of Zoning Bias." *Star Ledger* (Newark), January 29.

Herbold, Hilary. 1994–95. "Never a Level Playing Field: Blacks and the GI Bill." *Journal of Blacks in Higher Education* 6, Winter: 104–8.

Herr, Philip B. 2002. "Zoning for Affordability in Massachusetts: An Overview." *NHC Affordable Housing Policy Review* 2 (1), January: 3–6.

Hill, Walter B., Jr. 2005. "Finding Place for the Negro: Robert C. Weaver and the Groundwork for the Civil Rights Movement." *Prologue: Journal of the National Archives* 37 (1).

Hills, Patricia. 2010. *Painting Harlem Modern: The Art of Jacob Lawrence*. Berkeley: University of California Press.

Hinton, Harold B. 1949. "No Change Viewed in Work of F.H.A." *New York Times*, December 4.

Hirsch, Arnold R. 1983, 1998. *Making the Second Ghetto: Race and Housing in Chicago, 1940–1960*. University of Chicago Press.

——. 1995. "Massive Resistance in the Urban North: Trumbull Park, Chicago, 1953–1966." *Journal of American History* 82 (2), September: 522–50.

——. 2000a. "Choosing Segregation. Federal Housing Policy Between Shelley and Brown." In John F. Bauman, Roger Biles, and Kristin M. Szylvian, eds., *From Tenements to the Taylor Homes: In Search of an Urban Housing Policy in Twentieth Century America*, 206–225. University Park: Pennsylvania State University Press.

——. 2000b. "Searching for a 'Sound Negro Policy': A Racial Agenda for the Housing Acts of 1949 and 1954." *Housing Policy Debate* 11 (2): 393–441.

——. 2005. *"The Last and Most Difficult Barrier": Segregation and Federal Housing Policy in the Eisenhower Administration, 1953–1960*. Poverty and Race Research Action Council, March 22.

Hogan, James. 1996. *Scattered-Site Housing: Characteristics and Consequences*. Prepared for the U.S. Department of Housing and Urban Development, Office of Policy Development and Research, September.

Holliman, Irene V. 2008. "Techwood Homes." *New Georgia Encyclopedia* (edited by NGE staff in 2013).

Houlihan, Joseph. 2010. "Integrating the Suburbs: A Park Forest Case Study."

*Cities in the 21st Century* 2 (1), Article 4. Online at Macalester College Digital Commons.

Hoover, Herbert. 1931. "Address to the White House Conference on Home Building and Home Ownership." December 2. Online at the American Presidency Project.

Hoover, Herbert. 1932. "Foreword." In John M. Gries and James Ford, eds., *Planning for Residential Districts: The President's Conference on Home Building and Home Ownership*. Washington, D.C.: National Capital Press.

Hope, Andrew. 2011. *Tract Housing in California, 1945–1973: A Context for National Register Evaluation*. Sacramento: California Department of Transportation.

Houston, Charles H., and John P. Davis. 1934. "TVA: Lily-White Reconstruction." *Crisis* 41 (10), October: 290–91, 311.

Hoyt, Homer. 1939. *The Structure and Growth of Residential Neighborhoods in American Cities*. Washington, D.C.: Federal Housing Administration. Washington, D.C. USGPO.

HUD (United States Department of Housing and Urban Development). 2016. "HUD Announces New Approach to Expand Choice and Opportunity for Section 8 Voucher Holders in Certain Housing Markets." Press Release, HUD No. 16-173, November 15.

Hughes, Langston. 1940. *The Big Sea*. New York: Hill and Wang.

Hutchison, Janet. 1997. "Building for Babbitt: The State and the Suburban Home Ideal." *Journal of Policy History* 9 (2): 184–210.

ICP. 2008. *Inclusive Communities Project v. Texas Department of Housing and Community Affairs*, Civil Action No. 308 CV-546-D, filed in U.S. District Court, Northern District of Texas, Dallas Division, March 28, complaint.

Immergluck, Dan, and Geoff Smith. 2006. "The External Costs of Foreclosure: The Impact of Single-Family Mortgage Foreclosures on Property Values." *Housing Policy Debate* 17: 57–79.

Jackson, Kenneth T. 1985. *Crabgrass Frontier*. New York: Oxford University Press.

Johnson, Charles S. 1932. "Negro Housing: Report of the Committee on Negro Housing." In John M. Gries and James Ford, eds., *The President's Conference on Home Building and Home Ownership*. Washington, D.C.: National Capital Press.

Johnson, Charles S., Herman H. Long, and Grace Jones. 1944. *The Negro War Worker in San Francisco: A Local Self-Survey*. Race Relations Program of the American Missionary Association.

Johnson, Elaine D. 1960. "Survey of Peninsula Realtors to Determine Devices Used to Enforce Racial Segregation and Realtors' Attitudes toward Negroes." Exhibit 2 to "Prepared Statement of Mrs. Tarea Hall Pittman," Acting Regional Secretary, West Coast Region, National Association for the Advancement of Colored People. In USCCR 1960, 722–36.

Johnson, Marilyn S. 1993. *The Second Gold Rush: Oakland and the East Bay in World War II*. Berkeley: University of California Press.

Julian, Elizabeth K., and Michael M. Daniel. 1989. "Separate and Unequal: The Root and Branch of Public Housing Segregation." *Clearinghouse Review* 23: 666–76.

Kahrl, Andrew W. 2015. "Capitalizing on the Urban Fiscal Crisis: Predatory Tax Buyers in 1970s Chicago." *Journal of Urban History*, May.

Kantrowitz, Stephen. 2000. *Ben Tillman and the Reconstruction of White Supremacy*. Chapel Hill: University of North Carolina Press.

Katznelson, Ira. 2005. *When Affirmative Action Was White*. New York: W. W. Norton.

———. 2013. *Fear Itself*. New York: W. W. Norton.

Kennedy, Randall. 2013. *For Discrimination: Race, Affirmative Action, and the Law*. New York: Pantheon.

Khadduri, Jill, Larry Buron, and Carissa Climaco. 2006. *Are States Using the Low Income Housing Tax Credit to Enable Families with Children to Live in Low Poverty and Racially Integrated Neighborhoods?* Poverty & Race Research Action Council, July 26.

Kifer, Allen Francis. 1961. *The Negro Under the New Deal, 1933–1941*. Ph.D. dissertation, University of Wisconsin.

Kimble, John. 2007. "Insuring Inequality: The Role of the Federal Housing Administration in the Urban Ghettoization of African Americans." *Law and Social Inquiry* 32 (2), Spring: 399–434.

King, Desmond. 1995. *Separate and Unequal: Black Americans and the U.S. Federal Government*. Oxford: Clarendon Press.

Kingkade, Tyler. 2015. "Clemson Officially Denounces 'Pitchfork Ben,' A Racist Founder of the School." *Huffington Post*, July 20.

Kirp, David L. 1982. *Just Schools: The Idea of Racial Equality in American Education*. Berkeley: University of California Press.

Koch & Fowler, Consulting Engineers. 1928. *A City Plan for Austin, Texas*. Reprinted by Austin, Texas, Department of Planning, February 1957.

Krefetz, Sharon P. 2000–1. "The Impact and Evolution of the Massachusetts Comprehensive Permit and Zoning Appeals Act: Thirty Years of Experience with a State Legislative Effort to Overcome Exclusionary Zoning." *Western New England Law Review* 22.

Kushner, David. 2009. *Levittown: Two Families, One Tycoon, and the Fight for Civil Rights in America's Legendary Suburb*. New York: Walker & Co.

Kushner, James A. 1979. "Apartheid in America: An Historical and Legal Analysis of Contemporary Racial Segregation in the United States." *Howard Law Journal* 22: 547–685.

Lamb, Charles M. 2005. *Housing Segregation in Suburban America Since 1960: Presidential and Judicial Politics*. New York: Cambridge University Press.

Lambert, Bruce. 1997. "At 50, Levittown Contends With Its Legacy of Bias." *New York Times*, December 28.

Lang, William L. 1979. "The Nearly Forgotten Blacks on Last Chance Gulch, 1900–1912." *Pacific Northwest Quarterly* 70 (2), April: 50–57.

Lapsansky-Werner, Emma J. et al. 2016. *United States History: Reconstruction to the Present*. Pearson Education.

Larrabee, Eric. 1948. "The Six Thousand Houses that Levitt Built." *Harper's* 197, September: 79–88.

Larson, Erik. 2011. *In the Garden of Beasts*. New York: Crown.

Lathers, Ellis. 1960. "From Segregation to Community." *Crisis*, October: 513–19.

Laurenti, Luigi M. 1952. "Effect of Nonwhite Purchases on Market Prices of Residences." *Appraisal Journal* 20 (3): 314–29.

Laurenti, Luigi. 1960. *Property Values and Race; Studies in Seven Cities. Special Research Report to the Commission on Race and Housing*. Berkeley: University of California Press.

Leler, Harold C., and Hazel Leler. 1960. "Statement." In USCCR 1960, 654.

Lemann, Nicholas. 1991. *The Promised Land: The Great Black Migration and How It Changed America*. New York: Alfred A. Knopf.

Leppert, Adele. 1959. Untitled statement, December 29. In USCCR 1960, 657.

Levine, Sheen S., et al. 2014. "Ethnic Diversity Deflates Price Bubbles." *Proceedings of the National Academy of Sciences of the United States* 111 (52), December 30: 18524–29.

Levine, Sheen S., and David Stark. 2015. "Diversity Makes You Brighter." *New York Times*, December 9.

Leviner, Sagit. 2004. "Affordable Housing and the Role of the Low Income Housing Tax Credit Program: A Contemporary Assessment." *Tax Lawyer* 57, Summer: 869–904.

Lilley, William, III. 1970. "Housing Report. Romney Faces Political Perils with Plan to Integrate Suburbs." *National Journal* 2, October 17: 2251–63.

Link, Terry. 1971. "The White Noose: How Racist Federal Policies Put a Stranglehold on the City." *San Francisco*, November: 26–29, 53–56.

Little (Arthur D. Little, Inc.). 1973. *A Study of Property Taxes and Urban Blight*. Prepared for the U.S. Department of Housing and Urban Development, January. Washington, D.C.: U.S. Government Printing Office.

Loewen, James. 2005. *Sundown Towns*. New York: Simon and Schuster.

Logan, John R., and Brian Stults. 2011. *The Persistence of Segregation in the Metropolis: New Findings from the 2010 Census*. Census brief prepared for Project US2010, Brown University, March 24.

Logan, John R., et al. 2015. "Creating the Black Ghetto: Black Residential Patterns Before and During the Great Migration." *Annals of the American Academy of Political and Social Science* 660, July: 18–35.

Long, Herman H., and Charles S. Johnson. 1947. *People vs. Property: Race Restrictive Covenants in Housing*. Nashville, Tenn.: Fisk University Press.

Lopoo, Leonard, and Thomas DeLeire. 2012. *Pursuing the American Dream: Economic Mobility Across Generations*. Washington, D.C.: Pew Charitable Trusts, Economic Mobility Project, July.

*Los Angeles Sentinel*. 1947a. "Five Negroes Killed in City's Worst Blast." February 27: 1–5.

———. 1947b. "Explosion Spotlights Ghetto Housing, Evils of Zoning Methods." February 27: 1–2.

———1947c. "Survey." *Los Angeles Sentinel*, March 6: 2.

Lyons, Christopher J., and Becky Pettit. 2011. "Compounded Disadvantage: Race, Incarceration, and Wage Growth." *Social Problems* 58 (2), May: 257–80.

Lyons, Arthur. 1982. "The Urban Property Tax and Minorities." In Illinois Advisory Committee to the U.S. Commission on Civil Rights, *Housing: Chicago Style—A Consultation*. October, 73–78.

Mandelker, Daniel R. 1977. "Racial Discrimination and Exclusionary Zoning: A Perspective on *Arlington Heights*." *Texas Law Review* 55: 1217–53.

Marshall, Thurgood. 1944. "Negro Status in the Boilermakers Union." *Crisis* 51 (3), March: 77–78.

———. 1949. "Memorandum to the President of the United States Concerning Racial Discrimination by the Federal Housing Administration." February 1, p. 18. Proquest History Vault, NAACP Papers. Group II, Series A, General Office File, 1940–1955: Housing; Folder: 001521-009-0592 (Racial discrimination and FHA loan policies), Library of Congress (NAACP).

Massey, Douglas S., and Nancy A. Denton. 1993. *American Apartheid: Segregation and the Making of the Underclass*. Cambridge, Mass.: Harvard University Press.

Massey, Douglas S., et al. 2013. *Climbing Mount Laurel: The Struggle for Affordable Housing and Social Mobility in an American Suburb*. Princeton: Princeton University Press.

Mazzara, Alicia, and Barbara Sard. 2016. Analysis of Data from "Picture of Subsidized Households," Center on Budget and Policy Priorities and Office of Policy Development and Research, U.S. Department of Housing and Urban Development.

McClure, Kirk, Alex F. Schwartz, and Lydia B. Taghavi. 2014. "Housing Choice Voucher Location Patterns a Decade Later." *Housing Policy Debate* 25 (2): 215–33.

McDonald, Hugh. 1970. "'Integrate or Lose Funds.' Warren was Given Romney Ultimatum." *Detroit News*, July 24.

McEntire, Davis. 1960. *Residence and Race: Final and Comprehensive Report to the Commission on Race and Housing*. Berkeley: University of California Press.

McGhee, Fred L. 2015. "Rosewood Courts Historic District." National Register of Historic Places Registration Form, U.S. Department of the Interior, National Park Service, April 1.

McGovney, D. O. 1945. "Agreements, Covenants, or Conditions in Deeds Is Unconstitutional." *California Law Review* 33 (1), March: 5–39.

McPherson, James Alan. 1972. "'In My Father's House There Are Many Mansions—And I'm Going to Get Me Some of Them Too': The Story of the Contract Buyers League." *Atlantic Monthly*, April: 52–82.

McPherson, James M. 1996. "Parchman's Plantation." *New York Times*, April 28.

McWilliams, Carey. 1949. "The Evolution of Sugar Hill." *Script*, March: 24–35.

Memphis and Shelby County. 2011. "First Amended Complaint for Declaratory and Injunctive Relief and Damages" in *Memphis v. Wells Fargo*, Case 2:09-cv-02857-STA-dkv, filed in U.S. District Court for the Western District of Tennessee, Western Division. April 7.

Merton, Robert K. 1941. "Intermarriage and the Social Structure: Fact and Theory." *Psychiatry* 4, August: 361–74. Reprinted in Robert King Merton, ed. 1976. *Sociological Ambivalence and Other Essays*. New York: Free Press, 217–250.

Metzger, Molly W. 2014. "The Reconstruction of Poverty: Patterns of Housing Voucher Use, 2000 to 2008." *Housing Policy Debate* 24 (3): 544–67.

Miller, Loren. 1946. "Covenants in the Bear Flag State." *Crisis* 53 (5), May: 138–40, 155.

———. 1964. "Government's Responsibility for Residential Segregation." In John H. Denton, ed., *Race and Property*, 58–76. Berkeley, Calif.: Diablo Press.

———. 1965a. "Testimony." *Transcripts, Depositions, Consultants Reports, and Selected Documents of the Governor's Commission on the Los Angeles Riots*, Vol. 10. October 7.

———. 1965b. "Relationship of Racial Residential Segregation to Los Angeles Riots." *Transcripts, Depositions, Consultants Reports, and Selected Documents of the Governor's Commission on the Los Angeles Riots*, Vol. 10, October 7.

*Milpitas Post* (probably, but unidentified). 1955 or 1956. "Loan Group Hits Public Housing Idea."

*Milwaukee Journal*. 1952. "Negro Sticks to New Home." March 6.

Mohl, Raymond A. 1987. "Trouble in Paradise: Race and Housing in Miami During the New Deal Era." *Prologue: Journal of the National Archives* 19, Spring.

———. 2000. "Planned Destruction. The Interstates and Central City Housing." In John F. Bauman, Roger Biles, and Kristin M. Szylvian, eds., *From Tenements to the Taylor Homes: In Search of an Urban Housing Policy in Twentieth Century America*, 226–45. University Park: Pennsylvania State University Press.

———. 2001. "Whitening Miami: Race, Housing, and Government Policy in Twentieth-Century Dade County." *Florida Historical Quarterly* 79 (3), Winter: 319–45.

———. 2002. *The Interstates and the Cities: Highways, Housing, and the Freeway Revolt: Urban Expressways and the Central Cities in Postwar America*. Washington, D.C.: Poverty & Race Research Action Council.

Monchow, Helen C. 1928. *The Use of Deed Restrictions in Subdivision Development*. Chicago: Institute for Research in Land Economics and Public Utilities.

Mondale, Walter F. 2015. "Former Vice President Walter Mondale on Housing Policy." C-Span.org, September 1.

Moore, Elizabeth. 1963. "I Sold a House to a Negro." *Ebony* 18 (12): 92–100.

Moore, Shirley Ann Wilson. 2000. *To Place Our Deeds: The African American Community in Richmond, California 1910–1963*. Berkeley: University of California Press.

Morsy, Leila, and Richard Rothstein. 2015. *Five Social Disadvantages that Depress Student Performance*. Washington, D.C.: Economic Policy Institute.

———. 2016. *Mass Incarceration and Children's Outcomes*. Washington, D.C.: Economic Policy Institute.

Munzel, Steve. 2015. E-mail correspondence between archives director, Milpitas Historical Society and author's research assistant Jenna Nichols, September 4.

Myrdal, Gunnar. 1944. *An American Dilemma: The Negro Problem and Modern Democracy*. New York: Harper & Brothers.

National Coalition for the Homeless, et al. 2009. *Foreclosure to Homelessness 2009*. Washington, D.C.: National Coalition for the Homeless.

Nguyen, James. 2011. "Yield-Spread Premiums Prohibited Under New Loan Origination Compensation and Steering Rules." *Berkeley Business Law Journal Network*, March 7.

Nichols, Jesse Clyde. 1923. "When You Buy a Home Site You Make an Investment: Try to Make It a Safe One." *Good Housekeeping* 76 (2), February: 38–39, 172–76.

Nix, Mindy. Undated. "UAW Newsletter Article." In the Paul Davidson Papers, Collection Number 4250, Division of Rare and Manuscript Collections, Cornell University Library, "The Mahwah Project, Box 6, Folder 18."

Nixon, Richard. 1973. "Special Message to the Congress Proposing Legislation and Outlining Administration Actions to Deal with Federal Housing Policy." American Presidency Project, September 19.

Northrup, Herbert R. 1943. "Organized Labor and Negro Workers." *Journal of Political Economy* 51 (3), June: 206–21.

NPS. Online. *Rosie the Riveter WWII Home Front: History and Culture*. National Park Service, U.S. Department of the Interior.

NYCHA. 1970. "Minutes of Meeting with Woodside Tenant Council, November 23." New York City Housing Authority, Research and Reports Division, September 1, 1954. In NYCHA Archives (LaGuardia Community College), Box # 0067A2 Folder # 15; Folder Title: WOODSIDE HOUSES—MSGRS + SUPERINTENDENTS MEETINGS; PROJECT SURVEY RPTS; INCIDENTS RPTS. Date (Range): 1959–1975.

*NYT*. 1910. "Baltimore Tries Drastic Plan of Race Segregation." *New York Times*, December 25.

———. 1914. "President Resents Negro's Criticism." *New York Times*, November 13.

———. 1922. "F.D. Roosevelt to be Building Arbiter." *New York Times*, May 15.

———. 1936. "New Standard in Harlem Housing Is Set by Clinic and Amphitheatre." *New York Times*, June 14.

———. 1938. "120-Acre Housing Will Rise in Bronx as Private Project." *New York Times*, April 8.

———. 1947a. "1st Buildings Open in Housing Groups." *New York Times*, May 30.

———. 1947b. "20,000 Seek Homes. First 10 Chosen." *New York Times*, July 29.

———. 1947c. "Race Housing Plea Quashed by Court." *New York Times*, July 29.

———. 1950a. "Stuyvesant Town to Admit Negroes after a Controversy of Seven Years." *New York Times*, August 25.

——. 1950b. "4 Say Levittown Refuses Leases After Children Play With Negroes." *New York Times*, December 5.

——. 1951. "Bias Appeal Dismissed." *New York Times*, October 30.

——. 2016. "The Racist Roots of a Way to Sell Homes" (editorial). *New York Times*, April 29.

O'Dea, Colleen. 2015. "COAH Is History: State's Top Court Declares Troubled Agency 'Moribund'." *New Jersey Spotlight*, March 11.

O'Neil, Tim. 2010. "A Look Back—St. Louis Factory Loaded America's Weapons During World War II." *St. Louis Post-Dispatch*, June 27.

Ogden, Karen. 2007. "Uncovering Black History in Montana." *Great Falls Tribune*, February 5.

Oldman, Oliver, and Henry Aaron. 1965. "Assessment-Sale Ratios under the Boston Property Tax." *National Tax Journal* 18 (1), March: 36–49.

Oliver, William H. 1955. "Letter to Irving Bloom, enclosing draft of letter to Wilbur F. Warner," July 19. Wayne State University, Walter Reuther Archives, UAW Fair Practices and Anti-Discrimination Department Collection, Folder 65-18.

——. 1957. "Status of UAW Sponsored Housing Development—Sunnyhills." February 6. Wayne State University, Walter Reuther Archives, UAW Fair Practices and Anti-Discrimination Department Collection, Folder 65-10.

Oliver, William H., and Arnold Callan. 1955. "Letter to Eugene B. Jacobs, Deputy Attorney General." July 25. Wayne State University, Walter Reuther Archives, UAW Fair Practices and Anti-Discrimination Department Collection, Folder 65-29.

Olson, Lynne. 2013. *Those Angry Days*. New York: Random House.

Onkst, David H. 1998. "'First a Negro... Incidentally a Veteran': Black World War Two Veterans and the G.I. Bill of Rights in the Deep South, 1944–1948." *Journal of Social History* 31 (3), Spring: 517–43.

Orfield, Gary. 1985. "Ghettoization and Its Alternatives." In Paul E. Peterson, ed., *The New Urban Reality*, 161–93. Washington, D.C.: Brookings Institution.

Palm Beach. Online. "African American Communities." Historical Society of Palm Beach County.

Pates, Gordon. 1948. "West Coast Restricted." *San Francisco Chronicle*, January 4:2.

Pelo, Rose O. 1922. "Industry's New Doctors." *New York Times*, June 4.

PG&E. 1954. "Ford Factory Covers 44 Acres." *P.G. and E. Progress* 31 (6), May. Pacific Gas and Electric Company. In uncatalogued files of the San Francisco Office of the American Friends Service Committee.

Pietila, Antero. 2010. *Not in My Neighborhood: How Bigotry Shaped a Great American City*. Chicago: Ivan R. Dee.

Plotkin, Wendy. 1999. *Deeds of Mistrust: Race, Housing, and Restrictive Covenants in Chicago, 1900–1953*. Ph.D. dissertation, University of Illinois at Chicago.

Polikoff, Alexander. 2006. *Waiting for Gautreaux*. Evanston, Ill.: Northwestern University Press.

Postal Record. 2011. "Same Work, Different Unions". *Postal Record*, National Association of Letter Carriers, June: 8–13.

Powell, Michael. 2010. "Blacks in Memphis Lose Decades of Economic Gains." *New York Times*, May 31.

Power, Garrett. 1983. "Apartheid Baltimore Style: The Residential Segregation Ordinances of 1910–1913." *Maryland Law Review* 42 (1): 289–328.

———. 2004. "*Meade v. Dennistone*: The NAACP's Test Case to '. . . Sue Jim Crow Out of Maryland with the Fourteenth Amendment.'" *Maryland Law Review* 63 (4): 773–810.

PRRAC. 2005. "An Analysis of the *Thompson v. HUD* Decision." Washington, D.C.: Poverty & Race Research Action Council, February.

PWA. 1939. *America Builds*. Public Works Administration, Division of Information.

Quinn, Frank. 1960. "Statement of Frank Quinn, Executive Director, Council for Civic Unity." In USCCR 1960, 545–622.

Quivik, Frederic L. Undated. *Rosie the Riveter National Historical Park, Richmond Shipyard No. 3*. National Park Service, Historic American Engineering Record (HAER) no. CA-326-M.

Rabin, Yale. 1987. "The Roots of Segregation in the Eighties: The Role of Local Government Actions." In Gary A. Tobin, ed., *Divided Neighborhoods: Changing Patterns of Racial Segregation*, 208–26. Thousand Oaks, Calif.: Sage.

———. 1989. "Expulsive Zoning: The Inequitable Legacy of *Euclid*." In Charles Haar and Jerold Kayden, eds., *Zoning and the American Dream: Promises Still to Keep*, 101–21. Chicago: Planners Press.

Racioppi, Dustin, and Stephanie Akin. 2015. "N.J. Supreme Court: Judges Taking Over Enforcement of Affordable Housing." Northjersey.com, March 10.

Radford, Gail. 1996. *Modern Housing for America: Policy Struggles in the New Deal Era*. Chicago: University of Chicago Press.

Randle, William. 1989. "Professors, Reformers, Bureaucrats, and Cronies: The Players in *Euclid v. Ambler*." In Charles Haar and Jerold Kayden, eds., *Zoning and the American Dream: Promises Still to Keep*. Chicago: Planners Press.

Reagan, John. 1967. "Testimony of John Reagan, Personnel Manager of the Kroehler Furniture Manufacturing Company, Fremont." In USCCR 1967, 589–598.

Record, Cy W. 1947. "Characteristics of Some Unemployed Negro Shipyard Workers in Richmond, California" (mimeo), September. Archived at Intergovernmental Studies Library, University of California, Berkeley.

Robertson, Stanley G. 1952. "Police Reveal 'Leads' in Bombings. Local, State, Natl. Agencies Delve Into West Adams Blasts." *Los Angeles Sentinel*, March 20: A1.

Rollingwood Improvement Association Board. 1952. "Fellow Residents of Rollingwood." March 4. In Papers of the California Federation for Civic Unity, Bancroft Library, University of California, Berkeley, BANC-MSS 274, Carton 1, Records 1945–1956.

Romney, George W. 1969. "Nomination of George W. Romney. Hearing before the Committee on Banking and Currency, U.S. Senate, Ninety-First Congress, First Session, on the Nomination of George W. Romney to be Secretary of the Department of Housing and Urban Affairs," January 16. Washington, D.C.: U.S. Government Printing Office.

Roosevelt, Anna Eleanor Roosevelt. Online. *First Lady Biography: Eleanor Roosevelt*. National First Ladies' Library.

Rosenhaus, Sharon. 1971. "UAW Starts Suburban Zoning Fight." *Washington Post*, January 29: A2.

Rosenthal, Jack. 1971a. "President Reaffirms Opposition to Forced Suburban Integration." *New York Times*, February 18.

———. 1971b. "U.S. Sues Suburb on Housing Bias." *New York Times*, June 15.

Rothstein, Richard. 1998. "Bilingual Education: The Controversy." *Phi Delta Kappan* 79 (9), May: 672, 674–78.

———. 2004. *Class and Schools: Using Social, Economic, and Educational Reform to Close the Black-White Achievement Gap*. New York: Teachers College Press.

———. 2013. *For Public Schools, Segregation Then, Segregation Since: Education and the Unfinished March*. Washington, D.C.: Economic Policy Institute.

Rotman, Michael. Online. "Lakeview Terrace." Center for Public History and Digital Humanities, Cleveland State University.

Royko, Mike. 1971. *Boss. Richard J. Daley of Chicago*. New York: Signet.

Rubin, Lillian B. 1972. *Busing and Backlash; White Against White in a California School District*. Berkeley: University of California Press.

Rubinowitz, Leonard S., and Imani Perry. 2002. "Crimes Without Punishment: White Neighbors' Resistance to Black Entry." *Journal of Criminal Law and Criminology* 92 (2): 335–428.

SAI. 1972. "Fully Integrated New Community Planned for Mahwah." *Suburban Action News*. Suburban Action Institute, April 24. In the Paul Davidson Papers, Collection Number 4250, Division of Rare and Manuscript Collections, Cornell University Library, "Mt. Laurel, Box 6, Folder 32."

*San Francisco News*. 1955. "UAW to Start Homes Tract Near Milpitas." August 20.

*San Jose Evening News*. 1955. "UAW Official Claims Tract Political Roadblock Target." May 4: 4.

*San Jose Mercury*. 1955. "UAW Tract Sewer Fee Protested." May 17.

*San Jose News*. 1957. "UAW Inter-Racial Tract to Add Another 522 Homes." September 27.

San Lorenzo Village. Mid-1950s. *10 Reasons Why Your Home in San Lorenzo Is a Safe Investment*. California Federation for Civic Unity Records, 1945–1956, Bancroft Library, University of California (Berkeley), BANC MSS C-A 274, Carton 1: File 13.

Santow, Mark, and Richard Rothstein. 2012. *A Different Kind of Choice: Edu-*

*cational Inequality and the Continuing Significance of Racial Segregation.* Washington, D.C.: Economic Policy Institute.

Sard, Barbara, and Douglas Rice. 2014. *Creating Opportunity for Children: How Housing Location Can Make a Difference.* Washington, D.C.: Center on Budget and Policy Priorities, October 15.

———. 2016. *Realizing the Housing Voucher Program's Potential to Enable Families to Move to Better Neighborhoods.* Washington, D.C.: Center on Budget and Policy Priorities, January 12.

Sard, Barbara, and Will Fischer. 2008. *Preserving Safe, High Quality Public Housing Should Be a Priority of Federal Housing Policy.* Washington, D.C.: Center on Budget and Policy Priorities, October 8. Including unpublished technical appendix provided by the authors.

Satter, Beryl. 2004. "'Our Greatest Moments of Glory Have Been Fighting the Institutions We Love the Most': The Rise and Fall of Chicago's Interreligious Council on Urban Affairs, 1958–1969." *U.S. Catholic Historian* 22 (2), Spring: 33–44.

———. 2009a. *Family Properties. How the Struggle over Race and Real Estate Transformed Chicago and Urban America.* New York: Henry Holt.

———. 2009b. "Race and Real Estate." *Poverty and Race* 18 (4), July–August: 1–2, 8–11.

Schill, Michael H., and Samantha Friedman. 1999. "The Fair Housing Amendments Act of 1988: The First Decade." *Cityscape: A Journal of Policy Development and Research* 4 (3): 57–78. U.S. Department of Housing and Urban Development, Office of Policy Development and Research.

Schwartz, Gary T. 1976. "Urban Freeways and the Interstate System," *Southern California Law Review* 49 (3), March: 406–513.

Schwartz, Heather. 2010. *Housing Policy Is School Policy: Economically Integrative Housing Promotes Academic Success in Montgomery County, Maryland.* New York: Century Foundation.

Self, Robert O. 2003. *American Babylon: Race and the Struggle for Postwar Oakland.* Princeton: Princeton University Press.

Seligman, Amanda I. 2005. *Block by Block: Neighborhoods and Public Policy on Chicago's West Side.* Chicago: University of Chicago Press.

Sewall, Gilbert T. Online. *Widely Adopted History Textbooks.* American Textbook Council.

Sexauer, Cornelia F. 2003. *Catholic Capitalism: Charles Vatterott, Civil Rights, and Suburbanization in St. Louis and the Nation, 1919–1971.* Ph.D. dissertation, University of Cincinnati.

Sharkey, Patrick. 2013. *Stuck in Place: Urban Neighborhoods and the End of Progress Toward Racial Equality.* Chicago: University of Chicago Press.

———. 2014. "Spatial Segmentation and the Black Middle Class." *American Journal of Sociology* 119 (4), January: 903–54.

Sides, Josh. 2003. *L.A. City Limits: African American Los Angeles from the Great Depression to the Present.* Berkeley: University of California Press.

Silva, Catherine. 2009. *Racial Restrictive Covenants: Enforcing Neighborhood*

*Segregation in Seattle*. Seattle Civil Rights and Labor History Project, University of Washington.

Simons, Grace E. 1947. "Judge Stanley Mosk Rules Race Covenants Illegal, 'Un-American': Upholds Negroes' Rights." *Los Angeles Sentinel*, October 30.

Silver, Christopher. 1997. "The Racial Origins of Zoning in American Cities." In June Manning Thomas and Marsha Ritzdorf, eds., *Urban Planning and the African American Community: In the Shadows*, 23–42.Thousand Oaks, Calif.: Sage.

Simkins, Francis Butler. 1944. *Pitchfork Ben Tillman: South Carolinian*. Baton Rouge: Louisiana State University Press.

Smart Growth America. 2016. "Adopt Fair-Share Requirements for Affordable Housing." Smart Growth America.

Smith, Leo F. 1967. "Testimony of Leo F. Smith, Personnel Manager of the Fremont Plant, Trailmobile." In USCCR 1967, 598–605.

Smith, Mark M. 1994. "'All Is Not Quiet in Our Hellish County': Facts, Fiction, Politics, and Race: The Ellenton Riot of 1876." *South Carolina Historical Magazine* 95 (2), April: 142–55.

Smothers, Ronald. 1990. "Hate Crimes Found Aimed at Blacks in White Areas." *New York Times*, April 28.

Spear, Allan H. 1967. *Black Chicago: The Making of a Negro Ghetto, 1890–1920*. Chicago: University of Chicago Press.

Spratt, John M., Jr. 1970. "Federal Tax Exemption for Private Segregated Schools: The Crumbling Foundation." *William and Mary Law Review* 12 (1), Fall.

Squires, Gregory D., Derek S. Hyra, and Robert N. Renner. 2009. *Segregation and the Subprime Lending Crisis*. Briefing Paper no. 244. Washington, D.C.: Economic Policy Institute, November 4.

Stainton, John, and Charleen Regan. 2001. *Protecting the Commonwealth's Investment: A Report Prepared for the Boston and Cambridge Housing Authorities*. Boston: Citizens Housing and Planning Association.

Stegner, Wallace. 1947. "Four Hundred Families Plan a House." *'47: The Magazine of the Year* 1 (2), April: 63–67.

Stevenson, Alexandra, and Matthew Goldstein. 2016. "Wall Street Veterans Bet on Low-Income Home Buyers." *New York Times*, April 17.

Stevenson, Frank. 2007. Oral Interview, April 29, 2003. Conducted by Esther Ehrlich for the Rosie the Riveter World War II American Homefront Oral History Project. Regional Oral History Office, Bancroft Library, University of California, Berkeley.

Streator, George. 1949. "Housing Bias Curb Called Minor Gain." *New York Times*, April 27.

Stiles, Elaine B. 2015. "Every Lot a Garden Spot: 'Big Dave' Bohannon and the Making of San Lorenzo Village." San Lorenzo Heritage Society.

Sugrue, Thomas J. 1993. "The Structures of Urban Poverty: The Reorganization of Space and Work in Three Periods of American History." In Michael B. Katz, ed., *The Underclass Debate: Views from History*. Princeton: Princeton University Press.

———. 1995. "Crabgrass-Roots Politics: Race, Rights, and the Reaction Against Liberalism in the Urban North, 1940–1964." *Journal of American History* 82 (2), September: 551–78.

———. 1996, 2005. *The Origins of the Urban Crisis: Race and Inequality in Postwar Detroit*. Princeton: Princeton University Press.

Swarns, Rachel L. 2015. "Minority Sheet Metal Workers in New York Get Back Pay After Decades of Bias." *New York Times*, December 21.

Taylor, Quintard. 1994. *The Forging of a Black Community: Seattle's Central District from 1870 Through the Civil Rights Era*. Seattle: University of Washington Press.

Tegeler, Philip. 2013. "New Report Demonstrates Persistence of Housing Discrimination But Understates the True Extent of It." *Huffington Post*, June 17.

Tegeler, Philip, Megan Haberle, and Ebony Gayles. 2013. *Affirmatively Furthering Fair Housing at HUD: A First Term Report Card*. May. Poverty and Race Research Action Council.

Thompson, David. 2014. "As a UCLA Student George Brown Jr. Shared his Room with History." *Cooperative Housing Bulletin*, Winter: 1, 4–5.

Thornbrough, Emma Lou. 1961. "Segregation in Indiana during the Klan Era of the 1920's." *Mississippi Valley Historical Review* 47 (4), March: 594–618.

Time. 1951. "ILLINOIS: Ugly Nights in Cicero." *Time*, July 23.

———. 1959. "Suburbia: High Cost of Democracy." *Time*, December 7.

———. 1960. "Races: Caws in the Wind." *Time*, January 4.

*Toledo Blade*. 1952. "Negro Family Defies Jeers of White Crowd." March 6.

Treib, Marc, and Dorothee Imbert. 1997. *Garrett Eckbo: Modern Landscapes for Living*. Berkeley: University of California Press.

Turner, Sarah, and John Bound. 2002. "Closing the Gap or Widening the Divide: The Effects of the G.I. Bill and World War II on the Educational Outcomes of Black Americans." Working Paper no. 9044, Cambridge, Mass.: National Bureau of Economic Research, July.

Tygiel, Jules. 1983. *Baseball's Great Experiment: Jackie Robinson and His Legacy*. New York: Oxford University Press.

UAW. 1979. "Biographical Sketch of William H. Oliver." *News from the UAW*. Public Relations and Publications Department, United Auto Workers, February 26. Wayne State University, Walter Reuther Archives, Biographical Files.

Ungaretti, Lorri. 2012. *Stories in the Sand: San Francisco's Sunset District, 1847–1964*. San Francisco: Balangero Books.

Unger, Nancy C. 2015. "Even Judging Woodrow Wilson by the Standards of His Own Time, He Was Deplorably Racist." *History News Network*, December 13.

UPI. 1971. "Court Upholds Public Housing Referendum." *Lodi News Sentinel* (California), April 27: 2.

USCCR (U.S. Commission on Civil Rights). 1960. *Hearings Before the United States Commission on Civil Rights. Hearings Held in Los Angeles, California, January 25, 1960, January 26, 1960, San Francisco, California, January 27, 1960, January 28, 1960*. Washington: U.S. Government Printing Office.

——. 1961. Book 4. *Housing. 1961 Commission on Civil Rights Report*. Washington, D.C.: U.S. Government Printing Office.

——. 1967. *A Time to Listen… A Time to Act. Voices from the Ghettos of the Nation's Cities. A Report of the United States Commission on Civil Rights*. Washington: U.S. Government Printing Office, O–227–91.

——. 1973. *Understanding Fair Housing*. Clearinghouse Publication 42, February. Washington, D.C.: U.S. Government Printing Office.

USHA. 1939. Bulletin No. 18, *Manual on Policy and Procedure*, U.S. Housing Authority, February 13,

Vale, Lawrence J. 2002. *Reclaiming Public Housing*. Cambridge, Mass.: Harvard University Press.

——. 2007. "The Ideological Origins of Affordable Homeownership Efforts." In William M. Rohe and Harry L. Watson, eds., *Chasing the American Dream: New Perspectives on Affordable Homeownership*, 13–40. Ithaca, N.Y.: Cornell University Press.

Velie, Lester. 1946. "Housing: The Chicago Racket." *Collier's*, October 26: 16–17, 110–13.

Vernon, John. 2008. "Jim Crow, Meet Lieutenant Robinson. A 1944 Court-Martial." *Prologue: Magazine of the National Archives* 40 (1), Spring.

VerPlanck, Christopher. 2008. "We're Sitting Pretty in Daly City: A Critical Analysis of Suburban Planning in Henry Doelger's Westlake Subdivision, Daly City, California." Draft of paper for presentation at annual conference of Society of Architectural Historians, Cincinnati, Ohio, March 20.

"Vitchek, Norris." 1962. "Confessions of a Block-Buster." *Saturday Evening Post*, July: 15–19.

von Hoffman, Alexander. 2000. "A Study in Contradictions: The Origins and Legacy of the Housing Act of 1949." *Housing Policy Debate* 11 (2): 299–326.

Wang, Wendy. 2012. *The Rise of Intermarriage: Rates, Characteristics, Vary by Race and Gender*. Washington, D.C.: Pew Research Center, Pew Social and Demographic Trends, February 16.

Wang, Wendy, and Kim Parker. 2014. *Record Share of Americans Have Never Married: As Values, Economics and Gender Patterns Change*. Washington, D.C.: Pew Research Center, Pew Social & Demographic Trends, September 24.

Warren, Elizabeth. 2007. "Unsafe at Any Rate." *Democracy* 5, Summer.

Waters, Mary C., and Marisa Gerstein Pineau, eds. 2015. *The Integration of Immigrants into American Society. Panel on the Integration of Immigrants into American Society*, Washington, D.C.: National Academies Press.

WBR. 1948. *"Real Estate in Forty-Eight*: The Negro Population. Its Effect on Real Estate." *Washington Business Review*.

Weart, William G. 1957. "Police Guard Site of Race Violence." *New York Times*, August 15.

Weaver, Robert C. 1948. *The Negro Ghetto*. New York: Russell & Russell.

Wehle, Louis B. 1915. "Isolating the Negro." *New Republic* 5, November 27: 88–90.

Weiss, Marc A. 1987. *The Rise of the Community Builders: The American Real Estate Industry and Urban Land Planning.* New York: Columbia University Press.

———. 1989. "Richard T. Ely and the Contribution of Economic Research to National Housing Policy, 1920–1940." *Urban Studies* 26: 115–26.

Weiss, Nancy J. 1969. "The Negro and the New Freedom: Fighting Wilsonian Segregation." *Political Science Quarterly* 84 (1), March: 61–79.

Wells, Amy Stuart, Lauren Fox, and Diana Cordova-Cobo. 2016. *How Racially Diverse Schools and Classrooms Can Benefit All Students.* New York: Century Foundation, February 9.

Wenkert, Robert. 1967. *An Historical Digest of Negro-White Relations in Richmond, California.* Berkeley: University of California, Survey Research Center, September.

Whelan, Deborah C., et al. 1997. *Historic Context for Department of Defense World War II Permanent Construction.* R. Christopher Goodwin and Associates, Inc., for the U.S. Army Corps of Engineers, June.

White, Alvin E. 1942. "Four Freedoms (Jim Crow)." *Nation*, February 21: 213–14.

White, Martin. 1956. "Housing Opportunities—Summary and Report of Program." May 31. American Friends Service Committee files, San Francisco.

Whitten, Robert H. 1922. "Social Aspects of Zoning." *Survey* 48 (10), June 15.

Wilhelm, Mark O. 2001. "The Role of Intergenerational Transfers in Spreading Asset Ownership." In Thomas M. Shapiro and Edward N. Wolff, eds., *Assets for the Poor: The Benefits of Spreading Asset Ownership*, 132–61. New York: Russell Sage Foundation.

Wilkerson, Isabel. 2010. *The Warmth of Other Suns: The Epic Story of America's Great Migration.* New York: Random House.

Will, Herman. 1949. "Affidavit, January 6." Attached to Marshall 1949.

Williams, Franklin H. 1959. Letter to Julian H. Zimmerman, Acting Commissioner, Federal Housing Administration, Re: FHA Proceedings Against Gerald S. Cohn, May 6. Proquest History Vault, NAACP Papers. Group III, Series A, Administrative File: General Office File--Housing, Papers of the NAACP, Part 05: Campaign against Residential Segregation, 1914–1955, Supplement: Residential Segregation, General Office Files, 1956–1965; Jan 01, 1958 – Dec 31, 1963: Folder: 000004-003-0786, Library of Congress.

Williams, Franklin N. 1960a. "Keepers of the Wall." *Frontier: The Voice of the New West*, April: 9–11.

Williams, Franklin. 1960b. "Statement of Franklin H. Williams, Assistant Attorney General, California Department of Justice." In USCCR 1960, 479–485.

Williams, Michael Paul. 2015. "Williams: Richmond's Segregation is by Design." *Richmond Times-Dispatch*, April 20.

Williams, Norman, Jr. 1950. "Racial Zoning Again." *American City* 65 (11), November: 137.

Williamson, June. 2005. "Retrofitting 'Levittown'." *Places Journal* 17 (2).

Wirt, Frederick M. 1974. *Power in the City: Decision Making in San Francisco.* Berkeley: University of California Press.

Wolgemuth, Kathleen L. 1959. "Woodrow Wilson and Federal Segregation." *Journal of Negro History* 44 (2), April: 158–73.

Wollenberg, Charles. 1981. "James vs. Marinship: Trouble on the New Black Frontier." *California History* 60 (3), Fall: 262–79.

———. 1990. *Marinship at War.* Berkeley, Calif.: Western Heritage Press.

Wolters, Raymond. 1969. "Closed Shop and White Shop: The Negro Response to Collective Bargaining, 1933–1935." In Milton Cantor, ed., *Black Labor in America*, 137–52. Westport, Conn.: Negro Universities Press.

Wood, Lewis. 1949. "Truman Puts Ban on All Housing Aid Where Bias Exists." *New York Times*, December 3.

Woodington, Donald DeVine. 1954. *Federal Public War Housing in Relation to Certain Needs and the Financial Ability of the Richmond School District.* Ph.D. dissertation, University of California.

Woofter, Thomas Jackson, 1928. *Negro Problems in Cities: A Study.* Garden City, N.Y.: Doubleday, Doran & Co.

Wright, John Aaron. 2002. *Discovering African American St. Louis: A Guide to Historic Sites.* St. Louis: Missouri History Museum.

Yardley, Jonathan. 2009. "Jonathan Yardley on 'Levittown': What Happened when a Black Family Tried to Live the Suburban American Dream." *Washington Post*, February 15.

Zineski, Tony, and Michael Kenyon. 1968. "Where the Racism Really Is—In the Suburbs." *Detroit Scope Magazine*, August 31: 6–10.

# PHOTOGRAPH CREDITS

covenants, the FHA continued to subsidize projects that penalized sellers of homes to African Americans. In Westlake, Daly City, California, the total fine, $16,000, was greater than the typical home sale price. Daly City History Museum.

92    Chicago, 1970. When federal policy denied mortgages to African Americans, they had to buy houses on the installment plan, which led to numerous evictions. Photograph by Paul Sequeira.

98    In the Lawndale neighborhood of Chicago, community opposition to evictions of contract buyers was so strong that sheriffs were often needed to prevent owners and neighbors from carrying belongings back in. Photograph by Paul Sequeira.

100    Denver, 1961. When a few African Americans moved to a middle-class white neighborhood, speculators panicked white homeowners into selling at a deep discount. Photo by Ed Maker, the *Denver Post* via Getty Images.

111    Before the 2008 burst of a housing bubble, lenders targeted African American and Hispanic homeowners for the marketing of subprime refinance loans. When the economy collapsed, many homes went into foreclosure, devastating entire neighborhoods—like this block of boarded-up homes on Chicago's Southwest Side. Photo by John Gress, Corbis via Getty Images.

114    Miami, 1966. Mayor Chuck Hall sends the first wrecking ball into homes of African Americans near downtown, fulfilling the city's plan to relocate them to a distant ghetto. Wolfson Archives.

130    After Miami-Dade mayor Chuck Hall sent the first wrecking ball to destroy an African American neighborhood, buildings were demolished to make way for I-95, as children look on. Top photo: Wolfson Archives. Bottom photo: Wolfson Archives.

139    Levittown, Pennsylvania, 1954. A crowd mobilizes before proceeding to harass the first African American family to move into the all-white development. Special Collections Research Center, Temple University Libraries, Philadelphia.

149    Top: Charlotte, Rosemary, and Andrew Wade, after rocks were hurled through the windows of their Shively, Kentucky, home in 1954. Wisconsin Historical Society, WHI-55227.

149    Bottom: A policeman inspects damage after the Wades' house was dynamited. Wisconsin Historical Society, WHI-55226.

152    Sausalito, California, 1943. Joseph James (front, at table, second from right) organized the refusal of black shipyard workers to pay dues to a segregated and powerless union auxiliary. Courtesy of the Sausalito Historical Society.

162    First Lady Eleanor Roosevelt supported civil rights leader A. Philip Randolph's demand that war industries be required to hire black workers. She was his emissary to her husband, but also

her husband's emissary to Randolph, urging him to call off the threatened June 1941 march on Washington. Bettmann Collection, Getty Images.

164 Joseph James, leader of African American shipyard workers in the San Francisco Bay Area, singing the national anthem at a launching in 1943. Yet his union denied him the chance for promotion, and he received few fringe benefits. Courtesy of San Francisco Maritime NHP.

166 "We Fight for the Right to Work as well as Die for Victory for the United Nations." In 1942, demonstrators protest the refusal of the St. Louis Small Arms Ammunition Plant to hire black workers. *St. Louis Post-Dispatch.*

177 St. Louis, 1947. To construct its Gateway Arch, the city demolished a downtown African American neighborhood, displacing residents to new black areas like Ferguson. Jefferson National Expansion Memorial Archives.

192 As public housing towers like Pruitt-Igoe in St. Louis were taken down in the early 1970s and their sites redeveloped, residents were forced into other segregated neighborhoods. U.S. Department of Housing and Urban Development Office of Policy Development and Research.

194 Plano, Texas, 2016. Attorney Elizabeth Julian (left) successfully sued HUD and Dallas over intentional discrimination. A settlement enabled Bernestine Williams (right) to move to this middle-class integrated neighborhood, where she raised two college-bound children. Courtesy of Betsy Julian.

214 A New Deal housing agency drew maps of metropolitan areas nationwide. Neighborhoods where African Americans resided were colored red to caution appraisers not to approve loans. This map is of Detroit. National Archives.

218 In the 1930s and 1940s, University of Chicago trustees (chairman Harold H. Swift, center) instructed chancellor Robert Maynard Hutchins (right) to ensure that neighborhoods near the campus were segregated. His father, William James Hutchins (left), president of the interracial Berea College in Kentucky, unsuccessfully advised his son to reject the demand. Special Collections Research Center, University of Chicago Library.

# INDEX

----------------------